Mothers Making
Latin America

Viewpoints/Puntos de Vista:
Themes and Interpretations in Latin American History

Series editor: Jürgen Buchenau

The books in this series will introduce students to the most significant themes and topics in Latin American history. They represent a novel approach to designing supplementary texts for this growing market. Intended as supplementary textbooks, the books will also discuss the ways in which historians have interpreted these themes and topics, thus demonstrating to students that our understanding of our past is constantly changing, through the emergence of new sources, methodologies, and historical theories. Unlike monographs, the books in this series will be broad in scope and written in a style accessible to undergraduates.

Published

A History of the Cuban Revolution
Aviva Chomsky

Bartolomé de las Casas and the Conquest of the Americas
Lawrence A. Clayton

Beyond Borders: A History of Mexican Migration to the United States
Timothy J. Henderson

The Last Caudillo: Alvaro Obregón and the Mexican Revolution
Jürgen Buchenau

A Concise History of the Haitian Revolution
Jeremy Popkin

Spaniards in the Colonial Empire: Creoles vs. Peninsulas?
Mark A. Burkholder

Dictatorship in South America
Jerry Dávila

Mothers Making Latin America: Gender, Households, and Politics Since 1825
Erin E. O'Connor

In preparation

Mexico Since 1940: The Unscripted Revolution
Stephen E. Lewis

Emancipations: Latin American Independence in a Global Context
Karen Racine

Mothers Making Latin America

Gender, Households, and Politics Since 1825

Erin E. O'Connor

WILEY Blackwell

Registered Office
John Wiley & Sons Ltd, The Atrium, Southern Gate, Chichester, West Sussex, PO19 8SQ,
UK

Editorial Offices
350 Main Street, Malden, MA 02148-5020, USA
9600 Garsington Road, Oxford, OX4 2DQ, UK
The Atrium, Southern Gate, Chichester, West Sussex, PO19 8SQ, UK

For details of our global editorial offices, for customer services, and for information
about how to apply for permission to reuse the copyright material in this book please see
our website at www.wiley.com/wiley-blackwell.

Library of Congress Cataloging-in-Publication Data

O'Connor, Erin, 1965–
    Mothers making Latin America : gender, households, and politics since 1825 / Erin E.
O'Connor.
        pages cm
    Includes bibliographical references and index.
    ISBN 978-1-118-27143-8 (cloth) – ISBN 978-1-118-27144-5 (pbk.)   1. Women–Latin
America–History.   2. Motherhood–Latin America–History.   3. Sex role–Latin
America–History.   4. Feminism–Latin America–History.   5. Latin America–History–
1830-   I. Title.
    HQ1460.5.O36 2014
    306.874'3–dc23
                                                                                              2013046058

A catalogue record for this book is available from the British Library.

Cover image: Mother and Child, photograph by Pamela Castro

Set in 10/12.5pt Minion Pro Regular by Toppan Best-set Premedia Limited
Printed in Malaysia by Ho Printing (M) Sdn Bhd

1   2014

Contents

Series Editor's Preface

Each book in the "Viewpoints/Puntos de Vista" series introduces students to a significant theme or topic in Latin American history. In an age in which student and faculty interest in the Global South increasingly challenges the old focus on the history of Europe and North America, Latin American history has assumed an increasingly prominent position in undergraduate curricula.

Some of these books discuss the ways in which historians have interpreted these themes and topics, thus demonstrating that our understanding of our past is constantly changing, through the emergence of new sources, methodologies, and historical theories. Others offer an introduction to a particular theme by means of a case study or biography in a manner easily understood by the contemporary, non-specialist reader. Yet others give an overview of a major theme that might serve as the foundation of an upper-level course.

What is common to all of these books is their goal of historical synthesis. They draw on the insights of generations of scholarship on the most enduring and fascinating issues in Latin American history, and through the use of primary sources as appropriate. Each book is written by a specialist in Latin American history who is concerned with undergraduate teaching, yet has also made his or her mark as a first-rate scholar.

The books in this series can be used in a variety of ways, recognizing the differences in teaching conditions at small liberal arts colleges, large public universities, and research-oriented institutions with doctoral programs. Faculty have particular needs depending on whether they teach large lectures with discussion sections, small lecture or discussion-oriented classes, or large lectures with no discussion sections, and whether they teach on a semester or trimester system. The format adopted for this series fits all of these different parameters.

In this eighth volume in the "Viewpoints/Puntos de Vista" series, Professor Erin E. O'Connor uses motherhood as a lens through which to view gender and family in modern Latin American history. *Mothers Making Latin America: Gender, Households, and Politics since 1825* provides a sweeping overview of both the enduring and the changing aspects of motherhood. The volume covers nearly 200 years, from the time of the macho, militaristic caudillos of the early and mid-nineteenth century to the present day, which features women presidents (all three of them mothers) in Argentina, Brazil, and Costa Rica. Geographically, the book includes examples from all of the major regions of Latin America as well as the Caribbean. By means of this analysis, readers come to understand the struggles of women to earn their rightful place in a patriarchal world. They also learn to appreciate the ways in which patriarchal structures change rather than disappear, notwithstanding the fact that women now serve in prominent political, economic, and cultural roles.

A particular feature of this book is the dialogue between captivating case studies and insightful interpretation. These case studies include women from different social classes and ethnic/racial origins, from an Argentine political activist organizing to protest the fate of her "disappeared" son, to a Brazilian *favela* (shantytown) dweller who wrote her diary on scraps of paper. Moving back and forth between these case studies and overarching analysis, Professor O'Connor has crafted a sophisticated, yet highly accessible book that will be of interest to scholars, students, and a general audience alike.

Jürgen Buchenau
University of North Carolina, Charlotte

Acknowledgments

The story of this book dates back to the 2011 meeting of the American Historical Association, when Jürgen Buchenau asked me if I might be interested in proposing a book for the *Viewpoints/Puntos de Vista* series. He did not know it at the time, but Jürgen was inviting me to submit exactly the kind of book proposal I'd wanted to make for a long time, though I had only recently realized it. I am grateful to Jurgen, and to Peter Coveney at Wiley-Blackwell, for making it possible for me to write the book that has been percolating in my teacher-scholar consciousness for many years. The process, from day one, has been a joy.

Bringing scholarship to the classroom in a meaningful and manageable way is a huge undertaking, and my greatest debts are to the students who continually inspire and challenge me to become a better teacher. These debts date back many years, and to more institutions than my current one; sadly, that means that the number of student names would be far too long to list here. However, I do want to give heartfelt thanks to students who took my courses – both surveys and colloquia – on gender in Latin American history over the years at Bridgewater State University (BSU). I taught Latin American Women's and Gender history at BSU in 2004, 2006, 2010, and 2012; Gender, Race, and Nation in 2007, 2008, 2010, and 2013; and Gender and Nation in 2011. The students in these classes, mostly history majors, went on journeys of history and historiography with me that have made me a better scholar as well as a better teacher. I must give particular thanks to my classes in Latin American Women's and Gender history in Fall 2012 who read an early draft of the manuscript in class with me. I was, and remain, thoroughly impressed and deeply moved by how seriously they took their job as my class testers for this book. Their likes, dislikes, observations, and confusions allowed me to make this a better book than it would otherwise have been.

I have been fortunate to have several colleagues to whom I have been able to turn for support, insights and ideas, and constructive criticisms, and I only have room to name a few of them here. I owe a debt of gratitude to Leo Garofalo, not only for his input on my initial ideas for this book, but also for his inspiration and camaraderie in coediting an earlier project that introduced me to the art of writing for undergraduate audiences. Mrinalini Sinha taught me how to do gender analysis and has been very patient with the fact that I have claimed as a lifelong mentor. Minnie encouraged me when I conceived of this project and bolstered me when I felt uncertain about it; her belief in me is invaluable. Nick Racheotes listened to my every complaint and joy in the process of writing, and he kept me laughing through it all. My greatest academic debts with this project are to Nicola Foote and Marc Becker, who read each of these chapters and commented honestly on them even when I did not want them to do so. They also both helped me (Marc most especially) to obtain sources that I needed in order to revise the manuscript while I was living and researching another project in Quito. I owe Nicola particular thanks for having discussed each chapter with me, and for introducing me to Jürgen back in 2011. Tanja Christiansen, Nicola Foote, and Margaret Power also shared primary-source documents with me for the book. I must also thank the anonymous reviewers for Wiley-Blackwell who engaged so meaningfully with the manuscript. I did not follow every one of their suggestions, but their ideas, praise, and criticisms inspired and challenged me to strengthen this book in very important ways. As always, the shortcomings in this book are my fault alone.

I am lucky to work at BSU, a teaching institution that values and supports scholarship, and where I find myself in a community of teacher-scholars who inspire me on a daily basis. Writing groups at BSU helped me to keep moving forward even when the semester was underway, and I am grateful to my writing group peers, Paula Bishop, Michelle Mamberg, Minae Savas, Stacey Sheriff, and Sarah Wiggins, for their encouragement and insights as I moved forward with this project. Ann Brunjes and Maggie Lowe at BSU have always been encouraging and helpful whenever I needed to think through the particulars of making good pedagogy out of scholarship, or good writing out of pedagogy.

I believe that empathy feeds historical studies, and my own experiences as a daughter and a mother have profoundly shaped how I approach the world, including how I analyze history. My mother, Martha O'Connor, taught me that a religious woman can also stand up quite firmly for her rights. I did not follow the kind of life that she envisioned for me, but the values and love that she gave to me so willingly continue influence me and my work every day of my life. My father, Gerald O'Connor, taught me through his actions, even more than his words, that men can and should respect women. Dad died in 2009; I miss him still. I also owe a tremendous debt to the family that made a mother of me. My husband, Howard Brenner, puts in a lot of extra parenting time to make sure that I can survive the juggle motherhood and academia. I could not have managed this book without his support and encouragement. Our children, Anya and Samuel, put up with absences from me as I holed up to write, but mostly they were a (much needed) distraction from work that kept my life in perspective. Mothering them, in both its joys and challenges, has given me a much better understanding of and appreciation for the women that I present in this book.

Source Acknowledgments

The author and publisher gratefully acknowledge the permission granted to reproduce the copyright material in this book:

1.1 Extract from Jo Fisher *Mothers of the Disappeared*, Boston, Southend Press, 1989. Reproduced with permission of Southend Press.

1.2 Translation of an excerpt from Bachelet's victory speech. Reproduced from Erin E. O'Connor and Leo J. Garofalo, eds., *Documenting Latin America Volume 2: Gender, Race, and Nation* (New Jersey: Prentice Hall/Pearson, 2011). Reproduced by permission of Pearson Education, Inc., Upper Saddle River, NJ.

2.1 Extract from Vicente Grez, *Las mujeres de la indepencia* (Santiago: Imp de la "Gratitud Nacional", 1910).

3.1 "Lorenza Cabrera vecina de Cajamarca litigando con el capitán de gendermería Don José María Cortés sobre entrega de la menor Manuela Chávez quien fue regalada al susodicho por Tadea Casas y José Manuel Goyocochea", Archivo Departamental de Cajamarca, Corte Superior de Justicia, Casos Criminales, legajo I, 19-1-1862. Translated by the author.

4.1 Extract from Gertrude M. Yeager ed., *Confronting Change, Challenging Tradition: Women in Latin American History* (Wilmington: SR Books, 1994). Reproduced with permission.

5.1 Extract from Nichole Sanders, "Improving Mothers: Poverty, the Family, and 'Modern' Social Assistance in Mexico" in Stephanie Mitchell and Patience A. Schell eds., *The Women's Revolution in Mexico, 1910–1953* (New York: Rowman and Littlefield, 2007). Reproduced with permission.

6.1 Extract from the transcripts of the Peasant Autobiographies Project, National University Library, Heredia, Costa Rica. Courtesy Dr N. Foote.

7.1   Extract from Fidel Castro's speech, reproduced from *Granma Weekly Review*.

8.1   Extract from Matilde Mellibovsky, ed., *Circle of Love Over Death: Testimonies of the Mothers of the Plaza de Mayo* (Willimantic: Curbstone Press, 1997). Reproduced with permission.

9.1   Extract from a document presented at the International Tribunal of Crimes Against Women in Brussels, March 1976. Reprinted in Ana Rima Rivera Lassen and Elizabeth Crespo-Kebler eds., *Documentos del feminism en Puerto Rico: facsimiles de la historia* (University of Puerto Rico Press, 2001).

9.2   Extract from Nathalie Lebon and Elizabeth Maier, eds., *De lo privado a lo publico: 30 años de lucha ciudadana de las mujeres en America Latina* (Siglo Veintiuno in collaboration with the Latin American Studies Association and the United Nations Development Fund for Women, 2006).

1

Introduction

Gender and Latin American History, or: Why Motherhood?

Two Tales of Women and Politics

Aída de Suárez did not begin her life as a political activist. She only became politicized when her son was "disappeared" – abducted by the military government without charges or due process. His disappearance turned her world upside down, particularly when she could not find out what happened to him. She described what it was like when she tried to find answers about what happened to her son:

> I had a neighbour who was a doctor and after they took my son I went to him and he gave me an injection to calm me down. They come into your house and they take your child like that – you think you've gone mad. The injection didn't calm me at all. At seven in the morning I was in the police station. A guard at the entrance asked me what I wanted. I said my son had been taken away and I didn't know by who or why. I cried so much he let me in. They took my statement. As I was leaving a policeman at the door said to me, "Señora, there's no point in coming here. Go to the military regiments, they're the ones who are taking people. Don't waste your time here. We have orders so keep out of the zones of their operations." I went straight to the regiment. They didn't want to see me. They said that they didn't know anything and that I should go to the Ministry of the Interior. Then one man told me to try the regiment at Ciudadela. I want there and they said I'd come to the wrong place and that I had to go to the First Army Corps in Palermo. That day I went to all those places but I didn't find out anything.[1]

Mothers Making Latin America: Gender, Households, and Politics Since 1825,
First Edition. Erin E. O'Connor.
© 2014 John Wiley & Sons, Inc. Published 2014 by John Wiley & Sons, Inc.

Aída de Suárez was like many middle-aged and older women whose adult children were disappeared when the Argentine state terrorized its own population from 1976 to 1979 in what eventually came to be known as the Dirty War. Although military violence against civilians began in the 1960s, the Dirty War started during Isabel Perón's presidency, from 1974 to1976, and it escalated rapidly after military forces overthrew her and established an authoritarian government. By the time that the military regime fell from power in the early 1980s, tens of thousands of Argentine men and women – most of them young – had disappeared and were presumed dead.

De Suárez was among 14 women, mostly housewives who had never been involved in politics before, who met each other in various government offices while trying to find out what had happened to their adult children who had disappeared. Their trips to police, military, and government offices yielded no results, just more frustration and fear. The mothers decided to march silently together around the Plaza de Mayo, Buenos Aires's central square, in order to bring attention to their plight and, hopefully, to find out where their children were. The movement grew rapidly to include thousands of mothers and grandmothers from many different walks of life, religions, and political perspectives. Thought they came from a variety of backgrounds, the women in the movement emphasized their identities as supposedly traditional mothers who were willing to sacrifice anything for their children, and who were more interested in family and morality than in any form of politics. In the end, the Mothers were one of the few groups able to bring international attention to state terrorism in Argentina; other protestors typically ended up among the ranks of the disappeared. The mothers' silent marching undercut the military government's claims to legitimacy, which in turn played a role in the regime's dissolution in the early 1980s.

Fast-forward to 2006, when Michelle Bachelet was elected as Chile's first woman president. In her victory speech, Bachelet stated:

> Today we have witnessed the magic of democracy, amigos and amigas. Today we're all equal. The vote of the most humble person is worth the same as the vote of the most powerful. Democracy can help untangle the wishes and hopes of the people. . . .
>
> Starting right now, your hopes are my hopes, your wishes mine. To all the people who welcomed me into their homes, all the men and women who gave me the gift of a hug and a kiss, above all so many women who gave me my victory today, on this night. To all the people from the prov-

inces, I send my greetings and my assurance that I will fulfill the vow I took in the last days of my campaign, that we would remember them when we were here celebrating and surely they are all celebrating in each of their cities our great triumph tonight.

Amigos y amigas, starting March 11, Chile will have a woman president, but it will also be the start of a new phase where we will make sure that the successes we achieve in this great country make their way into the homes of all Chileans, because I want people to remember my government as a government of all, for all. Ours is a dynamic country, with the desire to be successful, that is becoming more and more integrated into the world, a country of entrepreneurs who create prosperity with their ingenuity and creativity. But for Chilean men and women to dare to be entrepreneurial and to innovate, they must also know that the society they live in protects them.[2]

Later, in her first annual address, Bachelet claimed that her political victory represented the "defeat of exclusion" not just for women, but for Chileans more generally.[3] Bachelet was the sixth Latin American woman to hold the office of president, but she was the first to become president who had *not* been married to a high profile male political leader.[4] Neither did Bachelet highlight her role as a mother to grown children, as some other Latin American women leaders – most notably Violeta Chamorro in Nicaragua during the 1990s – had done. Bachelet had an ambitious sociopolitical agenda, promising to achieve gender equity in her cabinet and address women's issues in Chile as well as the needs of poor Chileans. Though she met only some of her goals, she maintained strong support throughout her presidency from 2006 to 2010, in no small part because she got Chileans through the hardships of the worldwide economic recession that hit during her term.

Since Bachelet's successful campaign in Chile, three other Latin American women have won the presidency in their respective countries. Cristina Fernández de Kirchner won the 2007 presidential election in Argentina, following in the footsteps of her husband, Néstor Kirchner, who was president from 2003 to 2007. Fernández de Kirchner proved herself politically capable in her own right when her husband died in 2007, leaving her to rule without his support, and she made her own mark on the history of women in politics when she became the first female president in Latin America to win reelection in 2011. Two other women – Laura Chinchilla in Costa Rica and Dilma Rousseff in Brazil – ascended to the presidency via elections in 2010. Rousseff, in particular, took power in a country with of one of the world's fastest expanding and important economies.

Women have often played significant roles politics in several Latin American countries since the 1970s. However, the nature of their participation and the roles that they have emphasized changed considerably over the course of about 25 years. These transformations in politics have coincided with other developments for women in Latin American societies. For example, fertility rates have fallen dramatically in many Latin American countries: overall, Latin American women have gone from having an average of 5.98 children in 1960 to 2.2 children in 2010.[5] This drop in fertility rates, however, has not occurred evenly throughout the region. The most dramatic decline in fertility rates has been in Brazil, where women averaged 5.33 children in 1970 and only 2.46 children by 1995. In other countries, the decline was not as dramatic, such as in Guatemala, where in the same time period, women went from having an average of 6.53 children to 5.12 children.[6] Women in many Latin American countries are also becoming more educated, particularly among the middling and upper classes.

The changes in women's lives raise important questions about Latin American history. The history of the Mothers' movement in Argentina makes one wonder: how could politically inexperienced housewives start a protest movement that helped to bring down a violent authoritarian regime? How and why did these women create a political movement by highlighting, rather than rejecting, their traditional roles as mothers and homemakers? What political, legal, social, and cultural trends in the Latin American past made it possible for such a movement to emerge? *Why* did these women – and later political figures, such as Violeta Chamorro in Nicaragua – emphasize motherhood in their political pursuits? What might have been the cost of this focus on motherhood in politics? Certainly, although one can find examples of women who used maternalist ideas to their benefit, motherhood also set limits on women's ability to gain an education, make a living, or enter political office. If maternity was a double-edged sword of both opportunity and limitation, why did so many Latin American women utilize this symbolism?

More recent developments identified here also raise questions. Does the recent rise of women presidents since 2000 indicate that Latin American women have broken the so-called glass ceiling in politics? How important is it that Bachelet and Rousseff, in particular, did not draw attention to their roles as mothers or wives, as many politically active women did before them? Does this shift, along with dropping fertility rates, indicate that motherhood no longer holds sway over Latin American societies and politics as it once did? What can the experiences of successful women politicians and rapidly falling fertility rates tell us about what it means to be a woman in Latin America – and what do these facts *fail* to reveal about women in Latin America? In what ways have contemporary Latin American women broken with the past, and in what ways are they building upon it?

Of course, none of the questions above has a simple or straightforward answer. Whether or not women are breaking free of motherhood and overcoming longstanding limitations placed on them depends on *which women* one discusses. In addition to regional or country-specific variations, one must also consider the impact of recent changes on women of different class and race backgrounds. This book seeks, then, not to "answer" but rather to explore the questions above by examining the history of Latin American women from independence through the 1990s via the lens of motherhood. It examines both continuity and change over time, and takes class, race, and regional differences into account. In addition to deepening readers' understanding of the history behind recent developments for women in Latin America, this book also addresses broader questions pertaining to history itself. What can an examination of women – and mothers in particular – teach one about Latin American history? How can the history of Latin America teach one more about motherhood, and in particular, how does it complicate and historicize the term "mother"?

Although Chapter 2 briefly addresses issues of gender in the colonial period, my focus in this book is on the nineteenth and twentieth centuries, mainly after Latin American countries achieved their independence. During the colonial period, although motherhood shaped women's lives in a variety of ways, it remained more of a private or religious issue. It was only with independence that women's identities as mothers came to have particularly powerful significance in social and political movements. The trope of motherhood is tightly intertwined with the history of modern Latin America. When nineteenth- and early twentieth-century state officials denied women the vote, they often did so by asserting that women belonged in the domestic sphere as wives and mothers, rather than in the public sphere of politics (Chapter 2). Women from middling and upper social classes did not always reject the idea that motherhood was at the center of their identities, but they used this notion in a variety of ways that state officials had not anticipated, arguing for greater personal rights and for greater influence in public society (Chapter 4). Yet upper-class gender norms rarely reflected the lives of the majority of women, who were poor and often from non-European backgrounds. For these women, the public and private spheres were not neatly divided, and motherhood was not necessarily the only or even central aspect of their daily identities (Chapter 3). By the early to mid-twentieth century, the themes of motherhood and home life helped political and economic elites to address the dilemmas and fears regarding the dramatic changes that came with industrialization, urbanization, or revolution. Though societies experienced rapid changes, including changes to women's roles in public, official gender discourses highlighted women's ongoing roles as mothers who would uphold morality and maintain traditions (Chapter 5). Thus, motherhood has been a central theme throughout changes in Latin America since independence, though its particular meaning at any given time was subject to change – as are all historical forces. Looking at Latin America through the lens of motherhood allows one to problematize simplistic divisions between public and private spheres, continuity and change, and private lives and political events.

Although motherhood has been an important theme throughout the course of modern Latin American history, it did not have the same meaning in all time periods, let alone in all regions of Latin America or among Latin Americans of different race or class backgrounds. Political, economic, and intellectual elites had a great deal of power to define the parameters of how gender and motherhood discourses developed, but they did not always agree with each other. Even more important, women developed many of their own ideas about what motherhood meant and how it should intersect with politics and the economy. Wealthy or middle-class women were the most likely to take advantage of elite notions about motherhood, in part because it was these women whom politicians and intellectuals identified as "good mothers." Poor women and those of indigenous or African descent utilized certain aspects of elite gender norms regarding motherhood, but they also developed their own ideas about what made one a good mother, and what influence that gave women (or should give women) in society. The particular ways in which women and men of different class, race, and political perspectives engaged the theme of motherhood was further influenced by broader contextual changes in Latin American governments and economies.

Writing a book to address an all-encompassing theme like motherhood in Latin America since independence is an ambitious undertaking, and there is no way to "do everything." Indeed, it is a mistake to try to do so with such a broad topic. Therefore, while readers will find many themes and historiographical works discussed, I lay no claim to summarizing or including the entire field of historical gender studies for Latin America. Similarly, although I take examples from a variety of Latin American countries, I do not attempt to include all of them, nor do I address every revolution, women's movement, or class-specific issue. Some of these other topics are referenced in the bibliography, and all of those not included in this narrative offer a rich set of possibilities for educators' own lectures, or for students' research projects.

Gender as a Category for Historical Analysis

Though many people associate the term gender with women and presume it is based on biology, gender is instead a social construction that pertains to the ideas a particular society holds about what it means to be a man or a woman. More precisely, groups that exercise the greatest political, economic, and social control define the dominant gender norms in a given society. Gender lessons begin extremely early in a child's life, when parents buy clothes and toys that they deem "gender appropriate" for him or her, or when they react negatively if a child crosses over accepted gender boundaries in his or her behavior. Because one learns gender rules so early and consistently, and often subtly rather than directly, by adulthood, gender norms often seem "natural" rather than socially constructed. Motherhood, as a subcategory of gender, is no different. Although one often hears references to "mothers' instincts" and how motherly urges and agendas are natural, in fact, motherhood is as much socially constructed and learned as any other aspect of gender.

In the 1980s, historian Joan Scott developed the now-standard definition of gender when she described it as both "a constitutive element of social relationships based on perceived differences between the sexes," and "a primary field within which or by means of which power is articulated."[7] The first part of Scott's definition indicates that gender is learned rather than natural, and that it influences all of one's social relationships. That means that the relationships between men and women, or any individual's place within the family or society, were (and are) patterned by the gender norms learned in childhood. The second part of Scott's definition, that gender bolsters or expresses power, suggests that individuals and groups can manipulate gender ideas either to demonstrate or try to increase their power relative to others. Gender often functions this way in politics, and not only when women are involved. For example, many constitutions in nineteenth-century Latin America did not allow men to vote who were in a so-called dependent economic position, such as servants and indebted workers; this exclusion stemmed in part from the notion that these men's employers were not simply their bosses, but also father figures who could tell them how to vote. Therefore, ideas about manliness (and the extent to which an individual became a "true man" or remained in "child-like dependence") often influenced voting laws. Because gender is one of the main building blocks in both society and politics, understanding how gender functioned and changed over time is a crucial part of studying history, regardless of the world region or time period on which one focuses.

Motherhood, in particular, is a useful theme for examining "the reproduction of power and the power of reproduction."[8] Reproduction refers to much more than simply women's ability to bear and raise children. Reproduction is a powerful and sometimes contentious force because it is at the heart not just of maintaining and growing families or broader populations, but because it is essential to passing down social and cultural norms. Motherhood is also a means through which power, including political power, is debated, constructed, and maintained. Contraceptive and reproductive laws in Latin America often intersected, for example, with particular cultural agendas in politics during the twentieth century, although sometimes in surprising ways (Chapter 9). State officials' ideas about "good" versus "bad" mothers (which overlapped with their race and class prejudices) were also essential to the development of nineteenth-century nation-making agendas (Chapters 2 and 4). Medical, social, and moral arguments about so-called traditional motherhood were central to easing elite anxieties over the growth of cities and industry in the late nineteenth and early twentieth centuries (Chapters 5 and 6). Even revolutionary leaders manipulated motherhood images in order to advance their broader political agendas (Chapter 7). Finally, although women have sometimes achieved recognition in diverse political movements since the 1970s, and there have been several women presidents in Latin America, motherhood continues to complicate women's overall advancement in national politics (Chapters 8 and 10).

When discussing Latin American gender relations, one often hears about *machismo* and *marianismo*. Though these labels are extreme and problematic – it is difficult, for example, to find individuals (let alone groups) who embody all of the stereotypes associated with such identities – they are commonly used terms and therefore need to be addressed. To do that, it is important first to identify these stereotypes and then analyze the extent to which they do or do not reflect on Latin American gender realities. *Machismo* is perhaps the better known term in the United States, conjuring up images of hypermasculinity among Latin American (or Latino) men who take insult easily. While it is true that machismo is associated with exaggerated masculinity that denies men any access to supposedly "feminine" emotions or actions, the macho also often represents a caring and loving head of household, although often as a strict patriarch. *Marianismo* is in some ways the counterpart of machismo, while in other ways it refers to its own distinct identity. Taking the ideal of the Virgin Mary, who gave her life over to her son Jesus Christ, a marianista is a woman who is ultrafeminine (often described as submissive), self-sacrificing, modest, and deeply religious. She is focused entirely on her husband's and children's needs rather than her own. Motherhood is at the core of this identity; indeed, the idea of marianismo often suggests that a woman has no other identity than that of wife and mother. Children, and sons especially, often become devoted to their saint-like marianista mothers once grown.

As with most stereotypes, references to machismo and marianismo are overstated, oversimplified, and lack a sense of historical context and change. These particular labels appeal most to individuals and groups outside of Latin America, because they allow them to point to things that are supposedly "wrong" in another culture while ignoring similar problems in their own. Although an exhaustive discussion of these stereotypes is outside of the purview of this book, a few main points are important to establish. In addition to the extreme oversimplification of these stereotypes, these typecasts do not fit the evidence one finds in a closer examination of Latin American societies and histories. Although there is evidence dating back to the colonial period of men fighting with each other over access to women or individual pride, these were moments of transgression from ordinary life, not necessarily daily events that defined the men's identity.[9] Generalized references to machismo also fail to account for class and race differentials in male power and attitudes. Large estate owners, for example, made a regular practice of emasculating male workers by both punishing them like children for real or perceived transgressions, and by claiming sexual access to their male employees' wives, sisters, and daughters (see Chapter 2). Further, Latin American history offers examples of men who viewed women as partners and allies, rather than simply as objects of desire or a means to express power. The same man who fought with another at a bar over sexual access to a particular woman might at another time ally himself with both that man and woman in order to protest unfair taxes or other exploitation by powerful elites.

Marianismo is even more heatedly disputed among scholars of Latin America than machismo. Evelyn Stevens first coined the term in 1973 as a way of referring to ideals of the long-suffering woman in Latin America, asserting that this identity allowed women a certain spiritual superiority over men even as it encouraged them to be passive.[10] Other scholars picked up on Stevens' use of marianismo (which ordinarily would simply refer to the cult of the Virgin Mary) as a way of describing women and women's history in Latin America. Though some of them criticized Stevens' use of marianismo as too extreme to fit women's lives and views, they accepted many of her assumptions about marianismo. In 2002, however, Marysa Navarro contended that the concept of marianismo itself was "seriously flawed" as a way of describing women in Latin America, present or past.[11] Among her many arguments against using the term, Navarro asserted that Stevens' work was not well grounded in historical reality. Navarro was particularly critical of the concept of marianismo as both timeless and presenting Latin American women as powerless. She also took issue with Stevens referring to ideas of women's higher morality and spirituality (which she asserted as part of marianismo) as "female chauvinism," indicating that Stevens' work did not take feminist critiques of gender roles into account.[12] Navarro's criticisms of marianismo have a great deal of merit, but at the same time there are numerous examples in Latin American history since independence of political, intellectual, and religious elites who identified women with the home and with self-sacrifice, particularly with regard to their (supposedly natural and central) identities as mothers. Although women's lives certainly did not always fit this stereotype, and many women in Latin American history struggled against it, there were also many ways that women engaged the idea of themselves as long-suffering mothers in order to advance their own interests. Therefore, while Stevens' assertions might be flawed if we take them at face value, many scholars since her essay was written have used the term marianismo to refer to these stereotypes that powerful elites used to justify women's subordination, noting that even when women rejected all or part of this imagery, they were forced to grapple with it.

Therefore, while the terms machismo and marianismo rarely appear in *Mothers Making Latin America* due to their problems and the stereotypes they represent, they remain terms that both scholars and the general public, particularly outside of Latin America, continue to grapple with when trying to understand Latin American gender norms. It is my hope that the discussion and analysis of motherhood presented in this book might allow readers to push past simplistic stereotypes or labels in order to understand and appreciate the complexity of Latin American gender ideas, experiences, and struggles on a more meaningful level.

Even aside from using a term like marianismo, one must be careful when analyzing the politically charged topic of motherhood in modern Latin American history. Despite many elite references to women as long-suffering mothers who willingly sacrificed their own interests for others, there was and is no "natural unity" to women's experiences of motherhood in Latin America, past or present. Political scientist Lorraine Bayard de Volo captured this well in her book on motherhood and politics in Nicaragua from 1979 to 1999, when she wrote, "Because 'women's difference' implies a sense of connection and solidarity with women everywhere, the temptation to conflate gender identities into fixed, pre-political categories can be strong." Yet she warns that although women's identities, particularly around motherhood, may be ever-present, they do not reflect women's varied experiences and agendas. Bayard de Volo therefore asserted that "[i]nstead of focusing on whether women were more peace-loving, relational, and other-oriented than men, I examine when such claims are made, who makes them, and why."[13] *Mothers Making Latin America* takes the same approach: while not assuming that elite discourses on motherhood revealed "the truth" about women's experiences, this book does examine how and why particular elite discourses emerged, and how they changed over time. It also considers how and why women ignored, manipulated, rejected, or altered dominant social ideas about motherhood.

Patriarchy is another term that frequently comes up with reference to Latin American gender relations. Patriarchy indicates a set of social and legal structures in which men are dominant and privileged. Historian Bianca Premo notes that patriarchy "evokes the complex of legal and social relations of power that joined normative models of household governance to the larger legitimacy of [political] rule." In other words, ideas about the supposedly natural authority of parents (particularly fathers) over children, or husbands over wives, were often extended to justify broader political, social, and economic inequalities. One often sees this pattern with regard to slavery in Latin America: elites viewed African-descended slave adults as perpetual children who required the firm control of their so-called European-descended superiors just as children needed to be under their parents' rule.[14]

Unlike machismo or marianismo, patriarchy is a term that refers to a complex set of beliefs and experiences in society and history; it is therefore analytically useful to scholars who evaluate gender ideas and relations around the world. To identify a society as patriarchal does not necessarily indicate that men are all-powerful or that women are completely powerless, nor is patriarchy a fixed or unchanging category in history. Instead, like other aspects of gender, patriarchy is fluid and flexible: the gender laws, ideas, and structures supporting male power systems change over the course of time. In fact, it might be better to think in terms of *patriarchies* in the plural, because ideas and policies of male dominance not only change over time, but also vary according to region and culture. Patriarchy therefore does not refer to an unchanging "thing" in history, but rather to a set of structures and historical processes helping to shape social and political relations of power. It is intricately tied to, and a manifestation of, broader gender ideas and relations as defined by Joan Scott. For Latin America, historian Heidi Tinsman astutely noted that patriarchy has remained vital because of its ties to political power and principle, but in ways that have undergone constant revision and which are, often, contradictory in nature.[15] Although patriarchy is frequently associated more with certain societies and cultures than others, one finds variations of patriarchal models around the world. Consider, for example, that although women can enter any profession in the United States, they still typically make 77 cents on the dollar in relation to men, even in female-dominated fields. Moreover, the best-paying jobs and most powerful political positions are overwhelmingly staffed by men. One should be wary, therefore, of focusing on whether Latin America is "more" or "less" patriarchal than the United States or other regions. It is more analytically sound to attend to the ways in which patriarchy has developed in particular cultures, political situations, and economic conditions. Historians generally find that it is more useful – and results in better history – to analyze societies of the past in their own terms in order to understand how they functioned, rather than to judge them on moral or cultural bases. Gender is yet one more facet in which historians need to be careful to do this.

Relationships, Influences, and Terms

Gender cannot stand alone as a category of analysis, because race and class also helped to determine one's social relations, access to power, and rights within society. Race, like gender, is socially constructed rather than biological. Even when biologists and other scientists discussed race, their descriptions were always shaped by cultural assumptions. For example, scientists, doctors, and politicians who supported the early twentieth-century eugenics movements claimed that scientific methods "proved" the inferiority of nonwhite races, but in fact, the studies were conducted in a way in which the outcome was predetermined by racist assumptions (Chapter 5). Race is also distinct from phenotype, or color. This is particularly evident in Latin America, where a person who has dark skin – but is wealthy and educated – might be considered "whiter" than a lighter-skinned individual who is poor and uneducated. And although class is based on material conditions, how a person's wealth or poverty intersected with rights or reputation was, and remains, a definitively social process.

Thus, what it meant to be a woman, and how a woman was thought of in different parts of society, depended on her race and class status as well as her gender. For instance, in both the colonial period and in the nineteenth century, state officials considered an elite women of European descent as automatically "honorable," whereas they assumed that poor women of African or indigenous descent were dishonorable. This could influence a woman's ability to defend her interests in court, and in particular her rights and needs relative to men in her life: a poor indigenous woman would have to work hard, and provide many witnesses (particularly outside of her own class and race) to convince a judge that she had a good and honorable reputation, whereas the judge would be predisposed to seeing an elite European woman as honorable and therefore deserving of the court's assistance and protection (Chapter 2). Such rules were not absolute, however, and one can find evidence of judges and other administrative officials who intervened on behalf of poor, non-European women and men. Yet even when they did so, state officials' actions were often based on gendered notions about their responsibilities to protect weaker groups within society.

The history of gender in Latin America since independence has often intersected with concepts such as *progress, tradition,* and *modernity.* Anthropologists frequently refer to the fact that traditions are always changing – there are virtually no practices or customs that remain constant over time. Yet the perceptions and beliefs about tradition and modernity impact how people think of and categorize themselves and others. On the surface level, traditional motherhood in Latin America had to do with the idea that women remained in the home and tended to children, rather than going out into the workforce or being involved in politics. It also associated women with Catholic devotion and strict moral codes. Mostly, these ideas centered on the lives of women of the middling or wealthy sectors: poorer women had to work outside the home, so the public and private spheres continually overlapped for them. State officials and intellectual elites also often highlighted women's supposedly natural association with the home more emphatically in times of change when more women were going outside of the home to work, especially in factories (Chapters 5 and 6). Ideas about motherhood continued to influence women's engagements with politics, especially national politics, throughout the twentieth century, and in some ways into the present day (Chapters 8 and 10).

Progress and modernity are also dynamic, complex terms. For example, in late nineteenth-century Latin America, middle-class and elite notions of "progress" focused on emulating European (and US) economic, political, and cultural institutions and practices. These ideas about progress gave certain men of the middling and wealthy sectors new and broader roles in the public sphere, but their impact on women was quite mixed. Some women – mostly from the middling sectors in society – used notions of Europeanized progress to argue for better education and the right to work, and sometimes they succeeded in gaining new rights within marriage and the economy (Chapter 4). Yet in other ways, even middle-sector women were excluded from progress, and many women even experienced a tightening of male authority in their lives (Chapters 2 and 4). For poor women, particularly those of non-European heritage, so-called progress did more than simply leave them behind: elite-driven ideas about progress often identified them, especially in their roles as mothers who allegedly lacked integrity and honor, as threatening to drag the nation down into backwardness. These stereotypes did not necessarily reflect the reality of motherhood among nonelite women, but they did often determine the parameters of poor women's options to address their own or their children's needs (Chapters 2 and 3).

Between the late nineteenth and mid-twentieth centuries, many Latin American societies experienced processes of modernization, and middling and powerful groups often embraced ideas about *modernity*. Some countries, such as Mexico, Argentina, and Brazil, began to industrialize which, in turn, brought urban growth. New roads had to be built to accommodate the rising number of cars and trucks in countries. More consumer goods were available, from movies to modern clothing fashions to home appliances. Science gained extraordinary influence over public policy – and vice versa – as governments struggled to solve problems such as epidemics or urban waste, and to meet the medical needs of people in expanding cities. Doctors gained more power in local and even national government institutions than ever before, particularly with regard to newly created health or social service departments.

Even among elite groups, there were "winners" and "losers" in these processes of urbanization and modernization. In general, states and state officials benefited from these changes, because expanding state institutions – including welfare, education, and health – allowed states to reach into the everyday lives of citizens on an unprecedented level. Scientists and medical professionals also gained a great deal more respect and influence in formal politics during this period. It was not only powerful state, scientific, economic, or medical officials who benefited, however: the expanding state apparatus required a host of new lower- and mid-level officials to carry out new programs and policies, and to staff new state institutions. Because many medical and social welfare institutions concerned themselves with child health and family matters that elites considered part of women's natural domain, women (mostly from middling sectors) were often important contributors – and sometimes leaders – for initiating and maintaining new policies and state-run organizations. Other social and political sectors did not fare as well with urbanization, industrialization, and state expansion. One of the main groups to experience decline was the Catholic Church. It was not that Latin Americans were necessarily less religious than before these processes of modernization, but rather that the state took over many of the charitable and educative roles that the Church once held. Modern industrial and urban developments also had a mixed impact on the poor. On the one hand, movement from the countryside to the city meant, for some individuals, a release from long-standing social rules and community constraints. On the other hand, urban growth sometimes weakened built-in social obligations that could help one through hard times. Additionally, material conveniences and pleasures – such as new appliances, movie halls, or fashions – that allowed members of the urban middle and upper classes to measure their success or escape everyday reality were out of reach for poor urbanites. Instead, they often struggled with insufficient or unsafe housing, and underemployment or poor pay. It was also the urban poor who suffered the most from epidemics and other health problems. Furthermore, most people continued to live in the countryside, where it was far more difficult to receive new health, educational, and social services than it was in cities.

Women were often caught between tradition and modernity in this period. A so-called modern working woman, especially from one of the middling economic groups, often felt pressure to maintain traditional home-bound values: if she did not, she might face criticism for abandoning her moral and maternal duties (Chapter 5). A woman who stayed at home faced pressure to modernize her mothering by incorporating the latest scientific practices in child-rearing. In the early twentieth century, mothers might be expected to learn very specific and "modern" hygiene practices, and to buy newly available (and expensive) appliances and other consumer goods. In general, women typically faced more criticism than men if they embraced modern ways at the expense of their so-called traditional roles (Chapter 5). Poor mothers fared worse: new medical and state discourses often blamed poor mothers themselves for unhygienic or unsafe conditions that put their children in jeopardy, rather than looking to poverty as the cause for child illness and mortality (Chapter 6).

What's Feminism Got to Do With It?

Although scholars have long discussed and debated the relationships between motherhood and feminism, it is easy to find references – in newspapers, on television, or on the internet – that asserts a strong correlation between motherhood and so-called antifeminism. This association presumes that feminism is aimed primarily at rejecting all traditional gender norms and focuses on women's roles in the economy and politics. Yet both motherhood and feminism are more complicated than this, particularly in Latin America, where the term feminism is intertwined with multifaceted class–race and international issues, as well as with politics and values.

What, then, is feminism? The term first emerged in the mid-nineteenth century, though it did not take on its modern meaning until the early decades of the twentieth century. It was only with the First International Women's Conference in Paris in 1892 that the term came to be used regularly as a reference to those working to improve women's rights within society and to oppose women's oppression. Like motherhood, feminism has had many different definitions and meanings over the course of history, and even within a particular historical period or world region. Historian Karen Offen's article on divergent definitions and paths of feminism in the United States and Britain versus France and continental Europe in the late nineteenth and early twentieth centuries provides a particularly insightful discussion of how and why feminism is difficult to define. On the one hand, British and US feminists focused on what Offen labeled *individualist feminism*, in which women's rights advocates sought political, legal, and economic rights that were equal to those of men. Offen interpreted this as using the "standard of male adulthood" as the norm for women's goals. This approach to women's rights, and subsequent definition of feminism, resulted from historical contexts that were specific to Britain and the United States in the late nineteenth century, such as having a relatively large population of single, educated women who wanted greater individual autonomy in their lives. Also important was the fact that these two nations benefited from the growth of industrial capitalism that led to a prosperous middle class. On the other hand, in France and other parts of continental Europe, women's rights advocates concentrated on what Offen calls *relational feminism*, which emphasized giving women increased rights "as women" rather than trying to gain rights equal to men. This approach often emphasized women's roles as mothers, and accepted that women and men were inherently different and that their distinctive labors complemented each other. Relational feminists on the European continent were less concerned with winning equal rights as they were with improving women's rights as mothers and wives. By the twentieth century, Offen notes, these two divergent tracks of feminism conflicted more often, with individualist feminists accusing relational feminists of being "antifeminist" and upholding male privilege, whereas relational feminists often criticized individualist feminists for being egotistical and "unwomanly."[16] Ultimately, it was the British- and US-style individualist feminism that became the model on which definitions of feminism developed. The *Stanford Encyclopedia of Philosophy*, for example, defined feminism as working for women's rights based on the idea of equality between the sexes.[17]

Offen proposed a broader definition of feminism that could encompass these two divergent movements. She viewed feminism as an ideology in its own right (not simply attached to other sociopolitical movements) "based on a critical analysis of male privilege and women's subordination in a given society." Therefore, she considered that anyone who was a feminist who recognized the "validity of women's own interpretations of lived experiences and needs," sought to eliminate injustices of women by men, and challenged the gender status quo.[18] Although her definition and comparisons were based only on women's movements in Europe and the United States, Offen's analysis and definition of feminism provide a useful starting point for contemplating the role of feminists and feminism in Latin American history and, in particular, how they related to the theme of motherhood.

Latin American women's movements of the late nineteenth and early twentieth centuries had more in common with relational than individualist feminism. While one can find evidence of feminists who sought equal rights with men, far more women's rights advocates of the period emphasized women's motherhood roles as important to the nation and used this as the basis on which to argue for better education and rights within marriage (Chapter 4). By the early twentieth century, divisions emerged among women's rights advocates, with some groups beginning to emphasize gaining equal political and economic rights with men. The association of women's rights and importance with motherhood did not necessarily endure throughout the twentieth century among all feminist groups, but these historical foundations do help to explain the emergence of maternalist political movements in the late twentieth century (Chapter 8). However, one should be careful not to assume that Latin American feminists were simply following the path of relational feminists in

Europe. Instead, Latin American women's rights groups developed their ideas out of the specific historical, political, and social contexts in which they lived.

By the early twentieth century, socialist feminism had also taken root in many Latin American countries, especially those that were undergoing processes of industrialization. Unlike moderate feminists who sought only greater rights as women within existing political and economic systems, socialist feminists embraced Marxist (or Marxist-Leninist) arguments that in order to change social inequalities, it was first necessary to overthrow capitalism and the governments that buoyed capitalist production. In particular, socialist feminists paid more attention to the plight of working-class women, and especially women factory workers, than more moderate (usually middle-class) feminists generally did. However, although socialist leaders were in theory committed to women's equality, they often prioritized economic issues that were more relevant to men than to problems that they deemed exclusively "women's concerns."

Not all women's rights advocates have embraced feminism, either as a term for describing their goals or as a label on which to hang their identity. Resistance to the term came from both conservative and radical ends of the political spectrum. By the mid- to late twentieth century, most conservative women viewed feminism as going against woman's nature and flying in the face of what they saw as an "inherent" difference between the sexes. Even if they sought political power, these women were careful to identify themselves more with traditional women's roles, and particularly with home life (Chapter 8). Feminism also continued to be both central to and problematic within socialism, even (perhaps especially) in countries in which socialist revolutions occurred (in Latin America, this included Cuba, Nicaragua, and – briefly – Chile). Although socialist governments usually claim to seek gender equality, they have sometimes reinforced rather than eradicated gender differences (Chapter 7). Moreover, socialists often continue to reject the term feminism itself due to their association with a focus on women's rights as bourgeois.

Many poor women – particularly those of indigenous or African descent – likewise refuse to identify as feminists. Historically, there seemed to be no political space in feminist movements for indigenous or Afro-Latin American poor women. Feminists, usually from the middle sectors of society, often ignored the persistent economic problems that were central in poor women's daily lives, and most refused to acknowledge how racism affected women. Socialist leaders claimed to support women's equality, but in practice tended to marginalize these concerns. Many socialists – though not all – also ignored how racism influenced class and gender experiences. Since the 1970s and 1980s, however, ethnic-based political activism has been on the rise, especially among Latin American indigenous groups. These activists have combined class and cultural concerns, and women have sometimes achieved high leadership positions. Even so, feminism remains largely taboo among these groups, because they associate the term with western values and upper-class agendas. Many indigenous or Afro-Latin American women assume that "feminism" indicates a war between women and men, and they assert that they are interested in working alongside their male peers rather than fighting against them. Even though indigenous and Afro-American women's goals often overlap with feminist goals, the two groups have remained largely separate (Chapter 8).

Motherhood was an ever-present, though sometimes muted, part of these feminist organizations, both advancing their agendas and setting limits on their achievements. Nineteenth-century feminists, for example, celebrated women's roles as mothers and accepted that motherhood gave women a different destiny from men, one ultimately geared toward the private sphere (Chapter 4). In the twentieth century, feminists often conflicted more directly with notions that women should remain at home and identify mainly with motherhood. Their supposedly "modern" notions often came under criticism from conservative politicians and social thinkers (Chapter 5). Assumptions about motherhood also shaped resistance to feminism on the other end of the political spectrum. In Cuba, for example, socialist leaders rejected ideas about women staying in the home with children and pressured them to enter the wage labor force – promising structural support to enable mothers to work, but often falling short of providing adequate facilities (Chapter 7). Within indigenous organizations, motherhood is both highlighted and problematic: on the one hand, women's association with motherhood makes them important bearers of cultural continuity; on the other hand, motherhood responsibilities often make it difficult for women to participate actively in politics (Chapter 8).

Since the 1980s and 1990s, many Latin American feminists have strived to overcome earlier limitations, particularly around race and class dynamics, and one sometimes sees overtures rather than conflict between feminist and class- or ethnic-based political movements. All the while, motherhood remains an important undercurrent in Latin American politics, either by encouraging individuals and groups to overcome differences or by exacerbating political divisions.

Motherhood and the Course of Latin American History

Rather than indicate "only what happened in homes," the theme of motherhood challenges historians to think beyond neat divides between public and private spheres. In order to understand the significance of home life, and how women's experiences changed over time, one must place domestic concerns within the broader context of political, economic, social, and demographic changes over the course of Latin American history. Consideration of culturally specific gender and family ideas is also necessary. Yet broad historical shifts were themselves influenced by both ideas about motherhood and by mothers, and this too requires attention. The chapters that follow both question historical events and seek to deepen readers' understanding of them. Early chapters follow a roughly chronological order, paying close attention to class–race differences in the history of motherhood. Later chapters deal primarily with themes that have dominated gender history in Latin America in the mid- to late twentieth century, considering their influences on women of a variety of backgrounds within each chapter. All of these chapters aim to help readers better understand how this history helps to explain why motherhood – in Latin America and around the world – remains a politically important and charged subject in the current day, a concern which is addressed in the epilogue.

Notes

1 Jo Fisher, *Mothers of the Disappeared* (Boston: South End Press, 1989), 18–19.
2 The translation of this excerpt from Bachelet's victory speech is from Karin Alejandra Rosemblatt, "Verónica Michelle Bachelet Jeria: A Woman President," in Erin E. O'Connor and Leo J. Garofalo, eds, *Documenting Latin America, Volume 2: Gender, Race, and Nation* (Upper Saddle River, NJ: Prentice Hall/Pearson, 2011), especially pp. 264–265.

3   This quotation appears in Marcel Ríos Tobar, "Chilean Feminism and Social Democracy from the Democratic Transition to Bachelet," *NACLA Report on the Americas* 40:2 (March–April 2007), p. 25.

4   Susan Franceschet, "El triunfo de Bachelet y el ascenso politico de las mujeres," *Nueva Sociedad* 202 (Marzo–Abril 2006), p. 14. Other women presidents included Isabel Perón in Argentina (1974–1976), Violeta Chamorro in Nicaragua (1990–1997), and Mireya Moscoso in Panama (1999–2004). There were also two other women who filled the presidential seat on an interim basis: Lidia Gueiler Tejada in Bolivia (1979–1980) and Rosalia Arteaga in Ecuador (1997).

5   Samuel Schleier, "Latin America's Demographic Divergence," http://www.newgeography.com/content/002874-latin-america%E2%80%99s-demographic-divergence (last accessed November 7, 2013).

6   Alicia Adsera and Alicia Menendez, "Fertility Changes in Latin America in the Context of Economic and Political Uncertainty," at http://paa2006.princeton.edu/papers/61407 (last accessed November 7, 2013).

7   Joan Wallach Scott, "Gender: A Useful Category for Historical Analysis" in *Gender and the Politics of History* (New York: Columbia University Press, 1988), pp. 42, 45.

8   Marcia Stephenson, *Gender and Modernity in Andean Bolivia* (Austin: University of Texas Press, 1999), p. 20.

9   One of the ground-breaking examinations of masculinity and male violence is William B. Taylor's book, *Drinking, Homicide, and Rebellion in Colonial Mexican Villages* (Stanford, CA: Stanford University Press, 1979). Taylor does discuss masculine pride in fights and homicide between men, but he identifies this as taking place in "time out" situations while drinking, especially for men who were drinking outside of their home communities in Mexico City.

10 Evelyn P. Stevens, "*Marianismo*: The Other Face of Machismo," in Ann Pescatello ed., *Female and Male in Latin America* (Pittsburgh, PA: Pittsburgh University Press, 1973), pp. 89–101.

11 Marysa Navarro, "Against Marianismo," in Rosario Montoya, Lessie Jo Frazier, and Janise Hurtig, eds, *Gender's Place: Feminist Anthropologies of Latin America* (New York: Palgrave MacMillan, 2002), p, 257.

12 Navarro, pp. 267–268 for Navarro's reference to "female chauvinism" versus feminist discourses. Other claims were made throughout the essay.

13 Lorraine Bayard de Volo, *Mothers of Heroes and Martyrs: Gender Identity and Politics in Nicaragua, 1979–1999* (Baltimore: Johns Hopkins University Press, 2001), p. 15.

14 Bianca Premo, *Children of the Father King: Youth, Authority, and Legal Minority in Colonial Lima* (Chapel Hill: University of North Carolina Press, 2005), p. 10.

15 Heidi Tinsman, "A Paradigm of Our Own: Joan Scott in Latin American History," *American Historical Review* 113:5 (December 2008), p. 1368.

16 Karen Offen, "Defining Feminism: A Comparative Historical Approach," *Signs* 14:1 (Autumn, 1988), pp. 119–157.

17 "Topics in Feminism," from the *Stanford Encyclopedia of Philosophy*, available at: http://plato.stanford.edu/entries/feminism-topics (last accessed November 7, 2012).

18 Offen, pp. 151–152.

2

Motherhood in Transition
From Colonies to Independent Nations

Why Is Manuela Sáenz Problematic as a "Founding Mother" from Independence?

Manuela Sáenz was born in Quito (in what is now the nation of Ecuador) in 1797, the illegitimate daughter of parents of the elite class. Though her baptismal record listed her as an *expósita* (foundling), her father informally recognized her as his own, provided her with an education and a dowry, and expected her to marry the man of his choosing – English merchant James Thorne. Sáenz married Thorne according to her father's wishes and moved with him to Lima. There she became an early supporter of the independence cause, mostly in ways that were deemed acceptable for a woman of her standing: she gathered and sent to independence leaders any information on Spanish royalist actions and strategies that she could, and she held *tertulias* (intellectual gatherings) where independence sympathizers could gather and discuss their views. In 1822, she traveled with her father to her home city of Quito. There, she met independence leader Simón Bolívar, and the two began a passionate affair that lasted until Bolívar's death in 1830. In addition to their love affair, Sáenz acted as a spy and confidant for Bolívar, and she served as secretary for Bolívar's archive. She even saved his life on two occasions. Sáenz often followed Bolívar's army during the independence wars in her capacity as archival secretary. Most scholars agree that she also nursed wounded soldiers, and some believe that she fought on at least a few

Mothers Making Latin America: Gender, Households, and Politics Since 1825,
First Edition. Erin E. O'Connor.
© 2014 John Wiley & Sons, Inc. Published 2014 by John Wiley & Sons, Inc.

occasions. After independence, she lived with Bolívar for a time and continued to serve as an important link between Bolívar and those who wished to earn his favor. After Bolívar's death in 1830, she went into exile and spent most of her remaining years in northern Peru. From there, she continued to correspond with one of Ecuador's most important political leaders of the period, Juan José Flores, and assisted him in any way that she could by offering him advice and information from afar. She died in a yellow fever outbreak in 1856 and, along with other victims of the epidemic, was buried in a mass grave.[1]

Although Sáenz exercised considerable influence during the independence movement, she was largely forgotten following her death. Historians and nonacademic authors only rediscovered Sáenz in the twentieth century, at which time they referred to her either as an immoral and unfeminine woman who did little to help Bolívar, or as a heroine of independence whose love and devotion for Bolívar were without limits. In the 1980s, feminists also became interested in Sáenz, identifying her as a "precursor" to feminism and women's emancipation – a kind of mother figure for the women's movement as it were.[2] Manuela Sáenz was first ignored, and later either vilified or glorified, because she did not fit neatly into any stereotyped category of womanhood. Instead, authors made claims about Sáenz that fit their own gender and nationalist views and agendas. In contrast, historians of the early twenty-first century have pointed out that Sáenz was neither a powerless victim nor a pioneer for women's rights. Rather, she was a woman who was able to manipulate gender norms – sometimes adhering to them, at others rejecting them – in order to advance her personal *and political* interests.[3]

The controversies over how to evaluate Sáenz in Andean history highlights differences between "Fathers" and "Mothers" of nations. Although his peers and later historians recognized that Bolívar was a "ladies' man" who had numerous affairs with women, none of them gave this more than passing thought. What was more important to them was the fact that Bolívar was a skilled military leader and a political visionary – granted, his political visions for large federations in Latin America did not come to fruition, but he is recalled for these ideas just the same. It was completely different for Manuela Sáenz, whose contributions and skills were overlooked in favor of scrutiny of her morals and personal life. As a woman without children, and as one who rejected her assigned role in life as wife to James Thorne, her peers and later historians found her "unfit" to serve as a mother-figure to emerge from independence.

Even most of those who praised her simply saw her as a romantic figure, an appendage to Bolívar, rather than an active and intelligent patriot in her own right.[4] Most feminists also did not capture the reality of Sáenz's life, since did not fight for women's rights in any collective sense. In fact, her argument for allowing women some influence in politics rested on the idea that because women did not vote or hold office, they were disinterested enough to give sound advice to male political friends. Such reasoning assumed that women should not act directly in the political sphere.[5] Therefore, even historians and activists who claimed Sáenz as "mother" to nations did so by distorting who Sáenz was as an actual historical figure.

Sáenz may have been one of the most famous women to influence independence movements, but she was far from the only one. Women often played crucial roles in the Spanish American wars of independence. Some of them, especially among the elite and middle sectors of society, stayed within the bounds of "proper womanhood" in their actions and commitments. These women gave monetary support, served as spies, sewed uniforms, and sacrificed their husbands and adult sons to the cause. Other women followed armies and tended the wounded; they too were fulfilling accepted "feminine" roles by extending their supposedly natural instincts to nurture and sacrifice themselves when they nursed soldiers. Most of the women with the armies, though, were poorer women, usually indigenous or mestiza, known as *camp followers*. These women were the daughters, girlfriends, or wives of rank and file soldiers, not officers. They followed their men, feeding and consoling them as they marched and fought. Generally, these women remained within an accepted spectrum of actions according to their class, race, and status. Yet Manuela Sáenz was not unique in crossing over gender lines: Evangelista Tamayo, for example, fought under Bolívar and even earned the rank of captain before her death on the battlefield. Other women were willing to fight on behalf of independence but were turned away by military leaders who believed women were too weak to fight.[6] Bolívar himself wrote to his sister that women did not belong in politics, but rather the home. His views identified women with the domestic sphere, regardless of the fact that his lover was one of his political confidants, and that there were women in the ranks of his armies.

This tendency to identify women primarily with domesticity and motherhood continued in virtually all official and historical accounts of independence in the nineteenth century. Writers usually identified women as victims, bravely facing adversity during a war in which – according to the men who recounted independence events – royalist soldiers threatened not only to imprison, but also rape, honorable virgins and wives. They often spent as much, if not more, time discussing women patriots' beauty and romanticism as they did their actions, and emphasized that the women embraced the sacrifices that the situation demanded of them.[7] In this view, "good" women contributed to independence in a supportive role, leaving combat and politics to men. Such accounts identified women with a particular brand of self-sacrifice that was linked with either literal or figurative motherhood. If she was a mother, she sacrificed her sons to the cause. If she was a young, virginal woman, she willingly supported the cause in a proper womanly fashion, and she did so knowing that she might have to sacrifice being a wife and mother someday if the cause lost many young men. There was no room in these discourses for women who wanted to fight, or who failed to live up to elite notions of ideal womanhood.

Official accounts of women's relationships to independence raise a number of questions about how the transition from colonies to independent states affected Latin American women and gender relations. Why did these men identify women participants in independence as self-sacrificing maternal figures? To what extent did such classifications build on colonial gender norms? To what extent did they represent new ideas about gender, maternity, and family – or, at least, provide new significance for long-standing ideas about gender? What impact did independence have on women and their rights? What role did motherhood play in the transformations from colony to republic? In order to answer these questions, it is necessary to explore colonial gender norms, the centrality of gender to nation making, and developing ideas about the relationship between motherhood and nation over the course of the nineteenth century.

Gender and Power in the Colonial Period

When the Spanish and Portuguese colonized in the Americas, they brought their cultural values and rules with them, including gender norms. Gendered notions of power, protection, and privilege were essential components that shaped colonial laws and policies. They also had a great influence on individuals' lives, although in quite different manners on the European elite than on indigenous peoples or peoples of African descent.

Conquest and colonization were exceptionally hard on indigenous women, because Iberian gender norms were more restricting for women than those found in many indigenous societies. For example, although Aztec and Inca societies associated women with motherhood and with certain aspects of domesticity, women also maintained rights over land and often held important roles within their respective economies. In the Andes (home of the Incas), land was inherited through parallel descent, with daughters inheriting from mothers and sons from fathers. Religion was similar, with complementary male and female gods, and with powerful priestesses in charge of worship of goddesses. In Mexico (home of the Aztecs), women's access to political power was very limited, but they had strong roles in medicine and the marketplace. Moreover, a woman who died in childbirth was revered similarly to a warrior who died bravely in battle. In both empires, wives maintained identities and rights that gave them a certain amount of independence.[8] When the Spanish arrived and conquered these empires, they brought with them stricter gender norms than indigenous peoples had previously practiced. With the exception of times that male heirs were absent and a woman became queen, Iberian law kept women out of politics. Similarly, the Catholic Church allowed only men to serve as priests and in the Church hierarchy, whereas women were relegated to convents where they were (largely) secluded from society and had to answer to male Church officials. For indigenous women, Spanish conquest often meant the loss of independent rights, political influence, and religious prestige.

Motherhood was also at the center of the collision and blending of European and indigenous cultures. It was Spanish men who, with the help of indigenous allies, conquered the Aztec and Inca empires. During the process of conquest, Spaniards sometimes received indigenous women as "gifts" to forge alliances or at least good will. The most famous – and controversial – of such women was Doña Marina, or Malinche, who was a gift to Cortés, and who helped him as a translator during the process of the conquest of Mexico.[9] Moreover, Spanish men – like men in many cultures – viewed sexual access to women as one of the benefits of military victory. Even after conquest, few Spanish women arrived in the American empire during the sixteenth century, and Spanish men often sought indigenous women for sex. In some cases, real relationships developed, and in a few instances when Spanish men even married indigenous women of the high nobility. It was far more common, however, that indigenous women suffered rape or other forms of force and coercion when they became sexual partners to Spanish men. As a result of these practices, many indigenous women gave birth to Spanish men's children. These were the first *mestizos* in Spanish America, children of both European and indigenous heritage. Though mestizos were biologically mixed, in the early colonial period, most of them grew up as either Spanish (when recognized by their fathers) or as indigenous (in those cases when they were not). Many times, if a Spanish father recognized his child, he would separate the child from its mother. This was practiced regularly in Cuzco (Peru), where mestiza daughters were raised in convents in order to learn Spanish ways and, their fathers hoped, to make good marriages with Spanish men.[10] Over time, the mestizo population grew and became in important category in between the colonizing Spanish and the colonized indigenous peoples. Whether they raised these children or had to give them up to Spaniards, indigenous mothers of mestizos played a critical role in the cultural development of Spanish America.

Indigenous women also found themselves more limited in their property rights than they had been before conquest. Although Iberian law codes maintained that husbands and wives owned all marital property jointly, the law also gave husbands far more rights to control property than wives. Both sons and daughters were under their fathers' rule until they came of majority age or married (this was the *patria potestad*, or legal power of the father). Once they were of majority age or married, men had a great deal of autonomy in their economic transactions and were able to represent their own interests in civil matters. For women, however, this was different. Married women could own, inherit, and bequeath property, but their husbands had the legal right and obligation to administer their property and to represent their wives' interests in civil matters.

In both Spanish America and Brazil, husbands were legally required to manage marital finances in such a way as to advance their wives' interests. In Brazil, husbands were even supposed to consult their wives before engaging in financial transactions like selling property or goods that the couple owned. However, judges often assumed that a wife had consented to such transactions, and they rarely checked to confirm this with wives.[11] In Spanish America, however, wives did have some recourse if their husbands used their money improperly, especially with regard to their dowries. Although one often thinks of a dowry as a gift that a woman brought to her husband in marriage, Spanish law identified it as a woman's property which, although her husband was allowed to administer it, was supposed to be maintained in case a woman should find herself in financial need. Given that wives were often quite a bit younger than husbands in colonial Latin America, the dowry might be a critical resource for a widowed woman with children. On these grounds, women in colonial Quito were often able to go to court and gain independent control of their dowries, arguing that their husbands were not tending properly to their wives' economic interests. Widowed women, in both Spanish America and Brazil, had the right to control property and represent themselves in court.

Historical scholarship reveals that there was no unified "women's experience" in colonial Latin America, even with regard to women's rights before the law. Instead, these experiences differed according to region and by class or ethnic identity. For example, widowhood rights appear to have been challenged more frequently in Brazil than in at least some parts of Spanish America.[12] Also, since judges held the power to decide whether a husband maintained control of marital goods or if his wife gained some economic independence, practices might have varied widely around women's economic rights even within Spanish America. Furthermore, many women did not marry legally, and therefore their male partners did not have the same claim to power over them that married women's husbands did. Finally, women who entered into informal relationships rather than marrying maintained greater economic independence in business matters and rights to their children. However, most of these women were of middling and poorer classes who struggled to make ends meet, making their independence less powerful than it was for elite widows. Even some married women did not act in accordance with laws and gender norms. For example, there is some evidence that Iberian gender norms did not necessarily change indigenous women's roles in controlling property or businesses, at least in the Andes.[13]

Gender-specific Spanish and Portuguese notions of *honor* helped to shape both the laws described above and also colonial women's various lived experiences. An honorable man came from a good family (in the Americas, this was identified as having "pure blood," or *limpieza de sangre*), a distinction that was founded on the Iberian Peninsula during the centuries-long reconquest of territory from Muslim rulers. Limpieza de sangre was a reference to and individual or family that was purely of

Christian background. The term continued to have a religious meaning during the colonial period but, over time, it also had racial undertones, indicating that families were fully European, rather than containing any indigenous or African ancestry. A good man also had enough money to provide for a household without having to do any physical labor himself. He was in control of the dependents in his household, which included not only his wife and children, but also any servants and extended family that lived under his roof. As a powerful patriarch, he was also expected to treat his dependents fairly and provide adequately for them – among the elite, this would mean maintaining an expected level of comfort and luxury for his family members.

An elite woman's honor pertained in part to her devotion to the Catholic Church and prayer, but it was centrally focused on her sexuality: virginity before marriage, faithfulness during marriage, and chastity as a widow. Control of women's sexuality had a clear purpose: families, both nuclear and extended, were the means through which fortunes and status were made and maintained. In order for a man to be certain that the children his wife bore were his legitimate heirs who deserved a rightful share of inheritance, he needed to know that only he had sexual access to her. Over time, of course, Spanish and Portuguese elite honor codes developed many different facets and intricacies. Men, for example, had to uphold a virile public image, and it was a blow to one's honor to have to back down in a contest to fight another man. Honor also came to dictate that an elite woman could not be seen alone in public, lest someone suspect that she was having an illicit sexual affair. In short, honor was not just about one's actions but rather about his or her public reputation. Moreover, an individual's honor did not only affect him or herself. If an elite woman were to have sex before marriage, her actions would negatively impact her family's status in addition to ruining her own chances of making a good marriage. Although elite notions of honor affected both men and women, historian Karen Powers pointed out that while men could earn honor in the colonial period, women could only maintain or lose it.[14]

Motherhood was at the heart of female honor. If a woman was a virgin until marriage and was faithful to her husband, the children she bore to him (and these might be many in a woman's lifetime) not only expanded their family, but reinforced both her own and her husband's honor. While this honor derived from her sexual propriety and reproductive capacity, mostly it rested on having her elite peers recognize her as a faithful and honorable woman and mother. The reverse was also true: if a young elite woman had sex before marriage, it was not the act itself that would necessarily lead to scandal and dishonor, but rather the risk of pregnancy. A child outside of wedlock was clear-cut evidence of a woman's dishonor. Yet because honor was about reputation and public perception, there were choices available to an elite woman who found herself unmarried and pregnant. One option was to marry the man who had fathered her child, which often, though not always, was a man to whom she was engaged. Colonial records include baptisms for babies born to a couple only a few months after their marriage. Once a couple was married, that child was legitimate in the eyes of the law. If the baby's father would not marry the woman – or could not, either because he was already married or was in the priesthood – then the family had to take other action in order to maintain a woman's honor. This might be a case in which an elite woman would be willing to marry a man somewhat below her station if he would agree to raise her child as his own. Alternately, the young woman could make plans to travel for a period long enough to hide her pregnancy and give birth to her child away from the scrutiny of her social equals. In a case like this, the woman and her family might carefully select a couple to adopt the child and raise it, perhaps interacting with the child as a family friend as he/she grew up.[15] Other children were left in *casas de expósitos* (foundling homes) or deposited at convents – in the latter case putting virginal nuns in the position of mothering children.[16] Any of these alternatives, carried out successfully, would save a young woman from shame and scandal. Her honor would remain intact, because she had maintained the appearance of sexual propriety in the public eye. For this reason, many historians emphasize that honor was not an "all or nothing" category: lost honor was a significant blow, but it was in certain circumstances possible to overcome compromised honor in order to regain it either partially or fully.

Some individual elite women rejected, in whole or in part, the limitations placed on them. The most respectable way for a woman to escape marriage, motherhood, and living under a patriarch's direct rule was to enter the convent. Most famous woman who chose this option was Sor Juana Inés de la Cruz in Mexico. Sor Juana was an illegitimate daughter born to elite parents whose greatest desire was for education. Having learned at her brothers' side as a child, she often mastered material faster than they did. When she was 16, well-respected scholars in Mexico City examined her and were unable to stump her with their questions.

However, because she was female, university education and scholarly life were unavailable to her. Her only other honorable option, given that she was disinclined to marry or have children, was to enter the convent. There, women had greater access to education and independence, albeit within the hierarchical and male-dominated framework of the Catholic Church. Even in the convent, however, her superiors often forced Sor Juana to limit her studies, and she gave them up altogether shortly before dying.[17] Another famous "woman" who bucked the system was Catalina de Erauso, who was born to a lesser noble family in Spain. De Erauso was raised in a convent, which she escaped as a youth. She cut her hair, dressed as a man, and had many adventures in the Americas before confessing (in order to avoid execution for murder) that she was a woman. Instead of being punished, the Spanish king rewarded de Erauso for service in the Americas, and the pope allowed de Erauso to continue to dress as a man.[18]

Sor Juana and Catalina de Erauso were extreme examples of women who rejected limitations placed on them, but even they did not reject gender norms entirely. Sor Juana chose a respectable route for an elite woman when she entered the convent, and in the long term she succumbed to pressures to give up her studies. De Erauso rejected womanhood, but not gender norms: she/he embraced and performed a strictly male identity, and even referred to him/herself in the masculine in her/his memoir. Most women, however, resisted limits placed on them by working within the system rather than protesting against it. An elite woman might exercise influence in politics through family connections, avoiding impropriety by acting in an informal manner. Similarly, she might be actively engaged in business matters, but formally (on paper and in court) defer to her husband's role as provider and decision-maker, even if that was not his role in actuality. The convent also provided many women with the means to be technically secluded while having a great influence on the secular world through business transactions with and loans made to individuals in the outside world.[19]

If elite women were expected to remain chaste outside of marriage and faithful within it, elite men had no such limitations set on them. As long as an elite man kept his affairs discreet – again, honor was all about appearances – he could have a mistress, even a long-term one. As in the conquest period, concubines were usually of non-European descent and from relatively poor backgrounds. Indigenous servants or African slaves were often subject to their masters' sexual demands, without much recourse in cases of force. Sometimes, though, when there was mutual affection between an elite man and his mistress, he might help her out by providing her with money to keep her quietly and moderately comfortable. When children were born to such unions, an elite man could, at his own discretion, decide whether or not to recognize his child legally. Doing so might provide illegitimate children with an inheritance (though far less than any that his legitimate children would receive), or at the very least give them access to their father's financial and networking support in order to help sons to establish professions and daughters to marry well. Occasionally, especially if a mistress was of elite status, a father might decide to raise the child in his own household, alongside his legitimate children. This of course was complicated for the women involved – one having to give up her child in favor of his or her better opportunities in her lover's household, the other having to help raise a child born out of her husband's affair to another woman.

It was a far different matter for an elite woman to have an extramarital affair. In that case, the paternity of her child would be uncertain, which would put her husband into the most dishonorable position: a cuckold raising another man's child. Therefore, although Catholic doctrine taught that men and women should both be pure before marriage and faithful within marriage, elite society embraced a sexual double standard for men versus women. Spanish law reinforced elite double standards by stipulating that a man who caught his wife in the act of having an affair could kill both his wife and her lover without legal repercussions.[20] Such a rule applied most stringently to elite households; poorer couples certainly had their conflicts, and having an affair was complicated for a woman, because she might be abandoned by both men while pregnant. Yet poor, non-European women had greater freedom of movement and greater control over their own sexuality than elite women. Nonelite women were thus both disadvantaged and advantaged within the intricate web of colonial gender norms. On the one hand, whereas elite men (including court officials) considered elite women honorable unless proven otherwise, they presumed that nonelite women were dishonorable unless several, preferably elite, witnesses testified to a particular poor woman's honorable actions and reputation. On the other hand, nonelite women could act more independently in public and challenge their husbands' actions more directly than elite women were able to do.

The rigidity of elite double standards concerning honor and sexuality should not be taken to indicate that women and mothers were powerless in the colonial period. There is ample evidence that women were often active members of colonial society, particularly with regard to ensuring the rights and needs of their children. The ways in which colonial women exerted power or influence, however, depended on their class–race station in life. While technically men had legal power over their children until they reached the age of majority, mothers often had influence over their children as well. They might, for example, have power via the inheritance that they could leave to their children from their own assets. In some cases, husbands granted their wives guardianship over children in their wills. Elite widows were often powerful figures in colonial Latin America, able to wield independent economic power, and to preside over their extended families as powerful matrons protecting their children's interests.[21] Nonelite women had greater freedom to form and change their families, but they were also more vulnerable with their aims of protecting and providing for their children, both because they were typically in informal unions and because of economic need. Widowhood, for poor women, was a time of economic insecurity that rendered them and their children vulnerable.

The experiences and powers of colonial women therefore varied a great deal according to class and race, and the particular circumstances in which a woman found herself – especially with regard to the man with whom she married or set up house. The colonial state system was patriarchal, providing men with significant, but not absolute, power over their wives and children. Women had room to maneuver within this system and they, like men, were subjects of the king, who was the ultimate paternal authority. Women's association with the home and motherhood continued into the nineteenth century; however, the meanings of these associations were often transformed, as is evidence with legal developments of the postindependence period.

For Better or Worse? Gender, Law, and Nation in the Nineteenth Century

Historians have debated, sometimes quite heatedly, the extent to which the shift from colonies to independent republics changed women's lives and rights in Latin America. For a long time, scholars asserted that any limitations that women faced in the nineteenth century were the result of colonial-era laws; this suggested that gender history was static. Other scholars have argued that women gained more rights in the nineteenth century, and yet others asserted that any changes were typically detrimental rather than beneficial for women.[22] Most recently, there have been historians who have reexamined the colonial period and asserted that women had considerable ability to "work the system" in the colonial period, and that patriarchal restrictions tightened considerably only after independence.[23]

Though seemingly at odds, these different historical interpretations all add different pieces to the puzzle, allowing one to begin to put together a clearer and more meaningful picture of what the transition from colonies to republics meant for women in Latin America. The arrival of independence did, as historian Chad Black notes, accelerate "the long and contested slide in [women's] legal rights" resulting in a liberal commitment to rule of law and governments that more closely adhered to patriarchal rules and structures than in the colonial period.[24] Ironically, new republican laws, claiming to provide equality before the law often gave men greater patriarchal authority over women and children than the laws of the hierarchical colonial system had. Unlike the colonial system, in which women could seek state assistance to gain greater independence within their homes, in most nineteenth-century Latin American countries, laws identified the home as an inviolable sanctuary of male power. Women did not lose all rights to inherit, own, or bequeath land, but their ability to use those rights to advance their own interests declined. Why was this? The answer is twofold.

First, as Sylvia Arrom has pointed out, nineteenth-century politicians feared that offering true equality to women (or to indigenous peasants, or peoples of African descent) would encourage subjects to mutiny against established authority and therefore threaten the stability of the state.[25] Although central government officials – both liberal and conservative – maintained that they were putting an end to unjust colonial practices that differentiated rights according to one's place within a patriarchal and ethnic hierarchy, in practice, these state officials were elite men who benefitted from gender, class, and race inequalities. While they claimed to uphold equality before the law, they simultaneously feared that marginalized groups would rise up violently to demand equal rights.

Family law offered an important solution to state officials' dilemma over equality versus order, particularly in the politically turbulent decades of the early nineteenth century. As historian Elizabeth Dore noted, politicians "advocated a political model wherein male elders represented both the family to the state and the state to the family." Liberals, in particular, asserted that it was the "natural right of men of wealth or professional status to exercise political authority."[26] This male elite authority, state officials presumed, would maintain the social order. To highlight the differences between these inequalities and colonial hierarchies, new government leaders often differentiated between "active" citizens, who could vote and hold office, versus "passive" citizens, who would benefit from political rights but who lacked a direct political voice. Passive citizens included all women, and the vast majority of indigenous and African-descended populations. Importantly, however, it was not race that determined an indigenous or Afro-Latin American man's passive status; rather, it was his failure to meet either property or literacy requirements. Most statesmen apparently felt that it was not necessary to justify women's political marginalization: the law automatically excluded women from political participation regardless of their wealth, literacy, or proven loyalty to the new republics.

On the surface, it would seem that these tightened patriarchal controls contradicted liberal theories regarding equality before the law, suggesting that gender inequalities were a holdover from the colonial period. However, if one examines these issues more closely, it becomes apparent that the cause of the conflict lay not in Spanish colonial legal history as much as it did in the intertwined histories of liberal theory and British (and, to a lesser extent, French) family laws in the early modern period. Historically, in both liberal theory and practice, individual rights were based on preconditions, especially the ability to reason. Liberals, however, had long assumed that certain groups – women, the lower classes, children, or colonized peoples – lacked the ability to reason and therefore could be excluded from having a political voice. They could, in essence, be governed without their direct consent.[27] Nineteenth-century Latin American legislators therefore did not stray from liberal theory when they reinforced patriarchy and hierarchy, but rather adhered to it. Moreover, they borrowed many of their ideas from British legal history and from the Napoleonic Code in the French Revolution: both of these countries had historically limited women's rights, and advanced the rights of husbands and fathers as virtually absolute authorities. This differed significantly from the Spanish legal tradition which, while patriarchal, was more flexible with regard to women's rights as both individuals and as wives or mothers.

Part of the struggle over patriarchy in the transition from colony to republic was a conflict between Church and state as well. Many aspects of family life had been under the domain of the Catholic Church and ecclesiastical authorities throughout the colonial period. It was the Church that had registered baptisms and marriages, and that resided over funeral proceedings. The Church provided charities and oversaw most schooling at all levels. It was also through the Church that married couples could formally separate. During the nineteenth century, liberals and conservatives debated the proper role of the Church in their new nations. While most conservatives advocated an ongoing, strong position for the Catholic Church in their new nations, liberals sought to establish a strong secular state. Women's and family issues were often means through which arguments over the proper role of the Church were made, even though both Church and state officials maintained strongly patriarchal views of women and society.

Strict patriarchal family laws of the early to mid nineteenth century limited women's abilities to act independently in their own or their children's interests. This began to change, gradually, in the late nineteenth and early twentieth centuries when many Latin American countries revised family laws and nationalist discourses in ways that provided women with greater rights. These changes were subtle and partial, but important. One of the most important developments in this period was the creation of civil marriage laws that required couples to register their marriages with the state, which moved the oversight of marriage from the domain of the Church to that of the state. In most of Central America, as well as Ecuador and the Dominican Republic, civil marriage laws also included the right to divorce by the early 1900s. Eventually, most divorce laws allowed for divorce by mutual consent, which enabled couples to separate permanently without having to expose their troubles publicly. Exactly when countries granted the right to divorce differed greatly in Latin America. Some countries were quite late to grant any form of divorce, such as Colombia (1977), Brazil (1977), Argentina (1987), and Chile (2004). In others, divorce came earlier, but it was required couples to identify some compromising problem, such as adultery or domestic violence – requirements that were similar (if not the same) to Catholic Church prerequisites for separations. Although some countries, like Ecuador, allowed for divorce by mutual consent early (in Ecuador, it was in 1910), many did not grant this right until the mid-twentieth century or later.[28]

Legal reforms pertaining to women's control of money or rights over their children had a more significant impact on women's lives and options. Some countries developed new laws that allowed women to control all or a portion of the goods that they brought into marriage. This allowed wives a certain amount of economic independence from their husbands, although typically they had to provide state officials with a formal request to divide all or portions of their own goods from their husbands. If wives did not do this, their husbands would maintain control over all marital goods, regardless of which partner brought them into the marriage. Not all marriage laws worked to women's benefit: for example, most nineteenth-century legal codes no longer protected a woman's dowry as colonial laws had, which left wives financially vulnerable.[29] One of the more interesting revisions to family law that occurred in Mexico pertained to women's rights as mothers. Whereas Spanish-based laws of *patria potestad* only guaranteed women the right to act as their children's guardians until the age of seven in cases of separation or widowhood, Mexico's 1870 and 1884 civil codes allowed mothers to serve as guardians for their children until they reached the age of majority. Historian Sylvia Arrom observed that the law implicitly "conceded that most women had enough intelligence, education, and experience to manage their children's affairs."[30]

Laws alone were not the only way that women's relationships to their nations were changing in the late nineteenth century. New middle-class notions about both motherhood and childhood were developing that provided women – as mothers – with a (theoretically) more pivotal and respected role in the nation than they had previously enjoyed. By the late nineteenth century, members of the middle sectors in many countries (not just in Latin America) had developed new ideas about childhood. Until that time, children were often regarded as "small adults," and those from humble families had to work for a living starting at about the age of seven or eight. In the nineteenth century, however, middle-class men and women began to view childhood as a special and separate time in an individual's life, one that should be focused on play and learning rather than on work. At the same time, children were increasingly identified as the "future of the nation," whose upbringing would determine whether they would eventually make the nation stronger or bring it to ruin. In order to strengthen the nation, children needed to learn how to read and write, and they needed to learn good habits and patriotism.

Out of these new ideas about childhood came an increasing emphasis on *social motherhood* (sometimes also referred to as *republican motherhood*). Social motherhood theories emphasized that mothers played a critical role in children's development, for it was they could teach children (boys especially) to be good citizens. Proponents of social motherhood argued that the work that women did as mothers had a critical impact not only on their families, but on the nation as a whole. If women did their job poorly, the next generation of citizens would be inadequate, possibly leading to national ruin. If mothers excelled in the responsibility of raising their children, they would not only strengthen the nation, but perhaps even help to regenerate a nation in trouble. Although social motherhood ideas reinforced women's exclusion from formal political participation by associating them with the private sphere, they did offer more respect and dignity to motherhood and highlighted women's importance to national well-being. Further, although social motherhood perpetuated the elite notion that women belonged in the home, it placed this classification in a new sociopolitical context. Early feminists would use these ideas to argue for greater rights for women (see Chapter 4).

Why did this shift in gender policies and political discourses occur in the late nineteenth century? Why does one not find many such references and laws in the early nineteenth century? It is not that legislators cared less about social hierarchy and government stability in the late nineteenth century than their independence-era predecessors had, nor did their basic gender ideas change significantly. Even new laws that gave women more rights in (or to get out of) marriage merely took women out of the paternal care of their husbands or priests and put them under the supervision of men in the state. Moreover, although liberal state officials often made much of their conflicts with the Church, most liberal gender ideas were quite similar to Church-sanctioned marriage and gender ideas. Instead of changing gender norms, these legal reforms and new concepts about motherhood were made possible by the rise of stronger governments in the late nineteenth century, and by economic growth (mostly, but not only, in agricultural exports).

With governments better established than they had been earlier in the century, central state politicians aimed at developing true *nation states*. Nation states are much more than national territories or governments; they are also what anthropologist Benedict Anderson described as *imagined communities*, in which people from different regions, and of all class backgrounds and genders, would develop a sense of belonging to the national community, regardless of their differences with each other.[31] At the same time, stronger (and wealthier) governments were building bureaucratic institutions at a rapid rate, and they would need clerics in all of these. Together, the goal of building the imagined community of the nation plus the need for well-trained and patriotic state workers helped to create an atmosphere that, while not permitting dramatic rethinking of gender roles, was at least amenable to reorientations in how women's roles in the home related to the nation and expanding the roles that women could have in public.

Class and Race in Nineteenth-Century Gender Laws and Discourses

Although marriage laws and state-sanctioned gender discourses affected all women in nineteenth-century Latin America, they had a differential impact on women of different classes and races. First, marriage reforms did not necessarily benefit poor women in the same ways that they did middle-sector or wealthy women. For example, reforms that allowed women to separate the goods they brought into marriage did little to advance the needs of poor women, especially those who did not marry formally. Second, state officials did not view all women as equal. Unless they specifically indicated otherwise, whenever legislators or scholars discussed the category of "woman," and especially when they pondered women's contributions to the nation, they focused on the rights, roles, and needs of women of middling or elite classes. Politicians and other state officials did not view poor women of non-European descent as contributing to the national well-being. In fact, they usually saw poor women as weakening or threatening their nations.

State officials and scholars assumed that poor women had looser morals and were worse mothers than middle-class women. Even though notions of social motherhood indicated a new way of understanding gender and nation, the ideas also built upon elite notions of female honor. Whereas state officials assumed that elite and middle-class women maintained sexual propriety (which some did and others did not), they assumed that lower-class women, especially those of non-European descent, were sexually loose and therefore less deserving of government protections.[32] Moreover, they identified lower-class women as ignorant and uncaring mothers. Historian Laura Shelton captured this in her book on family and community in northern Mexico in the early nineteenth century. Shelton noted how missionaries and elites identified indigenous women as "savage" mothers and asserted that they had "given [their children] no useful instruction; they do not encourage them to goodness, and they do not correct them in their faults." They also identified indigenous mothers as "reckless" with their babies, regularly endangering rather than protecting them.[33] Similarly, elites often referred to poor urban women, who worked rather than tended full time to their children, as negligent and uncaring mothers. Although Chapter 3 will discuss how poverty and exploitation shaped poor women's motherhood roles, elites identified differences between middle-class and poor mothers as based on supposedly inherent moral qualities (or lack thereof, in the case of poor women).

Identifying poor women of non-European descent as bad mothers served a broader purpose in the nineteenth century. Just as legislators were uninterested in extending full political rights to women, they also denied voting rights to poor men, especially those of indigenous or African descent. In addition to justifying these exclusions through property or literacy requirements, they also regarded themselves as "civilized" and non-European peoples as "barbaric" in order to defend the political marginalization of indigenous and African descended men. As with voting rights more generally, arguments about civilization and barbarism were often gendered. For example, if raising children to be good citizens was primarily a mother's job, and it was essential to strengthening the nation, then indigenous and African descended mothers were failing the nation and therefore their sons should not have the right to vote. Other gender arguments also shaped discourses on civilization and barbarism. In Ecuador, state officials, scholars, and travelers claimed that indigenous men habitually beat their wives, a sure sign of their barbarism. Yet according to these same writers, indigenous women were accomplices rather than victims of rampant indigenous domestic violence.[34] Historical examinations of indigenous societies, however, do not uphold elite claims that indigenous peoples were any more prone to domestic violence than other groups, nor did indigenous women accept marital violence. Instead, domestic violence was a problem that affected all levels of Latin American society, from elite families to poor ones, just as it did (and does) in all societies around the world. Moreover, indigenous women sought to protect themselves from violent husbands, sometimes by seeking protection from relatives or neighbors, and sometimes by leaving abusive husbands altogether. The discrepancy between elite claims about indigenous domestic violence versus historical evidence about how indigenous women handled it highlights that elite stereotypes were just that: exaggerations that helped elites to justify, to themselves, indigenous peoples' exclusion from having an equal say in the nation. The stereotype also conveniently served to downplay how often domestic violence occurred among elites, because it identified domestic violence as a specifically "Indian Problem."

In slave societies, and particularly in Brazil and Cuba, slave motherhood became politically significant in the long march toward abolition in the mid- to late nineteenth century. In both regions, plantation owners and legislators were wary of sudden and complete abolition of slavery, given that their economies were almost entirely dependent on agricultural exports grown with slave labor. At the same time, Brazilian and Cuban elites felt mounting pressure both from within and without to put an end to the slave trade and slavery itself. Gradual abolition was elites' preferred strategy to balance their fears of economic ruin with pressures from powerful economic partners to end the slave system. By the middle of the nineteenth century, the transatlantic slave trade had been abolished in both Cuba and Brazil; therefore, the only way to increase the ranks of slave populations was through reproduction. In 1870 in Cuba and 1871 in Brazil, legislators took the next step toward abolition by passing "free womb" laws. These laws stipulated that all children born to slave mothers were free, though when they reached approximately eight years of age, their mother's owners could decide whether to free them entirely (for compensation) or receive their labor, for free, until the child reached the age of 18. Slave owners often chose the latter option so that they could have the children labor under essentially slave conditions despite their so-called freedom. This seems to have happened frequently in Brazil, where the free womb law prohibited the separation of slave parents from children under 12 years old.[35]

Motherhood was the linchpin on which the gradual abolition of slavery was successfully achieved. Yet for slave women, their experiences of motherhood changed little. Their own status was unaffected, and their children were either left to forage for themselves at a young age or they were beholden to obey their mother's master until adulthood. It must have meant something to these women that their sons and daughters would not know life-long slavery, but their thoughts on these matters are absent in the historical record. Existing documentation also shows little if any concern on legislators' part about what impact the new law might have on slave women. Slave women were, after all, little more than a means to an end: where once they were workers who helped to reproduce the slave system, they now provided a way to fulfill obligations to end slavery without overturning the plantation economy. For male legislators debating free womb laws, slave women were, literally, the vessels through which they found a compromise solution for their dilemma over abolition.

After the passage of free womb laws, legislators' interest in abolition died down because the end of slavery was inevitable. For slaves, however, the opposite was true. Slaves were increasingly disobedient on Brazilian plantations, often abandoning them by the 1880s. Historian Stanley Stein noted that hearing abolitionist ideas made slavery increasingly "less tolerable" over the course of the nineteenth century, and especially after the passage of the free womb law. Because of this, elite owners feared that slaves would resort to rebellion in order to attain freedom.[36] Partly in response to slave actions, the Brazilian government abolished slavery for slaves over 60 in 1880, and finally passed the "Golden Law" abolishing slavery in 1888 (slavery was abolished in Cuba two years earlier, in 1886). Once freed, former slaves did what they could to mark their change in status. Many plantation slaves migrated to cities, though not all of them could find work there. The majority continued to work on plantations, but usually they moved to work on different plantations than those on which they had labored as slaves. Gender also mattered in the transition from slavery to freedom: when possible, emancipated women avoided working in field gangs, or as cooks or house cleaners. And, when possible, slave couples had women stay at home, at least most of the year (many of them worked seasonally at harvest times), which was a choice that they did not have under slavery.[37]

Continuities, Changes, and Consequences

According to independence leaders and politicians in the nineteenth century, the transition from colony to republic marked a definitive forward movement. Instead of monarchy, hierarchy, and racial distinctions before the law, nineteenth-century military leaders and statesmen declared that they brought to the Americas a new age of representative government and equality before the law. In practice, their governments fell far short of their claims, revealing that although elite and middle-class men wanted to put an end to colonial inequalities that had limited their voices and powers in government, they were uninterested in giving up the privileges that they had enjoyed over women and lower orders. Women's status and rights within the new nations reflected this tension, and family laws were geared at either justifying the status quo or advancing state interests. Images of women were similarly manipulated: rather than being active participants in the politics of nation making, Latin American women – and especially mothers – symbolized both the hopes and fears of the men in charge of governments.

The changes that women experienced in the nineteenth century were subtle and limited, but important. Elite concepts about female honor, focused around sexual propriety, remained largely static in the transition from colony to republic, but this did not mean that gender was unaffected by independence. Early nineteenth-century gender laws reduced women's rights and independence primarily as a way to avoid social upheaval which might threaten elite men's privileges over others.[38] Later marriage reforms benefitted middle-class and elite women by providing them with more options in marriage, and new emphasis on the social relevance of their roles as mothers, than either colonial or early republican laws had done. Even so, these gains were always geared to serve the state and its interests. Poor women of non-European heritage gained least of all – marriage reforms offered them neither protection nor opportunities, and state officials saw them as aberrant mothers who would weaken rather than strengthen the nation.

While an examination of changing laws and dominant gender ideas in the nineteenth century identifies the parameters in which women acted, it leaves many questions unanswered. To what extent did women's lives reflect the gender assumptions embedded within elite-driven laws and discourses? How did class and race affect women's experiences not only of law, but also of daily life? When and how did women engage with legal reforms and elite gender ideologies? At what times did they choose to ignore or circumvent gender norms, and why? It is to these issues that the next chapters turn, examining motherhood and its meaning first for poor women, and then for middling- and upper-class women. Far from being merely passive symbols, women of different class and race backgrounds actively negotiated the terrain of nineteenth-century socio-politics in order to advance their interests and protect the needs and rights of their children to the best of their abilities.

Documents: Vicente Grez on Women and Independence

In 1907, Chilean Vicente Grez wrote a book about women's contributions to Independence in his country. In it, he described several women's heroism and emphasized the importance of their support for the patriotic movement. What patterns emerge with the women he described, and how do these relate to issues raised in this chapter? Even when the passages do not reference motherhood directly, how do they call upon images of women that elite discourses often identified with motherhood?

Mercedes Fuentealba: (Wife of José Miguel Carrera, a well-known Chilean patriot who spent time in exile in Argentina due not only to his independence cause, but also because of conflicts with other independence leaders.)

> His wife followed him through the whole length of the immense Argentine pampa, becoming a part of the army equipment, taking on all the tremendous danger of that situation, giving birth to her son in the middle of the desert, suffering from hunger and thirst – she, who had been born surrounded by all comforts and pleasures of good fortune! – she happily and contentedly put up with all of these terrible tests.
>
> Never did the annoyances of errant life, the loss of material pleasures, of fortune, of family, of her changed social position, upset the dream of this heroic woman: never did a complaint or reproach escape from her lips. At times sick, caring for two children, sleeping between two cradles, her soul suffering before the uncertain future for those children and the shadow over her husband's destiny. She loved this disgraced man [. . .]
>
> Carrera never sacrificed . . . the least of his projects, the smallest of his ambitions. [Fuentealba] understood this all too well and maintained a heroic silence . . . generous souls are always thus, preferring to sacrifice their own lives completely, in sublime tranquility and silence before the uncertainty of what might change in the future [. . .][39]

Paula Jara Quemada: (A woman who gave a place to stay an provisions to independence hero San Martín and his men at a critical point in 1818.)

a woman mounted on an elegant horse, a true Amazon, gave the word offering this group of brave men that they could replenish the casualties suffered by their ranks at their recent defeat.

This unexpected feminine apparition was Señora Doña Paula Jara Quemada, who was an opulent woman and an enthusiastic patriot, who knew about the surprising disgrace suffered by the Chilean army. She gathered together all the tenant farmers and overseers on her hacienda and placed herself at the head of them with her sons and daughters to go out and meet the defeated men, leading them with the example of her valor and selflessness.

And it was not just this small contingent of men that the Señora Jara Quemada offered to the defeated men, but also all of her estate, the magnificent horses and spacious houses, which were transformed into general quarters for the new and reorganized army.[40]

Notes

1 Discussions of the details of Manuela Sáenz's life can be found in Pamela S. Murray, *For Glory and Bolívar: The Remarkable Life of Manuela Sáenz* (Austin: University of Texas Press, 2010). Murray also has a shorter discussion of Sáenz in her article "Of Love and Politics: Reassessing Manuela Sáenz and Simón Bolívar, 1822–1830," *History Compass* 5:1 (2007), pp. 227–250. Also see Nicola Foote, "Manuela Saenz and the Independence of South America," *World History Connected* February 2010. http://worldhistory connected.press.illinois.edu/7.1/foote.html (last accessed November 8, 2013).

2 Pamela S. Murray, "'Loca' or 'Libertadora'? Manuela Sáenz in the Eyes of History and Historians, 1900–c. 1990," *Journal of Latin American Studies* 33:2 (May 2001), pp. 291–310.

3 Foote, pp. 9–11 out of 14.

4 Sarah C. Chambers, "Republican Friendship: Manuela Sáenz Writes Women into the Nation, 1835–1856," *Hispanic American Historical Review* 81:2 (2001), pp. 225–230.

5 Chambers, particularly pp. 247–252.

6 These examples, and many others, can be found in Evelyn Cherpak's pioneering essay "The Participation of Women in the Independence Movement in Gran Colombia, 1780–1830," in Asunción Lavrin, ed., *Latin American Women: Historical Perspectives* (Westport, CT: Greenwood Press, 1978), pp. 219–234.

7 Rebecca Earle, "Rape and the Anxious Republic: Revolutionary Colombia, 1810–1830," in Elizabeth Dore and Maxine Molyneux, eds, *Hidden Histories of Gender and the State in Latin America* (Durham, NC: Duke University Press, 2000), p. 136.

8 Pioneering examinations of gender in the Aztec and Inca empires were, respectively, Inga Clendinnen, *Aztecs: An Interpretation* (New York: Cambridge University Press, 1995), and Irene Silverblatt, *Moon, Sun, and Witches: Gender Ideologies and Class in Inca and Colonial Peru* (Princeton: Princeton University Press, 1987). A good synopsis discussion of gender and conquest is Karen Vieira Powers, *Women in the Crucible of Conquest: The Gendered Genesis of Spanish American Society, 1500–1600* (Albuquerque: University of New Mexico Press, 2005).

9 For an excellent scholarly discussion of Marina/Malinche, see Camilla Townsend, *Malintzin's Choices: An Indian Woman in the Conquest of Mexico* (Albuquerque: University of New Mexico Press, 2006).

10 For an excellent discussion of the role of convents in the process of mestizaje, see Kathryn Burns, *Colonial Habits: Convents and the Spiritual Economy of Cuzco, Peru* (Durham, NC: Duke University Press, 1999).

11 A very good source on women's legal rights to property is in Alida C. Metcalf, "Women and Means: Women and Family Property in Colonial Brazil," *Journal of Social History* 24:2 (Winter 1990), pp. 277–298, with reference to judges' assumptions on p. 285. Another good discussion of women's legal rights to property in Spanish America is in Kimberly Gauderman, *Women's Lives in Colonial Quito: Gender, Law, and Economy in Spanish America* (Austin: University of Texas Press, 2003).

12 For a discussion of widows' rights in Brazil, see Metcalf. For issues of dowry in Brazil, see Muriel Nazzari, "Parents and Daughters: Change in the Practice of Dowry in São Paulo (1600–1770)," *Hispanic American Historical Review* 70:4 (1990), pp. 639–665.

13 For a very good discussion of this in colonial Potosí, see Jane E. Mangan, *Trading Roles: Gender, Ethnicity, and the Urban Economy in Colonial Potosí* (Durham, NC: Duke University Press, 2005).

14 Powers, p. 123.

15 See Muriel Nazzari, "An Urgent Need to Conceal," in Lyman L. Johnson and Sonya Lipsett-Rivera, eds, *The Faces of Honor: Sex, Shame, and Violence in Colonial Latin America* (Albuquerque: University of New Mexico Press, 1998), pp. 103–126.

16 Burns has a particularly good discussion of nuns as mothers to foundlings in her *Colonial Habits*.

17 For Sor Juana's own discussion of her life and choices, see: Sor Juana Inés de la Cruz, *The Answer/La Respuesta*. Trans. Electa Arenal and Amanda Powell (New York: The Feminist Press, 2009).

18 Catalina de Erauso, *Lieutenant Nun: Memoir of a Basque Transvestite in the New World* (Boston: Beacon Press, 1997).

19 For an excellent discussion of this, see Burns.

20 For a court case that captures the interplay of honor, gender, and law around this issue in the colonial period, see Thomas A. Abercrombie, "Affairs of the Courtroom: Fernando de Medina Confesses to Killing his Wife," in Richard Boyer and Geoffrey Spurling, eds, *Colonial Lives: Documents on Latin American History, 1550–1850* (New York: Oxford University Press, 2000), pp. 54–75.

21 For a very good summary of these issues, and the experiences of colonial women more generally, see Susan Migden Socolow's textbook, *The Women of Colonial Latin America* (New York: Cambridge University Press, 2000).

22 For examples of scholars who identify more positive than negative changes, see: Sylvia M. Arrom, *The Women of Mexico City, 1790–1857* (Stanford: Stanford University Press, 1992), and "Changes in Mexican Family Law in the Nineteenth Century," in Gertrude M. Yeager, ed., *Confronting Change, Challenging Tradition: Women in Latin American History* (Wilmington, DE: SR Books, 1994), pp. 87–102; also Carmen Diana Deere and Magdalena León, "Liberalism and Married Women's Property Rights in Nineteenth-Century Latin America," *Hispanic American Historical Review* 85:4 (2005), pp. 627–678. For an essay that sees more negative than positive changes, see Elizabeth Dore, "One Step Forward, Two Steps Back: Gender and the State in the Long Nineteenth Century," in Elizabeth Dore and Maxine Molyneux, eds, *Hidden Histories of Gender and the State in Latin America* (Durham, NC: Duke University Press, 2000), pp. 3–32.

23 See Gauderman; also see Chad Thomas Black, *The Limits of Gender Domination: Women, the Law, and Political Crisis in Quito, 1765–1830* (Albuquerque: University of New Mexico Press, 2010). Although both Gauderman and Black assert that the colonial state was "not patriarchal," an interpretation with which this author does not agree, they both make very good cases that gender relations were complex in the colonial period, providing women with significant negotiating power, and sometimes independent authority.

24 Black, p. 202.

25   Arrom, "Changes in Mexican Family Law," p. 92.

26   Dore, "One Step Forward," pp. 15 and 9, respectively.

27   One of the earliest and best discussions of the exclusive nature of liberal theory is: Uday S. Mehta, "Liberal Strategies of Exclusion," *Politics and Society* 18:4 (December 1990), pp. 427–454.

28   Raul Francisco Andrade, *Gender, Marriage Markets and the Family* (Ann Arbor, MI: ProQuest, 2007), pp. 19–25.

29   In *The Women of Mexico City*, p. 84, Arrom explains that dowry had previously been taken out of a woman's inheritance, so in this sense women "broke even" – either they got a dowry, or they inherited more. However, if women could most easily protect and gain independent access to their dowries, versus other inheritance that the courts usually left under husbands' control, then loss of the dowry was a step backwards for women's options for financial independence.

30   Arrom, "Changes in Mexican Family Law," p. 91.

31   Benedict Anderson: *Imagined Communities: Reflections on the Origins and Spread of Nationalism*, revised ed. (New York: Verso, 1992 [1983]). It is important to note that deep race and class divisions inhibited the development of these "imagined communities" throughout Latin America in the nineteenth century, and challenge the goal to this day.

32   This is not to say that all notions of honor were static. For an excellent discussion of how male – especially plebeian male – notions of honor changed to emphasize conduct and labor over birth and purity of blood, see Sarah C. Chambers, *From Subject to Citizen: Honor, Gender, and Politics in Arequipa, Peru, 1780–1854* (University Park: Pennsylvania State University Press, 1999).

33   Laura M. Shelton, *For Tranquility and Order: Family and Community on Mexico's Northern Frontier, 1800–1830* (Tucson: University of Arizona Press, 2010), p. 41.

34   Erin O'Connor, *Gender, Indian, Nation: The Contradictions of Making Ecuador, 1830–1925* (Tucson: University of Arizona Press, 2007), pp. 67–71.

35   Katia M. De Queiros Mattoso, *To Be a Slave in Brazil, 1550–1888*, trans. Arthur Goldhammer (New Brunswick, NJ: Rutgers University Press, 1987), p. 110.

36   Stanley Stein, *Vassouras: A Brazilian Coffee County, 1850–1900: The Roles of Planter and Slave in a Plantation Society* (Princeton, NJ: Princeton University Press, 1986), pp. 146–147, 251–256.

37   Stein, pp. 262–268.

38   For a classic discussion of these processes, see E. Bradford Burns, *The Poverty of Progress: Latin America in the Nineteenth Century* (Berkeley: University of California Press, 1980).

39   Vicente Grez, titled *Las mujeres de la independencia* (Santiago: Imp. de la "Gratitud Nacional," 1910), pp. 66–68.

40   Grez, pp. 75–77.

3

Poor Women
Mothering the Majority in the Nineteenth Century

Varieties of Poor Mothers

Consider the lives of three women, all of whom lived sometime in the nineteenth century. Tadea Casas of Cajamarca, Peru, lost her baby shortly after it was born. Around the same time, three-month-old Manuela Chavez's mother died, leaving her without maternal care or breast milk. Casas nursed Chavez, raising her as her own daughter as long as she could, but later had to give the child up to a woman who could better afford to raise the girl. Meanwhile, in the Parahyba Valley of south central Brazil, a slave mother typically worked all day in the fields while an older slave woman tended to her baby; the only time she spent with her child during the work day was to nurse her at rest periods and lunch. This particular day, however, the slave woman was in the *tronco* (iron stocks) as a punishment for disobedience, so her baby came to nurse while she was immobilized in the stocks.[1] Marcela Bernal in Mexico fared better than either of these two women, though her life was also full of challenges. Bernal moved from Guanajuato to Mexico City after her husband died, looking for a way to support herself and her family. The only work available to women in Guanajuato was in domestic service, which she wanted to avoid for herself and her daughters due to its low pay and even lower status. Her move was successful: Bernal found factory work for her older daughters, which enabled her to stay at home tending to the house and to her younger children.[2]

Mothers Making Latin America: Gender, Households, and Politics Since 1825,
First Edition. Erin E. O'Connor.
© 2014 John Wiley & Sons, Inc. Published 2014 by John Wiley & Sons, Inc.

These three women, two of them real and one a composite based on historical evidence, make clear that even among the poor, there was no single or unifying "woman's" or "mother's" experience in nineteenth-century Latin America. Whereas Marcela Bernal had some choices and options open to her when she found herself widowed with children, the slave woman in Brazil lived subjected to the will of her owner, and while she did not have to find a job or housing, her work was tiresome and long, and her housing and nutrition were inadequate. Tadea Casas fell somewhere between these two – not among the poorest women in Cajamarca, but unable to afford to raise the young girl she had nursed after losing her own child (for more on Tadea Casas's story, see the document excerpt at the end of this chapter). These three women's lives do, however, point to some of the common challenges that poor mothers faced. Childbirth was dangerous, and infant mortality rates were high. Life was uncertain, and making ends meet was difficult. Work was necessary for most women, even after they had children. A husband or partner's death could mean ruin for an entire family even if the mother had a job and steady income.

It was ordinary women like these who did most of the working and living and mothering in nineteenth-century Latin America, yet finding and analyzing their experiences is incredibly challenging. There are far fewer sources on poor women, especially those of indigenous or African descent, than there are regarding the lives of middling and upper classes of women. Even when one can find evidence of poor women's lives, the document trail is typically fragmentary and raises at least as many questions as it answers. Historians are exceptionally hard-pressed to understand poor women's motivations and feelings regarding the challenges they faced and the choices they made. To understand and analyze what motherhood meant for the majority of women in nineteenth-century Latin America, it is critical to place such sources within context, especially the communities and economic realities in which individuals lived. Motherhood – its joys, sorrows, significance, and vulnerabilities – differed for women according to their class and race, their marital status, and whether they lived in a city or in the countryside. This chapter examines and analyzes what motherhood was like for ordinary women of different backgrounds and living in different situations. In doing so, it suggests that one must pay attention to the lives and mothering experiences of poor women in order to understand how the majority lived in nineteenth-century Latin America. Additionally, an examination of ordinary mothers' experiences reveals that their lives often did not reflect the elite perceptions of them.

Gender, Communities, and Contexts

Mothering never takes place in a vacuum. Where a woman lived, what her race and class status were, how she formed communities – these all affected her motherhood experiences. These circumstances help to identify the options, challenges, and obstacles that women faced when trying to mother. How much time women spent with their children, how much assistance they had in hard times, how well they could feed their children (and whether this would be enough to keep them alive) – all of these things depended on the conditions in which a family lived. Therefore, although the next few pages do not always discuss motherhood directly, the issues raised here are necessary to understand how most women experienced motherhood in nineteenth-century Latin America, as well as how the contours of motherhood changed in the twentieth century. These shifting experiences did not, of course, change overnight in 1900. Some changes began before that point, others not until almost 20 years later. Rather than indicating years that adhere neatly to calendar distinctions, the nineteenth century in Latin America often refers to the period between independence and the onset of modern economic and political institutions – roughly, from the 1820s or 1830s until about 1920.

The variety of women's and mothers' experiences in nineteenth-century Latin America was vast. But, for the sake of clarity, one can identify a few different circumstances in which most ordinary women lived and parented. Latin American economies in the nineteenth century were primarily agricultural, with most of the population living in the countryside. Though some middling and wealthy families lived in rural areas, most rural residents were poor. The rural poor in general can be referred to as *campesinos*, and they included rural dwellers that did various kinds of work. Many, but not all, campesinos were *peasants* who farmed their own small plots of land; others worked on large estates or were landless workers. Slavery remained legal and prominent until the 1880s in Brazil and Cuba, where the economies were almost entirely dependent on export crops. By the late nineteenth century, however, cities were growing – especially in countries such as Mexico and Argentina that experienced early industrialization. The shift from rural to urban life affected not only where people lived and how they worked, but also how they built communities and families. Yet as in the countryside, one's relative wealth or poverty, along with one's standing as free, servant, or slave, greatly influenced urban women's mothering practices and possibilities.

Living as a peasant or hacienda worker

Campesinos lived materially simple lives and, although some peasants had more (or more fertile) land than others in their communities, wealth differences were usually small. As the nineteenth century progressed, increasing numbers of campesinos lived and worked on the estates of the landed elite. Booms in export products, such as coffee, cocoa beans, or even hemp (for rope), led to the expansion of large estates, growth that often drove peasants off their lands. On some estates workers were technically wage laborers. However, on many estates, resident workers were indebted to such an extent that they were permanently bound to the estate and the owner. Whether peasants with their own land or workers on large estates, rural peoples lived by agricultural tasks, by the rising and setting of the sun, and by the seasons. Work was a family affair, and although adult men did the majority of daily agricultural labor in the fields, women and children provided necessary labor for household subsistence. Women and older children often took care of whatever animals the family owned, which was also essential to the family economy. Family members likewise helped with agriculture whenever men were away from home or alongside men during the labor-intensive sowing and harvesting times. Moreover, in some communities, women were as likely as men to inherit the land for the family to farm. The division between "home" and "work" was not always clear: cloth woven during evenings or slow periods could be sold, as could food or mildly alcoholic drinks (such as *chicha* in the Andes or *pulque* in Mexico).[3] Again, income from selling food or drink was often critical for family subsistence.

Women's duties and contributions within the household economy gave peasant women some negotiating power with their husbands, but peasant communities were patriarchal in so far as men systematically had more power than women. Practices varied in peasant communities throughout Latin America, of course, but one can find certain general patterns to gender relationships within peasant communities. If a wife had family within the community or in one nearby, her male family members might be able to intervene on her behalf in the case of marital conflict. The most vulnerable women were young wives without land or local family, but even they had recourse to addressing problems with their husbands. Gossip might be an effective tool against a husband who was spending too much money on alcohol or not living up to other duties, as it put social pressure on him to change his behaviors. In more dire cases, a woman might appeal to community leaders for justice or protection from an especially neglectful or violent husband. A woman's ability to win favor rested partly on her own reputation as a good wife, defined in most communities as a woman who fulfilled her own duties, was faithful, and obeyed her husband's authority. Her fate also rested on the extent to which local leaders thought that her husband had either punished her too harshly or failed to uphold his own obligations. If her peers and local authorities considered a husband habitually and cruelly abusive, they might accept (or at least tolerate) it if his wife left him to set up house with another man.[4]

On large estates, justice and gender rules were ultimately in the hands of the estate owners, to the detriment of women workers. In part, this power was economic. Indebted workers on haciendas needed loans for courtship, marriage, baptisms, or burials. On some estates, landowners even pressured men to marry and assume loans as both a means of ensuring their ongoing indebtedness and as a method of social control.[5] Moreover, when hacienda owners distributed subsistence plots of land to resident workers (typically the least fertile land on the estate), they only allotted this land to married men. Although women's work was required, it was only accounted for under their fathers' or husbands' names, and women lacked access to land.[6] Living and working in a male-oriented labor and land control system did not, however, necessarily mean that estate workers shared owners' extreme patriarchal values. Historian John Tutino found that in independence-era Mexico, when workers in the Bajío region took over control of land from large estate owners in the 1810s, they redistributed land (in peasant plots) to women as well as men. This suggests that even though they had been forced to live and work according to the landowners' rules until the independence uprisings, the estate workers had maintained essentially peasant ideas about gender, labor, and land rights.[7]

In addition to controlling labor and land, hacienda owners asserted power over workers through sexuality and, in particular, by maintaining sexual access to women workers whenever they wished. Such treatment, however, is difficult to document clearly for the nineteenth century because even if hacienda workers resented and resisted such practices, they rarely brought cases against estate owners to court due to the estate owners' influence in local politics and judicial systems. Using testimony from twentieth-century workers, however, offers a hint of how estate workers from earlier periods likely experienced and tried to manage the problem of sexual harassment and rape. Barry Lyons' interview with former hacienda worker "Mama Jacoba" in Ecuador during the 1990s is particularly revealing regarding these issues. Mama Jacoba told Lyons:

> When the *amos* [estate owners] saw a girl of fifteen, or thirteen or fourteen, they had her parents summoned to the hacienda. They told the parents, "Send her to take care of the saddle, so the dog won't eat it . . ."
>
> The girls would go, thinking they were going to watch the saddle. A girl would spend the night there and come home the next day with a load of meat . . . If the girl refused, her parents got a terrible beating . . .
>
> So, the girls would give birth to the amos' children.
>
> They would tell the married men, too, "Send me your wife. I need her for something." The husbands would just send their wives, my dad said. The married women, too, would just go . . .[8]

Mama Jacoba noted that, although husbands did not complain, they might, in a drunken rage, call their wives whores of the owner and beat them. She claimed that she herself refused to submit to the sexual advances of the hacienda owners and administrators, willing to pay the price of beatings. The estate owners' sons were also likely – even expected – to have their first sexual encounters with women workers on the estate, whether through the women's consent or by rape.

Although hacienda owners took advantage of their power on estates to gain sexual access to female workers, they simultaneously kept workers themselves to a very strict moral code. Owners or administrators of large estates often demanded that workers remain faithful to each other (except, of course, when the hacienda owner or his sons demanded sexual access to workers' wives or daughters), and that they fulfill their duties as good husbands and wives. If workers failed to live up to pre-scribed rules of conduct, estate owners or administrators would punish them. In theory, this could help to protect workers' wives from excessive abuse, because the hacienda owner or administrator could intervene to punish a cruel husband. In practice, estate authorities were likely to punish a wife for disobedience at the same time that they punished a husband for cruelty. Therefore, while hacienda owners might have laid claim to upholding morality and family values on their estates, not only did they break these rules themselves through their own sexual exploitation and violence toward women workers, but they also used rules of morality as a means to increase their own power, with workers gaining few if any benefits from them.

Gender and slavery on Brazilian plantations

Brazil was built on agricultural exports and slave labor, and as such it serves as a good example of another way in which ordinary women lived and worked in Latin America. Life for a slave woman on a plantation was typically filled with hard work and poor food and clothing rations. Women who worked in the fields had the most difficult physical labor and conditions, whereas female slaves who served as cooks, maids, or nannies in the slave owners' house usually received better clothing and food, and their work was not as physically demanding. However, life for a so-called house slave had its disadvantages: in particular, it was far more difficult for house slaves to build a sense of community with other slaves, and they were constantly under their owners' scrutiny. It is likely that, because of their accessibility, slave women who worked in the owners' house were also more vulnerable to sexual harassment and rape than women who worked in the fields.

Family life for slaves was inherently unstable insofar as loved ones could be sold away from each other at any almost any time. Legally, slaves who were formally married could not be parted, but slave owners often discouraged legal marriage, leaving them the right to separate slave men and women who were devoted partners to each other. When slaves did marry, they often had to do so in accordance with their owners' wishes about whom they married and when.[9] Slaves did not necessarily accept these limitations, and they were especially likely to run away to see loved ones from whom they had been separated. One can also find instances when slaves refused to do planters' bidding with regard to marriage or other long-term relationships. Historian Sandra Lauderdale Graham has documented the life of Caetana, a slave woman who refused to marry the man that her owner chose for her.[10] Fellow historian Stuart Schwartz related a similar story, in which a slave woman was sold away to another owner nearby, away from her chosen partner. He ran off to join her and, eventually, an "equivalent" male slave was sent back to the original owner to take the male partner's place.[11] In this latter case, it behooved the woman's original owner to sell her partner (in a trade) to the man to whom he sold her, because it was easier than continually tracking down and punishing her partner for running away.

Life as a slave in Brazil was also shaped by sex ratio imbalances. Male slaves outnumbered female slaves throughout the history of slavery in Brazil, although the particular ratios fluctuated over time. This imbalance resulted largely from plantation owners' preferences: most field workers were men, as were virtually all workers in the mills which transformed cane sugar into granular sugar. This gender discrepancy meant that it was much easier for a slave woman to find a marriage partner (whether legal or informal) than it was for a man, and almost two-thirds of married slaves were women.[12] Moreover, although there were fewer slave women on plantations, women were twice as likely as men to gain manumission. This was partly because women cost less to replace than men. Once freed, the former slave women often played a pivotal role in purchasing male family members' freedom.

As will be discussed later in more detail, the realities of slave women's lives made motherhood more complicated for them than for other groups of women. All poor women faced challenges feeding, clothing, and raising their children, but for slave women, these children were not even "theirs" per se, but rather the property of the slave owners. This contrasted with poor indigenous peoples and mestizos in the countryside in Spanish America where, even if they were indebted workers on large estates with few rights of their own, they and their children were, at least, not property of the landowner. Whether slave or free, however, women who lived in the countryside faced very different challenges and opportunities, in life generally and motherhood more specifically, from those who lived in cities.

Urban life and gender relations

Whereas life in the countryside – whether in peasant communities or on estates – was shaped by a strong sense of community identity and fairly strict rules of conduct, life in urban areas was both less confining and less secure. In cities, people from different classes and ethnicities came

together; granted, there were rich and poor neighborhoods, and some
that were shaped at least partly by ethnic or racial identity, but every day
requirements made it difficult for all but the wealthiest of individuals to
isolate themselves from other groups – and even they had servants in
their houses. By the late nineteenth and early twentieth centuries, many
cities were growing rapidly due to factors such as new railways connect-
ing urban centers to the countryside, the beginnings of industry that
drew workers from more rural regions, or because peasants driven off
their lands by large estate owners migrated to cities. After the abolition
of slavery in Brazil and Cuba, many former slaves left plantations for
cities in search of work.

Women's roles and experiences in cities varied greatly according to
the region and period in which they lived. Knowing their exact experiences is difficult not only because of lack of documentation, but also
because documents such as censuses reflect the biases of the state officials
who designed them or collected data. For example, the Mexico City
censuses of 1811 and 1848 identified any woman living with a man as
"married," making it difficult to gauge how many women married legally,
versus those who lived in informal unions.[13] The 1848 census in Mexico
City was also limited in that it counted only heads of households (rather
than entire household membership), and racial categories were no longer
identified. What the Mexico City censuses do make clear is that a large
number of women lived in the city, and that about one-third of all the
households in the city were headed by women, many of them unmarried.
Similarly, about 35–40% of the women in the Brazilian City of São Paulo
headed their own households.[14]

With the exception of the very wealthy, and sometimes women of
middling sectors, most urban women worked on a regular basis and for
most of them the lines between "home" and "work" were blurred. The
most common employment for urban women was work in domestic
service. Those who worked as full-time maids or cooks in houses often
lived with their employers. Live-in domestics were among the lowest-
status women involved in the formal labor market in most cities – as
evidenced at the beginning of this chapter by Marcela Bernal's determi-
nation to avoid this fate for her daughters. Though domestic servants
could be found in all Latin American cities, their numbers fluctuated
over time. In Mexico City, for example, although domestic service
remained the most likely occupation for women, the relative number of
women doing this work declined over the course of the nineteenth

century.[15] This shift was due to both the availability of other types of work as well as economic crises that forced many middle-sector families to cut down on or give up having servants. Other women lived apart from the people for whom they worked, or they provided domestic services out of their own homes, such as taking in laundry, ironing, or sewing.

Another common type of work for women in most Latin American cities was buying and selling goods on city streets and in urban market-places. Indigenous women were very well known as vendors in Andean cities from the colonial period forward, and they remain vital members of urban commerce to this day.[16] Women vendors also had an important presence in other cities, but in places like Mexico City and São Paulo, Brazil, nineteenth-century permit requirements for vendors made life for women sellers increasingly difficult.[17] Some women sellers were quite successful and entered the middling sectors of urban society, owning houses, lending out money, and collecting on debts. Others barely made a living and could fall easily into the ranks of the destitute.

Cities that industrialized early, such as Mexico City and Buenos Aires, also had a significant portion of women engaged in factory labor. Historian Susie Porter's study of working women in late nineteenth-century Mexico City showed that middle-sector and elite groups were concerned that working women's shifting job opportunities would undermine their morals through exposure to men. Partly for this reason, cigar industry owners were careful to segregate women from men on factory floors. Because factory work paid better than domestic work, and was more reliable than vending, women actively sought industrial employment.[18]

Slave women in Brazil often lived and worked as domestics in their owners' homes, but they also worked in a variety of other capacities in Brazilian cities. Though many slave women lived with owners, others did not. In fact, it was not uncommon for slaves to live on their own, sending back a portion of their earnings to owners whom they saw only occasionally. Slaves' work was especially important to humble Portuguese women in São Paulo in the early to mid nineteenth century. These women were under pressure to appear to have nothing to do (an outward sign of their status as "ladies"), yet who needed to bring income into their homes. Several of them emphasized that they made a so-called honest living through the work and wages of their slaves.[19] Sylvia Arrom found that Mexican middle-class women sometimes used their servants in a similar way, offering the example of a woman who was in the process of getting a formal separation from her husband and who, in need of cash, made sweet meats and did embroidery. However, rather than sell these goods on the street and lower her status, she had her maid go out to sell the goods.[20] In both cases, slave or servant women's labor was essential for upholding higher-status women's honor.

Urban women of the lower classes enjoyed more freedom of movement, and often more independence, than either their poor rural or middle- and upper-class counterparts. Yet this independence came with greater insecurity as well, and working women in cities strove to foster support networks in order to compensate for the lack of built-in communities one would find in rural areas. Their freedoms were considerable: urban women of the popular classes were largely able to move about on their own and engage directly in business matters (sometimes despite laws that gave husbands control of marital goods). Ordinary women who lived in cities also tended to have fewer set rules about sexuality and marriage than women in other areas or classes. For example, many women, whether they lacked money for a marriage ceremony or were unwilling to submit to a man's legally supported patriarchal will, often lived in consensual unions rather than marrying formally in the Church. Though some of these unions were fleeting, many were lifelong, with couples considering themselves "like married." Urban market women also frequently established female economic and social networks independent of men: these helped to assure their economic well-being and gave women a sense of community outside of direct male control. Similar to the countryside, women's economic contributions to their families gave them a certain amount of negotiating power with their husbands and male partners, and women were more likely in cities than in the countryside to provide the majority of family income. These social networks required constant maintenance, and they were sometimes not enough to enable a woman to pay her rent or feed her children adequately. Moreover, the extent to which a working-class urban woman controlled her own sexuality depended largely on the kind of work she did: for example, a domestic servant was as vulnerable to sexual abuse as a woman estate worker in the countryside, if not more so, given her constant proximity to male employers and their sons. Economically devastated women might be reduced to prostitution in order to make ends meet.

Motherhood exacerbated the complications for poor women everywhere – whether in cities or the countryside, as slaves or servants or free women. Poverty made child rearing particularly challenging, and led to greater instances of infant deaths. However, despite these universal realities, the context in which a woman lived and worked had great influence on how she raised her children, and the options available to her in times of difficulty.

Mothering One's Own Children

Childbirth and child rearing was the domain of women, but it was work for which women and babies often required support. Assistance with birthing often came from other women in the community known for their midwifery skills, perhaps based on knowledge passed down through generations. Childbirth was a dangerous undertaking, one which often resulted in maternal or infant death either during the birthing process or shortly thereafter. Babies born early had little chance of surviving, and even those born at full term were vulnerable to sickness. Mothers could die from blood loss or infection. It was not unusual for babies to lose mothers as their lives began, and to require another woman to nurse them. Such an infant was likely to be given to a woman who had an older child near weaning, or who had recently lost a baby of her own and was still producing milk. Sometimes, a nursing mother would adopt a child as her own.

Birth rates varied throughout Latin America over the course of the nineteenth century, and it is often difficult to determine how many children women had on average. Census data only reported how many individuals lived in a household, which would not include children who had died. Baptismal records also tell only part of the story, since many parents could not afford to have their children baptized. Similarly, although wills offer a great deal of information about families, including children who died young, they do not necessarily include references to illegitimate children. Moreover, most poor women (and men) could not afford to have wills drawn up. For example, Sylvia Arrom found evidence in Mexico City that the average age of marriage was 22.7, and that married women who left wills had given birth an average of five times by the age of 45, with 36% of those children dying before the women wrote their wills.[21] Except for the average age of marriage, which took women of different races and classes into account, one cannot assume that these averages necessarily applied to poor women who did not write wills. Poverty and limited nutrition likely led to higher mortality rates for poor infants and children, and although poor women may have also waited to enter partnerships (usually informal relationships), they were less likely than wealthy women to have widowhood limit the number of children they bore because they, unlike wealthier women, often paired up with other men after their first partners died.

We do know that birth rates were very low among Brazilian slaves. As with most matters concerning slave populations, exact reasons for this are difficult to gauge, but there are several overlapping factors that probably explain it. First, the unbalanced sex ratio among slaves, with lower numbers of slave women than men, almost certainly contributed to low fertility rates. Similarly, poor nutrition and overwork might have resulted in menarche (cessation of menstruation) among many slave women. Lengthy breast feeding also could have kept many slave women from conceiving soon after birth, since breast feeding sometimes delays the resumption of menstruation. Furthermore, slave women were more likely to be freed than slave men, and children born to freed mothers were free rather than counted among the slave population. Finally, there must have been many slave women who chose abortion or infanticide rather than to raise a child destined to slavery.[22] Until the slave trade was effectively abolished in the 1850s, Brazilian plantation owners had little incentive to address low fertility among their slaves, because they could make a profit off of adult slaves within several years' time and replace them with new slaves from Africa.

Slave women may not have had many children, but evidence suggests that they were willing to make great sacrifices to free those that they had. Slave mothers often worked to buy their children's freedom from their owners, even if it meant that they themselves had to remain enslaved. They might also postpone a child's baptism until he or she gained freedom, in order that the child would be formally recorded as "free" in the baptismal record. This was primarily a practical concern for the child's ongoing liberty, because freed slaves were often vulnerable to being forced back into slavery. Having a baptismal record that clarified the child's status as free would help to protect her or him from such a fate. One must also wonder if slave women sometimes abandoned children on purpose, because foundlings in Brazil were automatically presumed to be free.[23]

It is problematic to place too much emphasis on legitimate versus illegitimate births among poor women. Dominant gender norms, based on elite perceptions, assumed that poor women and women of non-European descent were inherently "dishonorable" and, as discussed in the last chapter, this meant that they questioned poor people's morals and sexual propriety. Because elites left behind the most documentation for historians to read and analyze, and because many poor women did enter into informal unions, for a long time historians assumed that illegitimacy indicated instability and the absence of fatherly influence. However, as Stuart Schwartz pointed out, "the formation of a conjugal unit and ultimately of a family did not depend on church-sponsored marriage for either slaves or freed persons," and that just because a child was born outside of wedlock did not necessarily mean that the father was absent from his or her upbringing.[24]

Most poor women could not leave the workforce once they had children, although in some cases, urban women changed the types of jobs they had once they gave birth. For example, a woman might leave a job in domestic service where she could not have her child with her and instead wash laundry or mend clothes out of her own home.[25] In most cases, poor women's children were woven into their daily routines, with infants being carried in slings throughout the day, heads bobbing along with their mothers' movements, to sleep or observe the world. They were only an arm's reach away when they cried of hunger, pain, or soiled clothes. Small children would toddle along with their mothers, likely mimicking adult duties and behaviors as young children are wont to do. As her children grew older, they began to do chores. Families valued, and needed, their various members to contribute work according to their abilities. Ideas that childhood should be a period of play, did not develop among middle-class or elite Latin Americans until the late nineteenth century and they do not exist in most peasant societies to this day.[26] What did develop strongly among poor mothers was a sense of community in child rearing. Sometimes this was built into an exploitative system, as with older women on plantations tending to slave children while their (younger, stronger) mothers worked. Many times, however, female support systems developed through women's own needs and initiatives. This was evident in many female-headed intergenerational households where grandmothers were highly involved in children's lives, and older siblings often tended to babies and small children while their mothers were busy doing other things.[27]

In rural, especially peasant, communities, motherhood was more than just another form of work. It was also a responsibility through which women (alongside men and fathers) taught younger generations about what it meant to be a man or a woman, and how one should act within the broader community. Mothers in particular were important transmitters of culture within indigenous peasant communities. It was with their mothers that indigenous children first learned language, and it was at their mothers' sides that girls learned how to cook, brew traditional beverages, and weave clothing that identified one's ethnic origins. Customs were handed down from one generation to another, and mothers were at the center of this intergenerational transmission. Fathers, too, had an important role to play, particularly with teaching boys and young men how to act within the community. In urban centers, indigenous mothers likely played a role of passing down customs and language, but these were not as strongly reinforced or central to everyday life as in rural communities.[28] Slave mothers on plantations were also likely to hand down important cultural beliefs, especially with regard to beliefs and customs of African origin.

Motherhood could also have an impact on women's struggles with their husbands (or partners, in the case of consensual unions). For example, an older woman's grown son might help her if she was in a domestic dispute, especially if the woman's partner was not the son's biological father.[29] In nineteenth-century Ecuador, when Manuela Atampala's husband, Antonio Chatín, began beating her, her son from a previous marriage came to her defense, resulting in a skirmish that proved fatal for Chatín. Many women were also careful to protect their families' economic interests at all costs if their husbands were having extramarital affairs. In a situation that threatened her financially and emotionally, rather than physically, a wife might act to guarantee whatever security she could. For example, when María Prudencia Quispi's husband had an affair and gave his mistress, Francisca Morocho, one of his cows, Quispi went to Morocho's land and took the cow back. It seems that even if she could not do anything to change her husband's behavior, Quispi was determined to protect the economy of her household unit by reclaiming the property that she considered rightfully hers.[30] Motherhood likely influenced women's decision to focus on economic needs rather than personal feelings, prioritizing their children's well-being. Similarly, a woman might enter a conflict to protect her child more directly, as did Matea Gallardo, a Peruvian woman whose daughter worked as a servant in Jesús del Campo's house. Gallardo was determined to defend her daughter when del Campo beat her, but ultimately her class status kept her from being able to protect her daughter effectively. When the altercation became heated, del Campo had Gallardo beaten and jailed.[31]

Not all poor mothers could afford to raise their children. Historian Elizabeth Dore discovered that in Diriomo, Nicaragua, unmarried parenthood was on the rise in the nineteenth century, resulting in a higher-than-usual number of child support cases which women brought against the fathers of their children. In some cases, these men were wealthier men in the local community (although not among the elite), and they agreed to fulfill their paternal financial obligations for these children in return for future custody of them. Though poor women in Diriomo sometimes resisted handing over their children once weaned, many poor women faced the painful necessity of giving away their children because they could not afford to raise them.[32] In urban areas, mothers and fathers without means to care for their children were likely to bring them to a foundling home (particularly if they were infants or young children) or to a poor house.[33] One woman who migrated from the countryside to Mexico City placed her six-year-old son in a poor house, explaining that she was "a poor and honorable woman, hardworking . . . who supports herself on the little she earns doing ironing." Her husband had left her, and she had not yet established a social network in the city. Without means to support her son, she did not know where else to take him.[34] Parents who placed children in institutional care in Mexico City sometimes tried to retrieve them later, as did Margarita García, who was able to call upon social networks (in particular the assistance of a local artisan) to help her reunite with the child she had deposited in a foundling home at age three.[35] Single mothers, particularly those without strong networks of support, were those most likely to have to hand over a child to an institution. If children were older when a mother hit hard times, she might instead hire them out, usually as domestic servants in wealthy households.

Patriarchal laws and judges also limited women's ability to mother their children effectively. As noted in the last chapter, many countries continued with *patria potestad* laws that gave fathers greater rights over children than mothers, including when couples separated. The idea behind this was that fathers could provide better for their children than mothers, with economic necessity being valued over emotional attachments. Historian Christine Hunefeldt, however, notes that by the end of the nineteenth century in Peru, middle-class ideas about childhood changed to weigh emotional needs more heavily, resulting in more cases in which even older children stayed with their mothers.[36] The times and extent to which laws changed to give mothers more rights over children varied in Latin America, but the new emphasis on the mother–child bond lay foundations that – along with women's own demands discussed in the next chapter – made the legal changes possible. Poor women, however, were not always limited by patria potestad laws, because they most often lived in consensual unions. If their partners were not officially married to them, they could not usually claim full patriarchal powers over women or children.

Informal unions, however, were no guarantee that a woman had secure rights over her children. Consider the case of María Dolores Alcoser in Arequipa, Peru. Her daughter's father won custody of the child, even though he refused to recognize her as his own. He persuaded the judge that Alcoser, who was a *chichera* (chicha maker/seller) would "exploit her daughter's labor, raise her on leftovers and chicha, and expose her to immoral and uneducated people."[37] Alcoser's former partner successfully painted her as an immoral woman who would corrupt her daughter, and she lost custody of the child. Similarly, when poor women in Mexico City tried to reclaim children whom poverty had forced them to put into the foundling home, welfare officials often made this difficult. State officials refused to face the fact that economic inequalities often forced poor mothers to send their children to foundling homes. Instead, they preferred to identify the women as "bad mothers" who had "abandoned" their children, and therefore stereotyped poor women as less deserving of family life than middle- class or elite women (who could afford to raise their children).[38] In this latter case, it is clear that emerging emphasis on the mother–child bond was not considered universal, but rather class (and race) specific.

If middling and upper classes excluded poor working women from their ideas about "good motherhood," it was also true that working women sometimes rejected dominant gender norms and the emphasis that motherhood was what defined all women's value. In her work on women workers in Mexico City from 1879 to 1931, historian Susie Porter found that women factory workers and street vendors displayed a view of their rights and worth as both mothers and as workers. Sometimes they emphasized their motherhood when seeking better pay, but in doing so they often referred to their roles as primary breadwinners, as Juana Gutiérrez did when she asserted that she was "a poor woman with children who by selling corn struggles for an honorable life," and therefore required a license to sell cooked corn on a street corner.[39] Female factory workers were even more likely to redefine gendered notions of honor when they discussed "the inherent dignity of our labor, and the support which the laws of our Motherland provide us" in protests against having to carry identification cards (*libretas*) in the 1880s.[40] As Porter rightly points out, it is not necessary (and in any case is likely impossible) to understand whether these working women accepted or rejected dominant gender norms, because the legal and economic realities of their lives forced them to engage dominant ideas about honor and morality. What most of these working women did, regardless of their own personal beliefs, was to reorient notions of honor and morality such that female honor could come out of work as well as motherhood.

Whereas women vendors and factory workers often had the economic and social independence to redefine how motherhood fit into their identities, servants and slaves lacked control over their personal lives, and they often found it difficult or impossible to raise their children themselves. Not only did a slave woman have to work most of the day while another looked after her small child, but a slave owner could decide to sell a slave woman's child any time that he (or she) wished. The slave system was also set up to deny the rights of slave parents in other fundamental ways. Slave children, for example, were taught at a young age to refer to the slaves owners as "mothers" and "fathers" – indicating clearly if indirectly that the true parental authority did not lie with their own parents.[41] Domestic servants were often just as vulnerable, though in different ways. Their wealthy employers did not want their servants' children around to distract them from work, and they often fired a female servant who got pregnant, particularly if it seemed that she would try to keep the child with her. Such actions were often bolstered by laws, such the "Regulation of Domestic Servants" in the state of Jalisco, Mexico, in 1888. Article 2450 indicated that one of the acceptable reasons for firing a domestic servant was "His/her vices, sickness, or bad behavior."[42] An unmarried woman's pregnancy easily fit within these very general bounds of "vices and bad behavior." This was true even if one of the members of the employer's household was the man who got the servant pregnant. Given this situation, domestic servants often had little choice but to send their children to be raised elsewhere. Similarly, women who worked as wet nurses at Mexico City's orphanage were required to "board their own babies in the countryside with other wet nurses."[43]

There are cases by the early twentieth century when working-class mothers had options other than putting their children into institutional care or hiring them out as servants. For example, in Quito, Ecuador, a day care center for children of working women opened in 1914. The center was founded by a police chief, Antonio Gil, and it was run by a semiprivate organization for child protection. Through his experiences in the police force Gil knew that although women who abandoned their children were often labeled "unfit mothers," the majority of them were forced to give up babies due to poverty, lack of assistance from their children's fathers, or their wealthy employers' demands.[44] Similarly, Mexican industrialist Carlos B. Zetina set up a day care center for his female workers' children in 1913.[45] In both of these instances, either public or private authorities recognized and responded to the needs of poor working mothers by trying to provide adequate child care facilities, indirectly recognizing that their inability to tend to their children full time was due to economic necessity rather than moral failings.

Mothering the Children of Others

Poor women frequently had the responsibility of tending to children other than their own. Women workers or slaves on large estates, in addition to tending to their own children and homes, sometimes tended to the household and children of the estate owner.[46] In cities, domestic servants – often women of indigenous or African descent – tended to the daily care of wealthy children. In some cases, babies and small children were more attached to these "hired caregivers" than they were to their biological parents because it was these women, and not their own parents, who regularly fed them when they were hungry, cleaned them when they were dirty, and comforted them when they were ill or hurt. Slave and servant women themselves probably had a variety of emotional reactions to their young charges, from maternal tenderness to resentment, perhaps with an individual woman experiencing a contradictory mix of these feelings on a regular basis. Regardless of the affective ties between wealthy children and their caregivers, slave and servant women did not receive formal recognition as "alternate mothers." In fact, as the next chapter will discuss, scholars and state officials considered middle-class and elite women inherently more nurturing than their lower-class counterparts, even though these same women handed over the less glamorous tasks of mothering – which is to say, the majority of tasks with young children – to such women.

In addition to the women who attended to the general needs of other people's children, there were also numerous wet nurses in nineteenth-century Latin America. There was no safe baby formula in this period: babies had no option other than to breast feed. Even around the turn into the twentieth century, when medical officials began to experiment with formulas, they were clearly inferior to breast milk. Historian Ann Blum, for example, found that when administrators of the Mexico City foundling home experimented with formula, due to a shortage of wet nurses, most of the formula-fed infants died.[47] Science had not yet come up with an adequate and safe substitute for Mother Nature.

Working as a wet nurse had both advantages and disadvantages for a poor woman. On the one hand, for a woman like Tadea Casas whose story appears at both the beginning and end of this chapter, being a wet nurse likely eased her pain after losing her own biological child. Casas was a mother without a child, and Manuela Chavez was a baby without a mother; they filled each other's biological, and possibly emotional, needs. Some women who nursed orphans were later able to adopt them into their own households. Whether they bonded strongly with infants under their care or not, women might find working as a wet nurse an important, perhaps even convenient, way to make extra money to meet their own household needs. This was work that sometimes (though not always) paid as well as other work, and it could often be done in conjunction with other household and economic chores. Working-class women were already used to laundering clothes or spinning cloth while tending to (and nursing) young children; adding someone else's child to the mix did not alter already familiar rhythms of work and life. However, sometimes things did not work out so smoothly. A wet nurse might be put in the ironic and difficult position of having to send her own child out to another (cheaper) wet nurse in order to make money necessary for herself and her older children. Alternately, if she nursed both her own baby and another's simultaneously (and some women nursed three or four babies at once, though it is not clear how frequently that happened), the health of all nursing children could be compromised.

By the end of the nineteenth century, the practice of wet nursing was coming under increasing scrutiny and criticism. Child welfare institutions, such as foundling homes and orphanages, began to supervise wet nurses more closely and, in particular, subjected them to frequent (and sometimes humiliating) medical examinations. One orphanage director noted that they never had any problems with the health of babies sent out to wet nurses precisely because "we always take care to inspect the wet nurses to ensure that they fulfill their duties."[48] Additionally, by the turn into the twentieth century medical doctors strongly advocated having a woman – particularly a middle-class or elite woman – breast feed her own child rather than hire a wet nurse. As Don Manuel Valle of Guatemala's Child Welfare Clinic (*Gota de leche*) proclaimed in 1907: "When will there be public action to preserve and protect the lives of children, who are the economic future in the life of the nation? . . . shouldn't criminal laws punish mothers who abandon their children?. . . ." He later added that "It is not only poor women, or unhappy or neglectful women who break from Mother Nature . . . rich and happy women have also denied their sons and daughters, some by necessity, some by error, the rightful nourishment of infancy, the milk of their [own] breasts."[49]

If critics (most of whom were men) called upon all women to nurse their own children, they held wet nurses in particular disdain. They identified them as "mercenaries" who were more interested in money than in the health of their own babies, who might suffer from lack of milk if their mother nursed another child. They also described wet nurses as dirty and diseased – in short, as women whose filth would harm rather than nourish the babies under their care. Such descriptions were rife with suggestions of class and race. Wet nurses were poor women who needed the income from nursing other people's children in order to tend to their own families' economic needs. This was a far different situation than the middle-class and elite stereotype that wet nurses lacked the moral and nurturing instincts attributed to middle-class women. Moreover, impressions of "dirtiness" and lack of hygiene suggested race as well as class, given that elites viewed peoples of indigenous or African descent as filthy people who lived in squalor.[50]

Despite the almost ubiquitous middle-class and elite disdain for "mercenary" wet nurses, anthropologist A. Kim Clark found evidence of wet nurses who became maternally attached to children that they brought into their homes. When the *casa de cuna* (children's shelter) in Quito, Ecuador rounded up children who had been placed with wet nurses in 1927, in order to raise them at the shelter, many wet nurses – usually through their literate husbands – petitioned to adopt the children.

Consider the petition, cited in Clark's work, made by carpenter Rosalio Cruz that Clark to the *Junta de Beneficencia* (the Social Welfare Office):

> My wife received the orphan A.G. one day after his birth and has cared for him for nine months. Yesterday the Junta de Beneficencia ordered that all orphans be returned, and among these is ours. We love him as if he were our own son, so we have decided to petition the Junta de Beneficencia to return to us the child A.G., and we relinquish any salary or other benefits that the Junta might offer to raise the child, committing ourselves to adopt him as our son, to clothe him, care for him as we have been doing, educated him, teach him a trade, and from our small legacy grant him a portion when that becomes necessary. We beg that the Junta de Beneficencia accept our petition for the good of the orphaned child as well as for our own consolation.[51]

Clark notes not only that such petitions call into question elite claims that wet nurses were mercenaries who were merely interested in profit, but she also highlights the differences between elites who "adopted" poor children and the petitioners here. Middle-class and elite families brought poor children into their homes in order to raise them "according to their class" and to put them to work in their households. These more humble petitioners sought to incorporate the children fully into their families, offering even whatever inheritance they might be able to leave them.

Elite Stereotypes, Subaltern Realities

The earlier discussion of wet nurses highlights discrepancies between elite perceptions of poor women's mothering skills and instincts (or, as they saw it, lack thereof) and the actual experiences and motivations of poor mothers. Middle-class and elite officials, scholars, and doctors identified poor women, especially those of indigenous or African descent, as dirty, inept, and largely uncaring mothers. Most of the evidence in this chapter, however, reveals that such claims were little more than unfounded stereotypes. Though it is challenging to uncover poor mothers' voices and viewpoints, available sources suggest that these women were as concerned about their children as wealthier women were; what they often lacked were the resources to provide adequately for their children. It was poverty, not moral character, that forced them to give up their children in most circumstances, just as it was poverty, and not ineptitude, that limited the cleanliness of some of their homes. Can one find evidence of poor women who did not love their children? Absolutely . . . just as one can find evidence of wealthy women who lacked affection for theirs. In fact, sometimes it was poor servant women who showed more caring for middle-class and elite children than their own mothers did, at least in terms of routine nurturing.

Why, then, did middle-class and elite scholars and officials describe poor mothers in such negative terms? In part, such classifications were based on colonial histories of exploiting peoples of indigenous and African descent, stereotypes used to justify the control and poor treatment of the conquered or enslaved. Moreover, elite notions of honor in the colonial period rested on ideas about wealthy women of Spanish descent as inherently moral and sexually pure; stereotypes of dirty, uncaring indigenous and African women offered as supposed "proof" of elite superiority and status. Elite and middle-class images of poor women continued to serve as a foil to claims about "good" middle-class women and mothers in the nineteenth century. However, although such impressions may have had colonial roots, they served new social and political purposes in the nineteenth century.

Many changes came in the century following independence in Spanish America (roughly 1825–1920). The stereotypes about poor women as dirty and unqualified (as well as uncaring) mothers was part of a broader set of elite and middle-class discourses that identified poor people of non-European descent as backward groups who required redemption before they could be included in the nation. Otherwise, elites asserted, their barbaric ways would drag the nation down rather than strengthen it. These stereotypes also helped elites to grapple with social and demographic changes that were occurring by the late nineteenth century in some areas, as historian Ann Blum noted for late nineteenth-century Mexico City. The population of the city was growing, mostly due to the migration of poor rural peoples who were driven off their own lands and sought employment in the capital city. Such change brought anxiety to wealthier city dwellers, who in part expressed their fears by identifying poor women as bad mothers whose children were rightfully taken out of their care.[52] Studying similar issues in Ecuador, A. Kim Clark notes that "it was always mothers . . . who were assumed to abandon their infants, while fathers seemed to have little connection to or responsibility for their children's well-being."[53]

Why were women, as mothers, at the heart of these national debates over how to deal with both children (the future of the nation) and poor peoples of indigenous or African descent? The answer lies in how nine-teenth- and early twentieth-century nations defined womanhood and connected middle-class motherhood with national growth and prosper-ity. It is to this matter that the next chapter turns.

Document: Tadea Casas, Accused of "Stealing" 11-Year-Old Manuela Chavez

In 1862, in the small city of Cajamarca, Peru, Tadea Casas tried to defend herself against charges that she "stole" 11-year-old Manuela Chavez (also known by the surname Cuculi) from her guardian, Lorenza Cabrera, and "given" the child to José María Cortés. Below, Casas defended her actions by explaining her relationship to Manuela Chavez, and her reasons for wanting the child to live with Cortés. This excerpt contains references to many different people, sometimes going by different names. What does this confusion suggest about what Manuela Chavez's childhood was like? Who were the "mother" figures in her life? How and why did mother-hood transcend biology in this document? What does this excerpt reveal about how poverty shaped experiences of family?

Tadea Casas's Testimony

"[Testimony of Tadea Casas], Natural resident of this capital city and about thirty years of age, single, and a spinner by trade."

". . . [She says] that it is true that she gave the aforemen-tioned minor to the Captain [José María Cortes]. She had raised Manuela Cuculi [Chavez], who had been given to her at the age of three months by her mother Estefania Cuculi who is dead. She presumes that the aforementioned minor, like her mother, had the surname of Chavez but she knew them by the common surname of Cuculi which she has indicated. The declarant raised the said minor until the age of two years, at which time she gave her to Doña Francisca García, because [Casas] was poor and could not care for [the child], even though she wanted to educate her, and loved her as if she were her own daughter. The aforesaid Francisca, called Lorenza, always gravely mistreated the minor . . . and [Casas's] aforesaid adopted daughter suffered. She trusted the offers that the said captain [Cortes] made that he could care for [the child] and hold her in high regard. [Then] the aforementioned Lorenza, upon returning to her house one night from a social gathering, threw the minor out of her house. [Casas] brought [Manuela Chavez] to Mr. Cortes, as she could not be indifferent to the suffering of the expressed minor who at that time was eleven years old. She had cared for [the child] properly and with the most natural compassion when being given charge of her when her godfather Martin Cuculi, now deceased, had brought [the child to her] on account of the fact that her mother Estefania had died after childbirth. [He did so because] the declarant, having lost a child in infancy remained able to nurse . . .

Testimony of Manuel Goyochea, 40-Year-Old Resident, Single, and a Farmer

Manuel Goyochea, Manuela Chavez's uncle, also bore witness in Tadea Casas's defense, explaining (and in some ways clarifying) the flow of events from the child's birth up to the events in which Casas and Goyochea decided that it was necessary for her to leave Lorenza Cabrera's home.

The expressed minor was orphaned from birth because her mother Estefania Chavez died in childbirth, and for this reason her godfather, who was Martin Cuculi, the deceased brother of the witness, brought her to be cared for by Tadea Casas, who kept her until she was two years old, after which age and, considering that the said Tadea was not able to continue to care for and feed the minor orphan due to her own poverty, gave her intentionally to the sister of the witness, Francisca Garcia. She [Garcia] died and passed the minor at four or five years old to the care of the daughter of

Francisca named Lorenza Cabrera, who repeated treated her extremely badly until one night when Lorenza had gone out to a social gathering to return late to her house and commanded the minor to light the candles. When she was slow in doing this, Lorenza beat her severely, and for that reason she felt obligated to flee to the home of her adoptive mother, Tadea. In these circumstances she begged [Casas] to talk to her uncle so that he could see where she lived and finally free her from her condition of suffering at the hands of the said Lorenza. The declarant was deeply shocked by his minor niece's tears and offered to look for someone who could take her and provide her with the caring that she deserved.[54]

Notes

1   This particular life was pieced together from descriptions of motherhood and slavery in Stanley Stein, *Vassouras: A Brazilian Coffee County, 1850–1900: The Roles of Planter and Slave in a Plantation Society* (Princeton, NJ: Princeton University Press, 1986), pp. 137, 164, 166.

2   Susie S. Porter, *Working Women in Mexico City: Public Discourses and Material Conditions, 1879–1931* (Tucson: University of Arizona Press, 2003), pp. 3–5.

3   *Chicha* is corn beer made in the Andes, and *pulque* is a fermented drink made from the maguey plant in Mexico. Each was a typical "indigenous peasant" drink, and each also served important roles in community gatherings' such as weddings, funerals, harvest celebrations, or celebrations of saint's days.

4   Divorce and remarriage were not options throughout Latin America for most of the nineteenth century, and sometimes well into the twentieth century. Peasant practices were informal rather than legally condoned.

5   For a discussion of some of these dynamics in southeastern Mexico, see Piedad Peniche Rivero, "Women, Bridewealth and Marriage: Peonage and Social Reproduction in the Henequen Hacienda of Yucatán, Mexico," in Heather Fowler-Salamini and Mary Kay Vaughan, eds, *Women in the Mexican Countryside, 1850–1990*, (Tucson: University of Arizona Press, 1994), pp. 74–89.

6   I have found some instances in Ecuador of estate records that included one or two women's names. I suspect that these women were widows. However, the general trend was to count labor, and distribute land, through men only.

7   John Tutino, "The Revolution in Mexican Independence: Insurgency and the Renegotiation of Property, Production, and Patriarchy in the Bajío, 1800–1855," *Hispanic American Historical Review* 78:3 (1998), pp. 367–418.

8   Barry J. Lyons, *Remembering the Hacienda: Religion, Authority, and Social Change in Highland Ecuador* (Austin: University of Texas Press, 2006), pp. 167–168. Also see Dore, p. 158.

9   Stuart B. Schwartz, *Sugar Plantations in the Formation of Brazilian Society: Bahia, 1550–1835* (New York: Cambridge University Press, 1985), p. 386.

10   Sandra Lauderdale Graham, *Caetana Says No: Women's Stories from a Brazilian Slave Society* (New York: Cambridge University Press, 2002).

11   Schwartz, p. 390.

12   Katia M. De Queiros Mattoso, *To Be a Slave in Brazil, 1550–1888*, trans. Arthur Goldhammer (New Brunswick, NJ: Rutgers University Press, 1987), p. 164.

13   Sylvia Marina Arrom makes extensive use of these censuses, and she also discusses their limitations, in her book *The Women of Mexico City, 1790–1857* (Stanford, CA: Stanford University Press, 1985). See particularly pp. 98–100 and 112–113.

14   Maria Odila Silva Dias, *Power and Everyday Life: The Lives of Working Women in Nineteenth-Century Brazil* (New Brunswick: Rutgers University Press, 1995). Accessed on Kindle, with this information appearing at 14% through the book.

15   Arrom, *The Women of Mexico City*, p. 161.

16   For two studies that include extensive discussions of women vendors in the colonial Andes, see Kimberly Gauderman, *Women's Lives in Colonial Quito: Gender, Law, and Economy in Spanish America* (Austin: University of Texas Press, 2003), and Jane E. Mangan, *Trading Roles: Gender, Ethnicity, and the Urban Economy in Colonial Potosí* (Durham, NC: Duke University Press, 2005).

17   Odila Silva Dias, 6%; Susie S. Porter, *Working Women in Mexico City: Public Discourses and Material Conditions, 1879–1931* (Tucson: University of Arizona Press, 2003), pp. 132–146.

18   Porter, particularly chapters 1–3.

19   See Odila Silva Dias, chapter 4.

20   Arrom, *The Women of Mexico City*, p. 170.

21   Arrom, *The Women of Mexico City*, pp. 124–126, 135.

22   Schwartz has a particularly nice discussion of these factors on pp. 354–363.

23   De Queiros Mattoso, pp. 111, 156, 171.

24   Schwartz, pp. 379 and 395.

25   Arrom, *The Women of Mexico City*, pp. 178–179.

26   For an excellent discussion of indigenous ideas about childhood and labor Ecuador circa 2000, see Kate Swanson, *Begging as a Path to Progress: Indigenous Women and Children and the Struggle for Ecuador's Urban Spaces* (Athens: University of Georgia Press, 2010), pp. 29–42.

27   A very good discussion of multigenerational households can be found in Odila Silva Dias, 5, 52, and 57%. Arrom, p. 182, also mentions how girls' wages were often important for family survival in households headed by single or widowed mothers, and Porter's example of Marcela Bernal on pp. 3–5, with which this chapter opens, shows that daughters often worked in order to allow their mothers to tend to younger children and other household duties.

28   Sarah Chambers mentions both mothers passing on ethnic identity and indigenous identity being weaker among urban than rural Indians in the Arequipa area of Peru in her book *From Subjects to Citizens: Honor, Gender, and Politics in Arequipa, Peru, 1780–1854* (University Park: Pennsylvania State University Press, 1999), pp. 71–72.

29   The notion of alternate patriarchs is one that was developed by Steve J. Stern in his discussions of "contested patriarchy" in *The Secret History of Gender: Women, Men, and Power in Late Colonial Mexico* (Chapel Hill: University of North Carolina Press, 1995).

30   Erin O'Connor, *Gender, Indian, Nation: The Contradictions of Making Ecuador, 1830–1925* (Tucson: University of Arizona Press, 2007), pp. 123–126. Also see Christine Hunefeldt, *Liberalism in the Bedroom: Quarreling Spouses in Nineteenth-Century Lima* (University Park: Pennsylvania State University Press, 2000), p. 214.

31   Tanya Christiansen, *Disobedience, Slander, Seduction, and Assault: Women and Men in Cajamarca, Peru, 1862–1900* (Austin: University of Texas Press, 2004), pp. 153–154.

32   Elizabeth Dore, *Myths of Modernity: Peonage and Patriarchy in Nicaragua* (Durham, NC: Duke University Press, 2006), pp. 65–66.

33   These were called *casas de expósitos*. Although they were technically for foundlings, or abandoned children of unknown parentage, by the nineteenth century, many poor parents brought the children there openly.

34   This example is from Ann S. Blum, *Domestic Economies: Family, Work, and Welfare in Mexico City, 1884–1943* (Lincoln: University of Nebraska Press, 2009), pp. 16–17.

35   Blum, p. 29.

36   Hunefeldt, pp. 162, 358.

37   Chambers, pp. 206–207.

38   Blum, p. 39.

39   Porter, p. 133.

40   Porter, p. 124.

41 De Queiros Mattoso, p. 112.

42 Jefatura Política del Primer Cantón del Estado de Jalisco, *Reglamento de Domésticos* (1888). This stipulation cited the Mexican civil code for regulating domestic servitude.

43 Blum, p. 73.

44 A. Kim Clark, *Gender, State, and Medicine in Highland Ecuador: Modernizing Women, Modernizing the State, 1895–1950* (Pittsburgh, PA: University of Pittsburgh Press, 2012), p. 48.

45 Porter, p. 168.

46 For an example, see Lauderdale Graham, *Caetana Says No*, p. 19.

47 Blum, pp. 96–99.

48 Clark, p. 64.

49 Don Manuel Valle, *Inauguración del Servicio: Discurso Oficial* (Guatemala: Tipografía Nacional, 1907), pp. 4–5, 7.

50 Ann Blum has an excellent discussion of turn-of-the century discourses on wet nursing in *Domestic Economies*, chapter 3.

51 This quote appears in Clark, p. 43. Her broader discussion of the relationship between wet nurses and their charges is on pp. 42–45.

52 See Blum's *Domestic Economies*.

53 Clark, p. 75.

54 Archivo Departmental de Cajamarca, Corte Superior de Justicia, Casos Criminales, legajo I, 19-I-1862. "Lorenza Cabrera vecina de Cajamarca litigando con el capitán de gendermería Don José María Cortés sobre entrega de la menor Manuela Chávez quien fue regalada al susodicho por Tadea Casas y José Manuel Goycochea." Many thanks to Tanja Christiansen for generously sharing her transcription of this court case with me for the purposes of including it in this book.

4

Middle-Class and Elite Mothers
Feminism, Femininity, and the Nation in the Nineteenth Century

Literary Women in Lima

Juana Manuela Gorriti was born in Argentina in 1818 to an upper-class family. At the age of 15, she married a Bolivian army captain, Manuel Isidoro Belzú (later president of Bolivia) and had three children with him. After several years, part of which time Gorriti and her husband lived in Lima, Peru, Belzú abandoned her. Gorriti continued to live in Lima, where she worked as a journalist and held many tertulias for literary men and women. She was a strong opponent of the Rosas dictatorship in Argentina, and became a supporter of Peruvian nationalism over the years. She also had a great deal of influence on younger Peruvian women writers. She published numerous essays and short novels in journals and newspapers in both Lima and Buenos Aires, and eventually returned to Argentina where, despite her scandalous marriage, she was welcomed and celebrated. Throughout her life, Gorriti was concerned with politics, and she consistently advocated for greater rights for women. Her literary works were both romantic and political, with women protagonists often playing the part of mediator between male political opponents. She often wrote women characters who were lone travelers, rebelling against restrictions placed on them while simultaneously upholding proper feminine behavior. Gorriti died in 1892 and was celebrated in her home country of Argentina.

Teresa González de Fanning was born in Peru in 1836 and grew up on a family-owned hacienda. She had a keen interest in the classics as

Mothers Making Latin America: Gender, Households, and Politics Since 1825,
First Edition. Erin E. O'Connor.
© 2014 John Wiley & Sons, Inc. Published 2014 by John Wiley & Sons, Inc.

she grew up and her intellectual passions ruled much of her life. She married a marine officer, Juan Fanning García and had two children with him. Her family life appears to have been happy until two tragedies struck. First, when resident workers on her family's estate rebelled, she fled with her children for Lima. However, the journey was difficult, and her two children died along the way. Later, her husband died in the War of the Pacific against Chile in 1881. González was an avid writer throughout her life, and after she was widowed she put much of her energy into running a girls' school and writing textbooks for it. She was also an ardent advocate for women's education and advancement, and was a regular attendant in the same literary meetings in Lima as Gorriti.

Clorinda Matto de Turner was born in 1852 in Cuzco, Peru, and spent most of her childhood on a nearby family estate. Intellectually hungry as a youth, she studied subjects that girls did not often take up, such as physics and natural history. In 1871, she married an English businessman, Joseph Turner. They had no children, and Matto continued to write during her marriage, founding the journal *El Recreo* in 1876, to which many well-known literary figures, including Gorriti, contributed. Matto also attended some of the tertulias that Gorriti held. When Joseph Turner died in 1881, leaving Matto in difficult financial straits, she continued to work as a writer and publisher, and in the 1880s took to writing novels. Her most famous novel was *Aves sin Nido* (*Torn from the Nest*), first published in 1889. The novel, like many of Matto's other works, was sympathetic towards Indians, but it also had references to affairs between white men and indigenous women, and it was highly critical of the priesthood – both issues that made the novel highly controversial. The Peruvian archbishop ultimately excommunicated Matto, who went into exile in 1895, spending a good deal of her time in Argentina, where she taught at a university. She died in Buenos Aires in 1909.

Teresa González de Fanning, Clorinda Matto de Turner, and Juana Manuela Gorriti's lives and literary interests overlapped in Lima's tertulias and publications. All three were intellectual women from well-to-do backgrounds. All three faced personal challenges in their lives and marriages. Though none of them self-identified as "feminist" – since the term was not used for women's rights advocates until the 1890s – they all sought to improve women's lives by both challenging and embracing the dominant gender norms of their time. In particular, all three women reinterpreted, rather than rejected, ideas that identified women with motherhood and the domestic sphere. They thus fit within the framework of *relational feminism* discussed in Chapter 1. These three women's lives and work offer important insights about motherhood, women's rights, and nation-state formation in nineteenth-century Latin America.

Unlike poor women, middle-class and elite women in Latin America experienced new opportunities in the late nineteenth century. Legislators and scholars considered middle-class women important contributors to the nation through their roles as mothers, and they therefore granted women protections and rights within their homes, over their children, and with money. They did not, however, challenge long-standing dominant gender ideas, nor did they propose that women should have any extensive role in the public sphere. Middle-class and elite women took advantage of their new symbolic importance, and some of them started movements to increase women's rights. Nineteenth-century feminists used discourses on social motherhood as a jumping-off point to argue for increased rights, and sometimes for more active roles in the public sphere. Those middle-class and elite women who were not drawn to feminism also found new ways to have a social impact. Many elite women, for example, became involved in charity work that had once been under the jurisdiction of the Catholic Church but which, with the rise of secular governments, required volunteers. Though men were sometimes the ultimate authorities overseeing these organizations, women did most of the work in these charities and, in a few countries, also ran them.

Despite the many activities in which upper-class women engaged from about 1850 to 1910, few of them – even among feminists – challenged the idea that women ultimately belonged in the home. While they reinterpreted social motherhood in order to expand women's opportunities and demand respect for women's work at home, they did not usually claim equality with men, and most did not seek the right to vote during this period. Likewise, although some middle-class and elite women were sincerely concerned with, and sought to help, poor women and children, few women of privilege questioned the dominant ideas about class and race. Most agreed with middle-class and elite men that the poor and peoples of non-European descent were backwards and in needed their wealthier "superiors" to guide and reform them.

The majority of these women – feminists and conservatives alike – centered their arguments on not only the home in general, but motherhood in particular. In her study of feminism in Argentina, Chile, and Uruguay, historian Asunción Lavrin observed that

It is not surprising that Southern Cone feminists opted for a feminism that would fit into their social milieu and be acceptable to other women as well as to the men who held the reins of power. Feminism oriented toward motherhood was more than a strategy to win favorable legislation, it was an essential component of their cultural heritage: a tune that feminists not only knew how to play but wished to play.[1]

One cannot expect nineteenth-century feminists to have been able to step outside of the cultures and ideas with which they lived on a daily basis, and from which many of them benefited considerably. However, even as they engaged (rather than rejected) dominant gender and class-race norms, they simultaneously lay the groundwork for more profound challenges that would come in the twentieth century.

Women's tendency to merge feminist goals with symbols of motherhood reflected the state of transition that Latin American societies were undergoing from about 1870 to 1910. Not only were women's legal rights in the process of changing as noted in Chapter 2, but other important transformations were taking place. Generally, the power and formal influence of the Church in politics and society was on the decline, creating a void that was not yet filled by government institutions in any systematic way. Governments were often stronger in the late nineteenth century than they had been immediately following independence, but in most cases well-established, state-run social welfare institutions were not created until the early decades of the twentieth century. Women's movements and activities in the late nineteenth century not only reflected and engaged with these broader transformations, but they also played a role in how governments would develop welfare institutions in the twentieth century.

Motherhood at the Crossroads of Feminism and Femininity

Feminists often embraced ,the idea that motherhood was central to womanhood, but they used this idea to argue that current laws or practices limited women's ability to fulfill this role and therefore needed to be changed.[2] The Baronesa de Wilson, a Spanish woman who spent a great deal of time in the Americas, and whose writings were often read in Latin America, warned that women's emancipation could never happen if women lost sight of "[woman's] most powerful influence as a mother, with a wife's necessary tenderness, her abnegation, her indulgence, her generosity, her grace and feminine ability, to conserve her purity and divine womanly essence."[3] Women's rights advocates claimed that better access to education, greater independent control of money, and the right to make decisions for their children would all enable mothers to raise stronger, healthier children who would contribute, in turn, to the national well-being.

Feminists' focus on maternity and rights came not only out of their adherence to dominant gender beliefs, but it also in order to deflect criticisms of their movements. Men – and women – who opposed women's rights often claimed that feminists were betraying their womanhood. They might claim, for example, that feminists "wanted to masculinize woman, to convert her into a mannish or butch woman (*marimacho*)" or that a feminist "aspires to see forever overturned the societal idea that woman requires man's protection."[4] Other antifeminists were afraid that if women entered the job force and politics, they would undermine male authority. Even proposals to give women the right to control some of the money they brought into marriage could provoke legislators' ire and fear. When such a reform was proposed in Ecuador in 1911, one senator claimed that allowing wives to control money during marriage would turn the whole notion of marriage itself on its head, resulting in a society where "marriage would be constituted of two husbands, rather than man and wife."[5] Though this assertion greatly exaggerated the economic power that wives would have if the law passed, many legislators shared his fears.

In the face of such attacks, many feminists were careful to define their movements within the bounds of what was "safe" and familiar territory for women – the home and motherhood. They asserted that feminism was aimed at

> elevating woman's condition, not just to guarantee her individual rights, justly extended in the name of personal human autonomy, but also collective [social] interests that relies on the collaboration of the two halves that make up our species; [to balance] the equation between the duties and rights within the family for the better distribution of power and functions, substituting the regimen of subjection for that of justice.[6]

Similarly, in her book *Torn from the Nest*, Clorinda Matto de Turner advocated companionate marriage and women's education through her heroine, Lucía, who was happily married to Fernando, a fellow member of the Lima elite. Yet in many instances, Matto made it clear that Lucía was subordinate within her marriage, and that her husband's fair rule, combined with his wife's good customs and education, were what made their marriage work. Women in the novel consistently upheld higher moral standards than men, even if the men were well educated. Their greatest concerns were maternal, either for children of their own or, as in the case of the childless young Lucía, through her concern for seemingly childlike Indians. By the end of the novel, young Lucía was pregnant with her first child, ready to meet her sublime maternal destiny full on.[7]

Some women's rights advocates, such as Teresa González de Fanning in Peru, reinforced long-standing male power within the context of liberal political ideas and goals, and identified feminism with the struggle against Church control in society. Gónzalez did so when she argued that women required a secular rather than religious education. Secular education, she claimed, would ultimately strengthen rather than weaken the patriarchal household. She asserted that religious education did the opposite, and accused some priests of undermining household order, writing:

> instead of procuring peace and unity in the family, [they] dislodge it and introduce anarchy and discord on the pretext of religion. Instead of [encouraging women] to fulfill their domestic duties, they authorize her to abandon them. Because of this, while a mother is on her knees in devotion at the temple . . . her house is like a ship without a rudder, swaying at the caprice of the servants, and the children, disheveled and unattended, go to bed late . . . And conjugal relations? . . . No one can ignore what happens when a husband finds his needs unattended . . . where his authority is nullified by the priest . . .[8]

In this passage, González identified bad priests, not women's advancement via secular education, as the source of marital unrest, chaotic households, and husbands' lack of authority in their own homes. In doing so, she strongly reinforced a patriarchal model for the happy and unified family. In one fell swoop, she combined women's rights with men's authority *and* a secular society – aims that liberal, middle-class and elite men would potentially find appealing.

Feminists identified educated, liberated mothers not only with the well-being of the family, but also with the good of the nation. As J. Adeláida Chéves commented, "Men make laws, but women make customs."[9] Feminists warned that without women's influence in the home to develop order, good customs, and morality, men's work in the public sphere of politics might come to naught. Yet mothers, they asserted, could only raise the next generation of citizens properly if they had adequate education, rights in the home, and control over money. Without that, they would fail. In Argentina, feminist Raquel Camaña indicated that once she gave birth, a mother attended to far more than the physical needs of her child. She wrote that a mother instantly realized that

> she must mold this little soul with spiritual tranquility, good character, wholesome happiness, and with never ending optimism . . . under the influence of the laws of love, she will improve herself as well as her child. This is the solution of the human condition, one that will create a vibrant democracy more important than political or industrial democracy.[10]

Thus, various feminists argued that the nation's prosperity or decline depended on whether women were granted the education and civil rights necessary to help them mother adequately.

Political rights, however, were another matter. Before the 1900, it was rare for feminist groups to seek voting rights. For example, feminists in the Southern Cone who argued for a political voice usually kept their demands to politics that affected "the family, the school, [and] the work-place, the three areas where women had a recognized presence." Some even stated that women should not hold political office, because the stresses of such work might compromise their ability to reproduce.[11] It would seem that feminists strategically chose the civil and educational advancements that would affect their daily lives most *and* which avoided questioning the dominant gender order. By 1900, when some feminist organizations began discussing the right to vote, they continued to merge feminism and femininity, particularly around ideas about women's pur-portedly inherent maternalism. Rather than emphasize that the vote would make women equal with men, many women's movements stressed that the right to vote would offer women another avenue through which to infuse society with their maternal morality. In this case, advocates of female suffrage argued that women should win the right to vote precisely because they were mothers.

Feminists thus asserted that motherhood was at the core of women's feminine nature, which in turn determined the health of the nation. Though this identity was most obvious when women gave birth and raised children, it transcended the physical acts of mothering one's own children. Women's proclaimed inherent, instinctive ability to nurture would be best developed via education, and it was the basis for which women should, they argued, enter into certain professions or run charity organizations. Even if they were single and childless, women could "mother" society and strengthen the nation. To do so, they required government support.

Education: The Linchpin of Social Motherhood

Perhaps the most agreed-upon goal among women of the middling and wealthy sectors, whether or not they identified with feminism, was their need for better education. It was also one of the arenas in which feminists were able to effect the most change. Their arguments for education were based strongly on social motherhood, stating that women needed to have a solid education in order to fulfill their "sacred mission" as mothers in order to raise the next generation of citizens. As the Baronesa de Wilson put it, if a mother "is not instructed, how can she transmit the principles of education to her children?"[12] Moreover, a number of women suggested that educational opportunities for girls and women would "strongly influence the future of families and their domestic bliss [as well as] the general interests of society."[13] Yet as Teresa González de Fanning lamented, "Even though being a mother is the most difficult profession, no one prepares us for it."[14] Seeking better educational opportunities and more respect for the work that mothers did, many women's rights advocates blended the longstanding ideas about motherhood and morality with more modern scientific approaches to the household and child rearing. This new emphasis on motherhood as a scientific endeavor offers a preview how discourses over motherhood would develop in the early to mid-twentieth century (Chapter 5).

Over the course of the nineteenth century, there was a shift in exactly what a "moral" education entailed. In 1830, the Argentinian women's periodical *Aljaba* advised mothers that their daughters required "an education that brings them to know God, who has created them, and who conserves life. . . . it is essential that they return to God for their road to moral education."[15] By the late nineteenth century, although advocates of women's education still claimed that girls needed a strong moral education, they often claimed that the most pressing need was to provide girls with a well-balanced secular education, not one focused primarily on religion. In the novel *Torn from the Nest*, for example, hero Fernando

Marín proposed to take his and Lucía's adopted (mestiza) daughters to Lima in order to "place them in the school that will best prepare them to be wives and mothers, without the false piety of constant rote prayers."[16] Similarly, Teresa González de Fanning criticized nuns' traditional education methods, though she was also careful to declare that girls should study Christ's life and moral teachings even in a secular classroom.[17] This shift from emphasizing religious to morally centered secular education typically merged well with liberal sentiments, since liberals wanted to replace Catholic educational and charitable organizations with secular ones.

As secular schools replaced religious ones, many middle-sector parents feared that girls would not only lose their moral foundation, but they would give in to inherent tendencies toward vanity and luxury. Proponents of women's education attempted to assuage such fears by claiming that motherhood itself would moralize women. The Mexican women's journal *Hijas del Anáhuac* went so far as to say that woman's "rehabilitation" would come through learning to be a good mother.[18] Women's journals and housewives' manuals (which became more common by the turn of the century) warned women against giving in to vices such as luxury, vanity, and frivolity. Instead, they claimed that virtue was a woman's real beauty, thrift an important contribution to the household, and responsibility essential to a woman's job as a mother. Such lessons came not only in essays, but also in stories and in pictures. Female heroines (such as Lucía in *Torn from the Nest*) were morally grounded and frugal. The message in such sources was clear: women needed to learn to be good homemakers and hard workers, lest they fall prey to vanity and ruin the entire family. Fears about women's vanity and materialism also related to changes going on in Latin American urban economies in the late nineteenth century. With the rise in export economies and lower tariffs, European fashions and other luxury goods were abundantly available and greatly desired among the middle and upper classes. Although showing off one's wealth was desirable in many ways, middle-class men and women were concerned that young women (and wives) needed to keep such displays and luxuries in check lest they lead to a family's economic ruin or dishonor.

Questions pertaining to the proper curriculum for young middle-sector or upper-class girls were also a topic of some concern. González de Fanning argued that girls needed to learn geography and history in order to foster nationalist sentiment in their children. She also contended that girls needed to learn mathematics in order to be able to manage their household shopping duties and to settle their servants' salaries.[19] It was *science*, however, that garnered the most attention in discussions of the proper curricula for girls. Both educational essays and housewives manuals indicated that a woman needed to understand many aspects of science in order to oversee the household properly; they also argued that household management itself was a science.

Given the rising emphasis on science and medicine in the late nineteenth century, it is not terribly surprising that teachers and doctors began to tout the importance of paying attention to science within the household. Hygiene was a favorite topic – experts discussed everything from ventilating the home to maintain air quality to cooking foods properly and making sure that the house got cleaned thoroughly. Infant and child cleanliness and nutrition were also frequent topics in manuals. As noted in Chapter 3, authorities encouraged women to breastfeed rather than hand over this motherly duty to a (supposedly dirty and potentially diseased) wet nurse, and they also paid a great deal of attention to how a child was fed once weaned. Additionally, supporters of women's education asserted that girls should learn chemistry and biology, at least to the extent that they would need them in order to fulfill their duties as wives and mothers, managing homes.

Women who wrote housewife manuals increasingly identified work in the home as a science. The reference to women's work in the home as the maintenance of a "domestic economy" (home economics as it were) suggested that women did more than love, nurture, or provide a moral foundation for their children. Managing a home and raising children meant that women engaged in "business" through budgeting, "medicine" when children were sick, and "science" in their roles feeding families and keeping houses clean. Identifying women's work as wives and mothers in scientific terms was, in part, an attempt to bring greater dignity to the work that women were already doing in their homes. It was also a means through which male doctors and scientists tried to assert indirect control over households. The assumption here was that customary practices or reliance on the backwards ways of domestic servants were insufficient for keeping a healthy and happy home. They argued that women – and mothers especially – should instead modernize their management of homes by listening to the sage advice of medical professionals who were mostly men. In the early to mid-twentieth century, this trend would culminate with *puericulture*, or scientific child rearing (Chapter 5).

Motherhood and "Appropriate" Work

The question of whether women should have the "right to work" was clearly a consideration only for women of some wealth. Working-class and peasant women had no choice but to work: their families depended on their labor and income for survival. For women of the middling and upper classes, matters were quite different because one of the signs of their status was that they did not have to work outside of the home. Yet in the nineteenth century, many – though not all – feminists argued that women could and should have the right, and the training, to work in certain professions. As with so many other facets of middle-class experiences and feminisms, arguments over women and work were shaped by ideas about motherhood.

The plight of widows offered a strong case for providing young women with an education that would enable them to enter the workforce one day should their circumstances make this necessary. González de Fanning made this point by discussing the life of Doña María Bisval, who was only a little over 20 years old when her husband died. Not wanting to remarry or burden her family of origin, she needed a way to provide for her three children. She committed herself to getting an education and then returned with her diploma to her native city, Huaraz, in order to find a teaching job there. Not finding employment there, she returned to Lima and went to school to become a medically trained midwife (*obstétrica*), a profession enabling her to provide for her children. Based on this story, González argued that, far from lowering a woman's status, work could in some conditions bring honor to her.[20] This honor, of course, all hinged on a woman's motherly concern for her children's well-being. In this sense, González and other feminists both built on long-standing notions of honor that identified women with the home, and at the same time they also reinterpreted and expanded notions of female honor to include work done outside of the home. González's argument reflected a reality that many women in Latin American faced: because they often married men older than them, women often found themselves widowed with young children. Not all of these women would have the necessary family wealth or inheritance to support their children without working.

Feminists were more divided on the question of whether women should be able to work before they married. Those in favor of a woman's right to work argued that women needed to have some kind of public experience before they married and became mothers. If they led sheltered lives, hardly ever leaving home and never learning what the working world was like, how could they teach their children – and most especially their sons – how to be good citizens and workers? They claimed that lack of experience, like lack of knowledge, could cripple a mother in her quest to raise good citizens.

Most early feminists carefully discussed the kinds of jobs that would be "appropriate" for a young unmarried woman of high status. Agriculture, industry, or domestic service were forms of work that were fitting only for poor women who lacked honor. Suitable positions for young women of standing were those that were an extension of their supposedly natural motherly tendencies, most prominently teaching and nursing, or (by the turn of the century) public health.[21] These professions, they argued, called upon women's supposedly natural instincts to teach young children or to tend to the sick. Work in health care or education would also provide women with valuable experience that they could take into their own homes once they married and had children of their own. Thus, some of the first university and professional degrees that women earned were in medical fields, which dovetailed with women's perceived inclination to nurture. Between about 1890 and 1940, many Latin American governments began to take over child and health care institutions (orphanages and hospitals) that had once been under the jurisdiction of the Catholic Church, and women – mostly young, single women – worked as professionals in these new state institutions. Women were, for example, often among the first health care inspectors in some countries.

For married middle-sector and elite women, however, options were limited. Not only did conservatives frown on women working once they married, but many feminists did as well. In fact, the success of feminist appeals to let young women work outside of the home often rested on the promise that once women married they would return to the domestic sphere and fulfill their destiny to be good wives and mothers. What, then, was a married woman of wealth and status to do? In addition to treating work in the home as a profession, some women found other ways to engage in public – yet respectable – activities. For Mexico, historian Jeffrey Pilcher discussed how some middle-class women took to writing cookbooks. By focusing on cuisine, and emphasizing nutrition, women found meaningful work that advanced new ideas about national identity, but they did so in a way that reinforced rather than repudiated their roles as wives and mothers.[22] By and large, however, the world of work lay beyond the reach of middle- and upper-class women. Yet some of them found a public niche for themselves in the world of charity work and other forms of "mothering society."

Mothering Society: Middle-Class Women and Social Reproduction

Motherhood extended beyond the nuclear family, and even beyond the job of raising the next generation of citizens. Motherhood also involved *social reproduction*. Historian Ann Blum explained that "[s]ocial reproduction entails childbearing and child care, household labor, and work outside the home that sustains the family."[23] This work outside of the home often entailed sustaining a family that was not a woman's own, as was evident in the last chapter with poor women who worked as domestic servants or wet nurses in the homes of the wealthy. It also pertained to middle-class and elite women who became involved in charity work or public health care, and even those women who viewed themselves as "mothering" their domestic servants. In all of these cases, wealthy women could build on their moral credentials in order to "mother society" and in particular lower-class children and families.

Charitable work was one of the few acceptable public activities available to married women of the wealthier classes.[24] Because they were not working for a salary, married women's philanthropic work did not threaten their husbands' standing as good providers and patriarchs, nor did it betray women's supposedly in-born maternal natures. It was, according to middle-class discourses, part of women's maternal nature to reach out and care for those in need. Housewife manuals often referred to a wife or mother's obligation to see to the well-being of those poorer than her, reminding women that they "should not forget to visit those who are poor and suffering from time to time . . . sometimes we can alleviate their [suffering] with sweet and caring words, bringing them some relief to soften their sad situation; but this class of visiting [the poor] must be done with delicacy and dignity . . . charity is modest and silent."[25] Another manual reminded women readers that modern cities include both rich and poor neighborhoods, and that it was a woman's duty to do what she could to advance the general interests of the poor.[26]

Practical concerns also allowed middle- and upper-class women to become more actively involved in charitable work. In the colonial period, most orphanages, poor houses, and hospitals were under the jurisdiction of the Catholic Church. When liberal governments came into power in the nineteenth or early twentieth centuries, they typically took such roles out of the hands of Church officials; yet these same liberal governments were often not yet ready to take over such functions themselves via state institutions. This made middle-class and elite women's charitable efforts particularly valuable, because they provided an important function during the transition between Church-based charity and state-run welfare systems. Sometimes religious and secular actors collaborated: in Ecuador, the Catholic *Hermanas de la Caridad* (Sisters of Charity, run by nuns) worked together with the new public health department, especially in matters concerning children, though sometimes the balance of power between the two institutions was a point of contention.[27] This indicates not only that the shift from Church to state-controlled institutions was gradual and uneven, but also to an important aspect of transitions with "mothering." State and intellectual officials tended to refer to lay women as social mothers in their societies, but they still relied upon virginal nuns to do some of the "mothering" within social and state-run institutions.

In Argentina, the Society of Beneficence (established in 1830) was a private philanthropic organization run by elite women; it did, however, receive state subsidies throughout the nineteenth century. The Society of Beneficence women took on a wide variety of charitable undertakings, most of which related to child and family welfare or education. The Society was a woman-led, influential institution in a world dominated by men. Though public health physicians tried to challenge the women's authority, the Society's leaders had their own medical doctors who could attest to the quality of care that they provided for orphans and other distressed groups.[28] The matrons of the Society of Beneficence may have been the largest and most powerful of philanthropic organizations in Argentina, but there were plenty of others, including a Jewish Beneficence society that served the needs of Jewish immigrants, a women's conference of the Catholic St. Vincent de Paul charitable organization, and the "Argentine Mothers" who helped to distribute vaccines. By contrast, however, most of these other organizations, though staffed by women volunteers, had male leadership. This was often the case in other parts of Latin America as well. Still, even when men directed these institutions, it was up to the women who staffed them to decide when and how to put policies into effect.[29]

Women's charity organizations formed throughout Latin America in this period. Wealthy Mexican women took pride in creating the *Casa Amiga de la Obrera* (Home of the Friend of the Working Woman), in which poor working women could bring their babies for free nutrition and care.[30] Mexico City also had a "Women's Visiting Committee" in its poor house for children, in which wives from influential families worked to place orphan girls in homes where they could be adopted as servants.[31] In the early twentieth century, *Gotas de Leche* (child welfare clinics) emerged throughout Latin America. Focused on offering assistance for lactating mothers (and for those who could not provide enough breast milk for their babies), the gotas de leche often also provided a variety of other medical assistance for mothers with infants. Sometimes, individual women acted on their own ideas about charity. The Mexican women's periodical *Hijas del Anáhuac*, for example, reported on a "virtuous mother" who invited several poor children to her "elegant house" to join in her son's birthday party. The article claimed that "The woman of the house was very emotional and could not refrain from crying . . . the poor creatures enjoyed their sweets, games, fruits, and clothing with such pleasure . . . and those poor mothers . . . blessed the caring [hostess] for having given them clothing for their little ones!"[32] This article, however, glossed over the power differential between the poor women and children versus their hostess; it also ignored the fact that clothing might help these individuals get through some cold weather, but it did nothing to address the causes of poverty that were the real source of these families' misery.

Wealthy philanthropic women, whether involved in formal organizations or acting on their own, rarely let go of ingrained stereotypes about the poor. Though they aimed to alleviate suffering, rarely did they attempt to address systems of inequality that persisted in their nations. In fact, they often actively perpetuated them. For example, many charitable schools for poor children carefully limited the curriculum to lessons "appropriate to the class and condition" of the poor students. This was occupational training, which for girls meant learning to sew, launder, and cook, whereas boys might learn a trade. Such training ensured that the poor would remain in low-paying jobs regardless of their academic abilities. Stereotypes shaped charitable encounters between wealthy women and the poor families that they helped. González de Fanning assumed that poor mothers knew nothing about basic hygiene and therefore had to be taught "the value of pure air, healthy food, hygienic cleansing with soap."[33] Again, the assumption here was that poor women were ignorant of healthy practices, not that their poverty kept them from being able to afford soap, clean water, or houses with good ventilation. This placed poor mothers in a child-like position relative to the wealthy women who ran charitable and educational institutions. In essence, wealthy women not only assumed that they had to teach poor women how to be good mothers, but also that they needed to "mother" these adult women as well.

Mothering across class lines was also evident in domestic instruction guides about how to handle domestic servants. These guides advised middle-sector and wealthy women to choose servants carefully and keep a close eye on them, because these household workers would inevitably have an influence on their own children. However, they coached women to treat these servants gently: just as servants should not have the right to hit children, the mistress of the house was not justified in hitting them.[34] Another manual suggested that a mother should not hand over child care to her servants – who were too vulgar to be trusted with such an important task – but that she should oversee their work quite closely to make sure that they fulfilled their duties properly. This manual also advised middle-class or elite housewives to "mother" their servants, because the servants' bad behavior was the result of ignorance and poor upbringing, not bad intentions. In other words, since their own mothers had failed them, the servants required their employers to mother them.[35] Manuals that instructed wealthy women to treat their servants like children not only reinforced middle-class notions about the so-called sacred mission of motherhood, but they also reinforced racial and class-based stereotypes about backwards, ignorant, dirty poor people of indigenous or African descent who threatened to drag the nation down if they were not reformed.

Who's Minding the Children?

As the nineteenth century passed and the twentieth century approached, national leaders in Latin America were increasingly concerned with the well-being of their nations, and in particular with infant and child welfare, because these would (in their view) determine not only the population of the nation, but also its relative health and strength. A healthy and fit population spoke of a modern and strong nation state. Yet as governments transitioned into an age of administration and secular governments, they often lacked funds to develop full-fledged social welfare or public health departments.

Middle-class and elite women helped to fill the gaps between the old Church-run charities and the new state-driven institutions through their charitable work. State officials and scholars also identified these women as models of social motherhood whose work promised to save the nation by raising a generation of fit, patriotic, moral citizens. Such emphasis on social motherhood, and need for women charity volunteers, gave women's organizations leverage to negotiate for marriage reforms, better education for women, and the right to work outside of the home before marriage. Middle-class women were symbols of progress that did not forsake morality and motherhood, and feminist groups manipulated this image to their own advantage.

Middle-class and elite women's association with motherhood and morality also made them prime candidates to supposedly "redeem" the poor through means such as charitable work, adoption of poor children, or overseeing servants in their households. Wealthy women's charitable work with poor infants and children is particularly interesting, since it was often undertaken by married women who already had children of their own. While their status as good mothers helped to justify their role in helping and teaching poor women in the art and science of mothering, their involvement in charitable organizations also took them away from their own children who were, more often than not, left in the care of servants. This created a convoluted web of interclass mothering in which poor women often had to hand over their own children to charitable or child welfare organizations in order to get and maintain jobs in elite households, where they would help to care for middle- and upper-class children. Meanwhile, the same wealthy women who demanded that their servants not bring children into their houses went out and reaped status and satisfaction by "mothering" poor infants and children whose own mothers had allegedly abandoned them.

The twentieth century brought challenges and changes that would reinforce middle-class and elite mothers' importance within the nation. Industrialization and urbanization upset previous demographic, economic, and social structures. It was also a century of political upheavals, military authoritarianism, and eventually turns to democracy. Most of all, the twentieth century was an era of modernity. Economic, demographic, and political transformations in the twentieth century affected mothers and children throughout Latin America, albeit in different ways according to one's race, class, and national identity. Motherhood itself underwent a form of modernization with the advent of puericulture (scientific child rearing) and new reproductive technologies. At the same time, deeply embedded notions about motherhood as a moral, even traditional, role in society continued to have strong appeal. Rather than try to follow these divergent themes with chapters that are entirely chronological, the following chapters take important issues pertaining to motherhood, modernity, and politics in Latin America and look at how they each changed over time and influenced the course of Latin American history in the twentieth century.

Document: González de Fanning on Motherhood and Education

One of Peru's most famous advocates of women's rights, Teresa González de Fanning, frequently combined arguments for increased women's rights while embracing motherhood as women's destiny. In the excerpt below, consider how Gonzalez de Fanning intertwined feminism and femininity (in this case, reinforcing women's difference from men and highlighting women's supposedly greater delicacy and morality). How and why did motherhood offer her a way to combine feminism and femininity?

Concerning the Education of Women[36]

> Ladies and Gentlemen, forgive . . . my audacity; excuse it in the name of the good intention that guides me, and allow me to ask you: Do you want to regenerate society? Do you want Peru to rise up powerful and vigorous, supported by its citizens who will enrich it with their virtue and make it occupy the place that it deserves among nations? Well, if you want it, then educate women. As long as there are mothers who do not understand the magnitude of their mission, you will

not have citizens who will be able to lift the motherland from the cruel prostration to which it has been reduced by its maladies. And their influence is so significant that you must observe that always, behind a great man, you will find a great woman – call her mother, wife, or sister – who has assisted and encouraged him along the way.

The family is to the state what the waves are to the sea, and the roots to the tree, the molecules to the body. Do away with the family and the state will disappear. Thus, it is mandatory that its regeneration should begin with the family. Educate woman, raise her moral level to make her understand that she is the priestess of good, the worker of the future, and, like a sound wave, her harmonious echo will reverberate in the family and in society, and Peru will be saved. [. . .]

Education must begin with life, and it is the mother, we insist, who is called to fulfill such a delicate mission. It is she who must shape the men of tomorrow, the future citizens, and those who must succeed them in the august priestliness of motherhood. Even when the child is in diapers and his halting tongue cannot express his thoughts without the help of mimicry, he already harbors little passions that time will ripen. The child is susceptible to wrath and envy, to revenge and jealousy. It is human nature with its virtue and vices in germinal form. These are the potential assets that, well combined, will produce a felicitous result. That is the task placed on the mother by nature. She must work so all the notes of the instrument will harmonize to produce a perfect combination.

Through example and perseverance, she must modify bad inclinations and strengthen good tendencies; she must be firm and energetic, without being harsh, sweet and benevolent, without being weak. How can it be expected for a child, whose mirror is his mother, to love the truth if he notices that his mother does not do it? How can he be peaceful and tolerant if he receives examples of impatience and wrath? [. . .]

A good education for women must have, at its base, religion, morality, and home economics. [. . .]

An egoist man is antipathetic; an egoist woman is a repulsive being, sort of a phenomenon outside the natural order. It is so much a characteristic of woman to sacrifice herself for the benefit of her people, to spread happiness and comfort around her, to suffer as long as she alleviates the suffering of those closer to her, to be the tutelary and providential angel to her children.

Her mission is to console, and she is never more beautiful or angelic than when she sacrifices her pleasure and even her necessary rest in favor of her people. The one who is not ready to sacrifice to fulfill these duties of elementary and sublime Christian charity does this because the poisonous plant of egoism germinates in her soul. To avoid egoism from taking root in the heart of her daughters, those who want to educate them well will never work too much. [. . .]

Notes

1 Asunción Lavrin, *Women, Feminism, and Social Change in Argentina, Chile, and Uruguay, 1890–1940* (Lincoln: University of Nebraska Press, 1995), p. 38.

2 Francesca Miller, *Latin American Women and the Search for Social Justice* (Hanover, NH: University Press of New England, 1991), p. 74.

3 La Baronesa de Wilson, *Perlas del Corazón: Deberes y aspiraciones de la mujer en su vida íntima y social* (Quito: Fundación de Tipos de Manuel Rivadeneira, 1880), p. 93.

4 A. López Decoud, *Sobre el feminismo* (Asunción: Imp. De Luis Tasso, 1902), pp. 9–10. López Decoud was actually summarizing such arguments against feminism in order to prove them wrong.

5 República del Ecuador, *Anales de Senadores*, Congreso Ordinario de 1911, Cámara del senado, September 15.

6 López Decoud, p. 48.

7 Clorinda Matto de Turner, *Torn from the Nest*. Trans. John H.R. Polt (New York: Oxford University Press, 1998).

8 Teresa González de Fanning, *Educación Femenina: Coleccion de artículos pedagógicos, morales, y sociológicos* (Lima: Tipografía de "El Lucero," 1905), pp. 60–61.

9 J. Adeláida Chéves, *Llave de Oro: Compendio de economía doméstica para uso de las niñas Centro-Americanas* (New York: La Revista Ilustrada de Nueva York Pub. Co., 1887), p. 14.

10 This quote appears in Donna J. Guy, *Women Build the Welfare State: Performing Charity and Creating Rights in Argentina, 1880–1955* (Durham, NC: Duke University Press, 2009), p. 67.

11 Lavrin, pp. 4, 201.

12 Baronesa de Wilson, p. 4.

13 Baronesa de Wilson, p. xxix.

14 González de Fanning, *Educación Femenina*, p. 21.

15 "Educación de las Hijas," *Aljaba* (Buenos Aires) No. 6, 3 de Diciembre de 1830.

16 Matto, p. 98.

17 González de Fanning, *Educación Femenina*, pp. 47–48.

18 "Higiene. Dedicado a las madres de familia," *Hijas del Anáhuac*, Año I, Tomo I, Núm. 10, 5 febrero 1888.

19 González de Fanning, *Educación Femenina*, pp. 46–47.

20 González de Fanning, *Educación Femenina*, pp. 33–34.

21 Lavrin, pp. 57 and 63 regarding women's occupations, and p. 30 on class and work.

22 Jeffrey M. Pilcher, *Que vivan los tamales! Food and the Making of Mexican Identity* (Albuquerque: University of New Mexico Press, 1998), pp. 47–49.

23 Ann S. Blum, *Domestic Economies: Family, Work, and Welfare in Mexico City, 1884–1943* (Lincoln: University of Nebraska Press, 2009), p. xxx.

24 Guy, pp. 8–9.

25 Chéves, pp. 24–25.

26 Teresa Prats de Sarratea, *Educación doméstica de las jóvenes* (Santiago: Imprenta A. Eyzaguirre I Ca., 1909), p. 80.

27 A. Kim Clark, *Gender, State, and Medicine in Highland Ecuador: Modernizing Women, Modernizing the State, 1895–1950* (Pittsburgh: University of Pittsburgh Press, 2012), pp. 35–36.

28 Guy, p. 46.

29 There were some countries, most notably Mexico, where charity work was primarily in the hands of men. See Sylvia Marina Arrom, *The Women of Mexico City, 1790–1857* (Stanford, CA: Stanford University Press, 1985), p. 45.

30 Discussions of this organization appear in *Hijas del Anáhuac*, Año I, Tomo I: Núm. 1, 11 diciembre de 1887; Núm. 10, 5 febrero de 1888; Núm. 24, 20 mayo de 1888.

31 Blum, p. 48.

32 Lucía G. Herrera, "Una fiesta de niños," *Hijas del Anáhuac*, Año I, Tomo I, Núm. 44, 7 octubre de 1888.

33 González de Fanning, *Educación femenina*, p. 66.

34 Teresa Prats de Sarratea, pp. 128–132.

35 Chéves, pp. 58–61, 133–139.

36 This excerpt is taken from: Gertrude M. Yeager, ed., *Confronting Change, Challenging Tradition: Women in Latin American History* (Wilmington, DE: SR Books, 1994), pp. 30–39.

5

Motherhood at the Crossroads of Tradition and Modernity, circa 1900–1950

The Peculiar Case of Gabriela Mistral

"*In my opinion, perfect patriotism in women is perfect motherhood. Therefore, the most patriotic education one can give a woman is one that underscores the obligation to start a family.*"[1] So wrote Gabriela Mistral, a Chilean teacher and poet who gained international fame as a voice for women in Latin America and, in particular, for the teacher-mother figure who upheld conservative gender norms that identified women with the home. Mistral also had the distinction of being the first Latin American (and only the fifth woman) to win the Nobel Prize in literature, in 1945. Mistral's own life, however, did not fit the mold of wife and (biological) mother that she so often suggested was not only a woman's personal destiny but also her greatest contribution to the nation state.

Gabriela Mistral was born as Lucila Godoy Alcayaga in 1889 in the Andean region of northern Chile. Abandoned by her father in 1892, Mistral grew up in poverty, and she first became a school teacher (after an irregular and limited formal education) before she turned 15. Mistral worked her way up through the Chilean school system while also writing poetry. In 1922, José Vasconcelos, Mexican Secretary of Public Education, who had met Mistral on a visit to Chile, invited her to come to Mexico in order to help establish its rural school system in the aftermath of the revolution there. It was with her move to Mexico that Mistral first became an international figure and a voice for women in Latin America.

Mothers Making Latin America: Gender, Households, and Politics Since 1825, First Edition. Erin E. O'Connor.

She lived the rest of her life in various parts of the world, including Brazil, France, England, and the United States. Though her life from 1922 forward was spent outside of her home country, Chileans claimed her as a national hero and buried her with great pomp and respect in Chile when she died in 1957. In her official capacity as an educational professional, and in many of her essays Mistral seemed to uphold conservative gender norms wholeheartedly. She often identified herself with motherhood (through her teaching), and state officials typically branded her as a woman who was so "married" to the state that she sacrificed her own personal happiness by never marrying or having children of her own (Mistral did have an adopted son, Juan Miguel Godoy, who committed suicide in 1943). For the state, she was the embodiment of female, motherly sacrifice and patriotism through her role as a teacher-mother.

Mistral's personal life and experiences were often at odds with these images of her as the conventional and conservative woman married to the nation. Mistral moved professionally in a mostly masculine world, and many observers noted that she was "mannish" in her appearance and mannerisms. Moreover, in addition to not marrying, her closest personal relationships – even the households she set up around the world – were made up of women friends and secretaries, independent of a male figure head. Mistral is purported to have been a closet lesbian, though there is no definitive proof of her sexuality one way or the other. And despite her image as a "teacher-mother" which identified her as happily giving herself over to the children of the nation, she once described the process of teaching as "tedium bordering on insanity."[2] Similarly, she was renowned as a defender of indigenous peoples and of the process of *mestizaje* (racial mixing), yet a close examination of her essays on this subject reveals that she viewed whites as superior and believed that indigenous peoples needed to assimilate into Hispanic-dominated culture. Her defense of "the Indian" also came at the expense of Afro-Latin Americans, who did not fit into her vision for Latin America. Women, as mothers, were central to her racial discourses, but mainly as receptacles through whom the nation would be strengthened, and who had to be taught to raise children scientifically according to the rules set forth by doctors, teachers, and state officials. In this, many of her ideas paralleled and reinforced those of Latin American eugenicists in the early twentieth century.

How can one make sense of the contradictions between Gabriela Mistral's personal life and public pronouncements? Of her independence as a woman versus her works that taught women to be maternal patriots? Of her claim to voice the concerns of Indians and women only to serve the interests of the state, which aimed at assimilating Indians, using mothers to inculcate blind patriotism, and manipulating maternalism to justify paying women low wages? It is impossible – and perhaps beside the point – to know for certain whether or not Mistral believed in her official message of maternalism, or whether she was sexually involved with other women. Yet despite the many unanswerable questions in her life, there is much to learn from Gabriela Mistral about women and nation, and especially motherhood and nation, in early twentieth-century Latin America.

Mistral's life presents both continuities and changes with regard to mothers' relationships to the state, and the contradictory ways that women were caught between discourses on tradition and modernity in the early to mid-twentieth century. That Mistral was identified through her work as a teacher with mothering the nation (and Latin America more generally) is similar to late nineteenth-century emphasis on social motherhood explored in the last chapter. Yet whereas women used notions of social motherhood to argue for better education and greater rights in the late nineteenth century, in the early to mid-twentieth century there was greater emphasis on mothers' obligations to serve the state and nation than on women's needs as social mothers. This is not to say that women's movements gave up on seeking rights, for in fact in some countries feminists sought (and sometimes won) the right to vote in the early to mid twentieth century.[3] Regardless of the ongoing movement for women's rights, the period was also one in which states – through public education and social welfare institutions – were able to intervene in the domestic sphere more deeply and consistently than they could in the nineteenth century. In particular, state officials defined mothers as requiring the intervention of medical and scientific professionals who would teach them how to raise modern-yet-moral children who would strengthen the nation and serve the state.

Mistral also reminds us that Latin American women did not necessarily live according to, or even believe in, their prescribed roles as domestically oriented mothers of the nation. Although state officials and intellectuals largely embraced industrialization, urbanization, and other forms of modernization, they also feared that these changes would bring race, class, and gender upheaval that might threaten to undermine elite privilege and power. As was so often the case, motherhood was at the center of these seeming contradictions in discourses on women and modernity. In her ground-breaking work on gender and modernization in early twentieth-century Brazil, Susan Besse observed that "Women were relegated to the difficult task of mediating between the past and the present, as well as between rational public standards of behavior, performance, and the rewards and almost religious domestic standards of devotion and self-sacrifice."[4] It was not simply that women were hard pressed to live up to these standards, but also that they learned to manipulate them to their own advantage in certain circumstances. Mistral's life, and other evidence presented in this chapter, forces us to recognize that many women did not completely accept or reject the dominant discourses on motherhood, modernity, and nation. Instead, women often upheld particular aspects of this discourse while ignoring or struggling against others. Sometimes, they used maternalist discourses strategically, reorienting them to their own individual or collective goals and needs.[5]

This chapter explores various dynamics behind the complex meanings of motherhood and modernity, with a primary (though not exclusive) focus on Chile, Argentina, and Brazil, where relatively early industrialization intensified both the promises and problems of modernity. The chapter centers on questions such as: How and why was motherhood so often at the center of elite men's debates over modernity? How did the eugenics movement influence ideas about mothers and nations in early to mid-twentieth-century Latin America? How and why was motherhood discussed in increasingly scientific terms, and why did this often result in government and medical intervention in the home? How did various kinds of feminists engage, negotiate, or reject modernized gender norms and government policies? In order to capture the atmosphere in which new ideas and policies on motherhood developed, this chapter focuses on elite and middle-class viewpoints that shaped national policies, whereas Chapter 6 will concentrate on the experiences of poor, indigenous, and Afro-Latin American mothers.

Dangerous "Modern Women" and the Need for "Traditional Mothers"

In the early twentieth century, several Latin American nations, including Brazil, Argentina, and Chile, underwent massive urbanization and industrialization. In Brazil and Chile, this included migration from the countryside to cities, whereas many of Argentina's new industrial workers and urban dwellers were immigrants from southern and eastern Europe. Either way, economic and demographic shifts had widespread implications. A new industrial elite emerged whose power eclipsed that of the large estate owners, and many middle-sector families benefited from the expansion of job opportunities in both the private and public sectors. Finally, modernity was coming to Latin American nations via new forms of entertainment and the availability of new consumer goods. With enough money, one could go to see movies, buy radios, or purchase the latest fashions or household appliances.

Although elites benefited from these changes, they were also concerned about their potential social and economic impacts of them. Workers often agitated for better pay, work conditions, and rights. They joined unions or – even worse in the eyes of political and economic elites – leftist parties to make their demands heard. Women were prominent in the new factory labor force, crossing the line between private and public spheres in greater numbers and more obvious ways than they had in previous generations. Middle-class women also entered the wage labor force. Jobs in the expanding health care and social service sectors offered important opportunities for young women or single mothers from lower middle-class backgrounds that needed an honorable way to earn a living.[6] Even married middle- and upper-class women more often appeared on their own in public buying the latest fashions, going out for entertainment or sunning themselves on beaches, and engaging in supposedly masculine activities like smoking. For wealthier women, being able to buy the latest electric appliances, and to dress and feed their families according to modern fashions, were outward signs not only of a family's economic success, but also of "good mothering," as will be discussed in detail in the next section.

For the poor, urban growth displaced people from their original homes and put them into strange new surroundings. As in the late nineteenth century, urban poverty often left mothers particularly vulnerable, especially if they had not yet established strong support networks. In the twentieth century, more women than ever were entering factory work, and more often worked alongside male as well as female coworkers. Moreover, some women workers were deeply involved in labor activism as it took off, particularly in Argentina and Mexico. Despite the pull of cities and industries, however, the majority still lived and worked in the countryside, and they were often the last groups to benefit from modernization, whether this was in the form of free public education, potable water and electricity, or social and health services. Even for poor women in urban areas, health care and social welfare benefits came with limits and costs.

For many elites, it seemed that the world had turned upside-down. They assumed that the influx of poor workers would lead to rising crime and violence, yet they also began to pay more attention to the suffering of the working poor, as they frequently encountered the poor in crowded city streets. They felt a strong need to get a handle on the lower classes, and to reestablish order.[7] Seeking not only to avert dangerous upheaval, but also to establish control over workers and women, elite groups identified the nation as being in a state of moral and medical danger, and women – especially mothers – garnered a great deal of their attention. How elites discussed the problems and potential solutions regarding women and modern society, however, depended on women's class–race status.

Elite discourses on the "modern woman" or "modern girl" typically focused on young middle- and upper-class women who were, in their view, lured by the façade of modernity. Colombian Gustavo Atuesta complained in 1940 that a modern woman was interested only in business, poker, and cinema. He claimed that she spent her time either taking in sinful modern entertainments or playing sports that "encourage immodesty in a woman [and deform] her body's proportions, [passing] down grotesque and brutish manners to the next generation." Instead of respecting her elders, critics asserted that the modern woman was irresponsible and engaged in all kinds of vices, including alcohol, nicotine, and caffeine. She went to dances and the beach, and she read supposedly "pornographic" literature.[8] She was acting like a man – and not a good one at that. In 1938, Argentine Roberto Campolieti summarized these fears when he warned that "Women themselves are the first victims of modernism," and he bemoaned their abandonment of the home and particular weakness for enslaving themselves to fashion, films, and consumerism.

Why did many elite men consider modern women's behavior dangerous, rather than simply unappealing? Because they thought that women's modern activities undermined the traditional order of the home and family. Campolieti noted that the modern girl's "preoccupation with imitating men in her activities, in her games, and worst of all, in her vices has made her unfit for marriage and family." Young women's failure to prepare for and fulfill their maternal destiny, critics claimed, threatened all of society. Campolieti even thought that modern women's activities might result in sterility, which would in turn lead to psychological disorders for the women unable to fulfill their destiny of motherhood. He warned that if a modern woman did have children, she would pass down weaknesses related to her unseemly activities. Not only would she have "grotesquely brutish" children if she was too athletic, but the "repugnant and androgynous" woman who overstimulated her brain would also have abnormal, sickly children.[9] Sickly children, critics warned, made for a sickly, weak nation.

When elites discussed working classes, they again focused on motherhood, but this time they emphasized how the poor were born and lived in filthy and crowded conditions. One critic wrote about an indigenous woman whom he claimed "feeds [her child] unconsciously, like a beast, and, very soon, abandons him to his free will, among the animals without any defense but his instincts."[10] Similarly, many elites reproached working-class women for allegedly abandoning their children in order to go out to work. Usually, they blamed poor conditions in working-class homes on men's drunkenness and failure to provide adequately for their families, though in some cases they highlighted mothers' alcoholism or irresponsibility.[11] Despite some sympathy for poor urban women, elites still identified the women as "unfit" mothers who allowed their children to wallow in filth and who failed to provide them with adequate care and nutrition. Moreover, crowded housing meant that poor children were being exposed to sex at a young age because adults and children slept in the same room together. In these cases, elite writers claimed that it was ignorance that led poor women to become bad mothers, rather than the selfishness that they declared that middle- and upper-class "modern girls" displayed.

If these discourses emphasized that so-called bad mothers had the ability to destroy modern nations, they also indicated that presumably "good" mothers had the ability to save nations from the evils of modernity. As Brazilian Maria Clava de Alvear wrote "It is incumbent on women to curb excesses, condemn abuses, and correct the errors of modernity." She claimed they would do so by staying at home with children, raising them in clean houses with nutritious food, and providing them with a strong moral education. Argentine Campolieti similarly suggested that if women embraced their roles in the home, they had the power to save Argentine society from the toxins of modernization and industrialization.[12]

These writers suggested that a woman, as a mother, could counteract the superficiality and immorality of modern urban life by providing a loving and moral home to which her husband would return each day, and in which her children would be raised. Her supposedly inherent and unchanging instinct to nurture others and sacrifice herself would ensure that her nation would grow stronger rather than dissolve into chaos. She was the harbinger of order and a reminder of the traditions that should not be cast aside for dangerous modern ways. At the same time, she had to have enough knowledge of the modern world to raise her children (her sons especially) to contribute to national advancement. Finally, her weakness for modern vices meant that she could not fulfill her duty on her own, but rather required the intervention of outsiders to guide her. Although few women's lives reflected either elite hopes for the ideal traditional-yet-modern woman or their fears about the dangerous modern-woman-run-amok, these extreme notions enabled some (mostly middle-class) women to identify their own goals as those that would make the nation stronger. To help poor mothers improve their homes, elites believed that they had to teach them to embrace values that they identified as bourgeois, including "responsibility, discipline, and initiative."[13] Women's supposedly traditional virtues of tenderness, morality, and discipline could be revived in order to rescue modern society from materialism and selfishness run rampant. Moreover, these authors argued that by saving the nation, women would also redeem themselves.

If dominant discourses required women to maintain traditional roles, they were supposed to do so via modern methods. Women were to listen to doctors (and in the case of poor women social workers), and raise their children according to modern scientific standards. They were also told that they should buy modern appliances if they could afford them. This would help them to bring the conveniences of modern technology within an appropriate home setting and enable them to lighten their workloads in order to attend more closely to their children's well-being. Consider the advertisement that appeared in the Argentine women's magazine *Damas y damitas* from 1946 in Figure 5.1.

The title in image reads "Protect your baby's skin with Palmolive . . . the soap that 86% of doctors recommend!" The description below the photographs suggested that protecting a baby's complexion with Palmolive would lead to a life of beautiful skin for the child, which "can influence the happiness and success of a woman's life!" In the photos, the women converse about the baby's health and cleanliness – which they

Figure 5.1   *Damas y damitas*, Año VIII, No. 386, 20 Noviembre de 1946.

could only ensure via the latest available (imported) soap. They are dressed modern-but-modest fashion, and merge the best of modernization with their traditional roles as mothers. Such advertisements were typical in middle-class urban women's magazines in the early to mid twentieth century, which sold everything from cleaning and baby care products to household appliances and the latest fashions. However, lest female readers become too materialistic and fritter away necessary household income, many articles encouraged them to be frugal and sew or knit clothes for themselves and their children. Other articles emphasized that women had a responsibility to uphold the strictest moral standards in their homes.

Twentieth-century elite discourses on the importance of good mothering to the nation were not merely holdovers of nineteenth-century notions of social motherhood, nor were they introduced only by the challenges of urbanization and industrialization. They were also caught up in the latest medical and racial ideas of the day, which alleged that women's reproductive and child-raising capacities were central to the strength and stability (and power) of nations and races. These ideas fell under the broad label of *eugenics*, although they were developed differently in Latin America than they were in the United States or Europe. To understand how doctors, governments, and social workers acted to reinforce motherhood in the name of national salvation, it is necessary first to explore eugenics and its global impacts in the early twentieth century.

Mothers and the Nation: Eugenics in Latin America

British scientist Francis Galton first used the term eugenics in 1883 to describe his theories about heredity. Literally, eugenics is taken from Greek and means "good breeding." If in nature the fittest survived to reproduce, then, according to Galton, human social practices of protecting the weak were counterproductive, because nature had destined the weak or "unfit" to die off before producing offspring. Galton failed to consider that among humans it was often economic or political power – not nature – that determined a person's or nation's relative strength. As Galton's ideas spread among members of the scientific community in Europe and the United States, his followers often identified their goal as improving the human race or purifying particular groups. In an era of imperialism and Social Darwinism, so-called fitness was defined as much by western notions of race as by physical or mental capacities. Many western European and US eugenicists wanted to disallow racial interbreeding, for example, based on the belief that it would weaken the stronger or more fit (i.e., white) race. In addition to reproduction, some eugenicists discussed the elimination of peoples they deemed unfit, though this proposal was less prominent than others.

The eugenics movement was not on the fringes of society, science, or politics in the early twentieth century. To the contrary, it was regularly taught at universities, had widespread support among the educated middle classes, and helped to shape social policies and laws. In the United States, for example, several laws kept those labeled "feeble minded" from marrying, and eugenics ideas served to uphold restrictions on immigration. Developmentally challenged individuals in the United States were also sterilized (without their consent) throughout much of the early to mid twentieth century. The most extreme, and tragic, example of eugenics practices was the Nazi extermination of millions of Jews (as well as homosexuals, gypsies, the mentally retarded, and others deemed unfit) in Germany. At the same time, Hitler offered incentives for Aryan women to have many children. After the horrors of the Holocaust, eugenics officially fell out of favor with most scientists and governments.

Although eugenics theories and policies were in the hands of political and intellectual elite men, they centered on reproduction and especially on motherhood. Advocates of eugenics focused on making sure that white, middle- and upper-class women did not fall prey to unfit (mentally deficient or nonwhite) men and have children with them. They supported sterilization policies for those whom they decided would weaken rather than strengthen the national gene pool. They encouraged supposedly "fit" couples to have many children. Women were thus at the center of European and US eugenics ideas and practices, but as subjects to be acted upon or told what to do, not as active participants in the process. Eugenicist scientists viewed women as passive participants because these theories were all about sexual reproduction and genetics – about nature rather than nurture, as it were – and because they assumed that women were sexually passive.

Early twentieth-century Latin Americans who were drawn to eugenics faced a dilemma. On the one hand, they were drawn to theories about racial fitness and national strength, and they believed that mothers were central to the production of strong populations. In Argentina, where the indigenous and African-descended populations were small, scientists often embraced western-style eugenics focused on biological reproduction. On the other hand, many Latin American nations had either a majority (or large minority) of peoples who were of African, indigenous, or mixed racial heritage. It was not feasible to aspire to "whiten" these societies by avoiding miscegenation and encouraging only whites to have many children, because miscegenation was already a fact in their countries and had been since the colonial period. To solve this dilemma, most Latin American eugenicists embraced so-called soft eugenic theories which assumed that "environmental change could cause genetic alternation . . . [and they] considered movements for sanitation and hygiene to be eugenic, that is, contributing to the improvement of the race."[14] Social policies could, they believed, make up for a lack of biological racial purity. Even in Argentina, where eugenicists were more prone to biological eugenics, Tomás Amadeo claimed that "education . . . neutralizes poor heredity, strengthening the personality and utilizing and amplifying the good inherited tendencies."[15] It was not necessarily that biology did not matter to Latin American eugenicists, but rather that they thought that any supposedly inherent racial weaknesses could be overcome with education, social programs, and government policies. Therefore, while US and European supporters of this movement focused on biological ("Mendelian") eugenics, most of their Latin American counterparts emphasized environmental ("Lamarckian") eugenics.

From 1920 to 1940, when eugenics was still quite popular, many Latin American scholars and politicians – most notably in Mexico and Brazil – rhetorically celebrated the racial mixture in their nations. They claimed that racial mixture did not weaken the white race, but rather it brought together the strengths of all races in the mix, developing a stronger rather than weaker population.[16] Although on the surface Latin American ideas about soft eugenics and celebrations about racial mixture apparently contradicted theories and policies in the United States and western Europe, when one examines them more closely similarities emerge. Both types of eugenics sought to strengthen what they saw as superior white races. Latin American glorification of racial intermixing, despite its democratizing claims, was really aimed at (in elites' view) improving indigenous, African, and racially mixed populations. Eugenicists believed that they could, in effect, regenerate their nations despite the presence of nonwhite populations whom they assumed threatened to degenerate their societies.[17]

Infant mortality was among state officials' main concerns in this era of eugenics. After all, mothers could not revitalize the nation unless their babies were born healthy and lived to adulthood. In some cases, women themselves were blamed for infant mortality if they failed to see a scientifically trained medical professional for pregnancy and childbirth, or if they drank alcohol while pregnant. Such accusations were typically aimed at poor women, especially those of indigenous or African descent. However, even in these cases, doctors and government officials had an obligation to try to offer adequate services for pregnant and laboring women, and one often finds the expansion of maternity hospitals and medically trained midwives in early twentieth-century Latin America.

In addition to their work to regulate pregnancies and labor, officials in Argentina, Brazil, and Mexico also developed laws requiring prenuptial medical examinations to ensure that a couple was fit (healthy) enough to procreate; in some cases doctors, also distributed eugenic pregnancy and child-rearing pamphlets to new couples. In Brazil, such examinations were voluntary, whereas Argentine and Mexican laws required them, and in 1928, Mexican law banned marriage licenses "to individuals with chronic and contagious illnesses and for those with conditions transmissible by heredity, as well as those with vices that could endanger the hereditary of offspring."[18] Although authorities in both Mexico and Brazil openly touted the benefits of racial miscegenation, their ideas about "transmissible vices" reveal underlying racist assumptions, because they emphasized that such vices were primarily a problem among poor people of non-European descent.

Latin American eugenics discourses focused primarily on the mother–child relationship rather than on reproduction alone. This encompassed a wide variety of concerns and practices that at the surface appeared universal but that in application were targeted at the poor and peoples of non-European descent. Essential to social eugenics was the notion that "women needed a rational, 'scientific' understanding of childhood development and modern principles of hygiene if they were to fulfill their new patriotic duty and social function of 'perfecting' the race."[19] Numerous handbooks on mothering came out that proposed to teach women the proper (and modern) ways to clean, feed, clothe, and generally tend to the health and welfare of their babies and children. These texts were seemingly appropriate for any woman, yet few working-class women had the time or ability to read such books. To compensate, governments set up policies by which outside experts would go to poor women's homes to teach maternal hygiene. Additionally, many eugenicists emphasized the importance of what they called "mental hygiene." This had not only to do with children's psychological health, but also with social pathologies that they associated with the poor and nonwhite populations, such as criminality, juvenile delinquency, and prostitution.[20] Again, the solution was the intervention of health care and social service officials.

As in Europe and the United States, eugenics in Latin America had a wide appeal among the middle- and upper-class women and men, and its supporters came from a broad range of political and ideological perspectives.[21] Uruguayan socialist feminist physician Paulina Luisi advocated eugenics medicine and state intervention to solve health problems, and Gabriela Mistral wrote an essay on social hygiene.[22] Due to their widespread appeal among the powerful, eugenics ideas and policies had a compelling influence on almost all aspects of motherhood in the early to mid-twentieth century, although as usual women's experiences were class and race distinct. Moreover, the Latin American eugenics movement brought medical professionals and the government into private homes on an unprecedented scale as social welfare states came into being around the region. Motherhood became both increasingly scientific (modern) and more deeply symbolic of tradition.

Doctors, Governments, and Motherhood

A 1940 Mexican radio program titled "Mother and Child" claimed that "It is a patriotic obligation to protect childhood." The program offered various infant-care instructions with an emphasis on hygiene and modern interventions like vaccines, advising that mothers should not "pay any heed to the advice or opinions of your female friends and neighbors regarding how to raise a child. Let your doctor's instructions guide you, or go to an infant hygiene center so that they can tell you what to do."[23] This advice reflected a trend throughout Latin America in the early to midtwentieth century in which medical and government institutions assumed unprecedented authority over infant care. The shift marked the rise of welfare states whose agencies intervened in citizens' personal and private matters, and it indicated the masculinization and medicalization of child rearing.

Eugenics paved the way for rising medical and government interventions in the home. Doctors and educators emphasized the need to introduce mothers to modern, scientific child rearing and household management, since this they deemed this the best path to strengthen and improve the population.[24] Whether emphasizing genetics or hygiene and morality, eugenics was the domain of medical and scientific professionals. Through their expertise on child welfare, doctors could claim to be indispensable to government social policies, and they often oversaw public health care initiatives and offices. Eventually, involvement in health care policies led some physicians to political careers.

The medicalization of maternity and the expansion of public health institutions made men into the ultimate authorities on motherhood and child rearing. Granted, there were some women doctors who presided over important child health and welfare conferences, but the field of public health was predominantly a male domain. This had a negative impact on women in several ways. Midwives and wet nurses were further marginalized and frequently brought under state scrutiny. For example, Dr. Emilio Fernández, former director of Bolivia's public mental hospital, in 1949 described indigenous midwives as "unhygienic hags who made women give birth in the 'praying position,' which caused hemorrhages and uterine inversions."[25] When possible, they imposed their own medically trained midwives over those that they deemed "backwards" traditional midwives. When they had to utilize women's services, such as with wet nurses, they often required them to remain under institutional supervision and to pass gynecological and other physical examinations; the only other group to be subject to such regulation was prostitutes. In Argentina, a 1937 article on "scientific wet nurses" even proposed that, ideally, wet nurses should be put in separate cubicles to express milk, wearing masks and headscarves during the procedure. This would not only ensure what physicians considered hygienic conditions, but it also guaranteed that wet nurses (who were from poor families) would not interact with infants.[26] State-run institutions, headed by medical doctors, also took over much of the work that elite women had done through charity and social mothering in several countries during the late nineteenth century.

The new emphasis on scientific motherhood and state-run public health organizations did offer opportunities for middle-class women. Although men were almost always in charge of the new institutions and policy development, women typically carried out these agendas. Not only were women among the first generation of health inspectors, but female social workers and nurses were crucial to enforcing new public health and social policies. Although most social workers were not (yet) mothers themselves, an association between women and mothering helps to explain why the vast majority of social workers were women. Historian Karin Rosemblatt noted for Chile that "social work continued to be portrayed as unscientific, more rooted in feeling than in planning."[27] Government policy makers and male heads of social and health care institutions therefore saw working with the poor as compatible with women's supposedly maternal natures. This assumption also explains the low pay and prestige for women who were on the front lines of public health initiatives.

Social work students received an education that highlighted the latest innovations in scientific mothering as well as on a wide range of other topics, from nutrition to accounting to civic education. Social workers would then hand on this information to poor women through individual counseling or in classes on such topics as domestic economy, moral education, and child rearing. Social workers helped to divert attention from the economic causes of workers' struggles, instead recasting them as moral concerns.[28] Visiting nurses served a similar purpose by making sanitary and health visits with new mothers.[29]

Social workers' attitudes toward their poor clients varied. Social workers' entire profession was based on the assumption that poor women were incompetent mothers who did not know how to keep their children clean and healthy, and who failed to provide them with adequate moral foundations. One can see this, albeit with good intentions, in a Brazilian student's speech before her peers at her graduation from a four-month puericulture program in 1941: "One aspect of life was revealed to us [during our studies] that had until now gone entirely unnoticed – the damages resulting from the ignorance that exists among our poor classes. This ignorance can be seen from the lack of awareness of the most elementary notions of hygiene to the use of primitive treatments – the survival of illusions and superstitions."[30] Puericulture was aimed at curing poor mothers of their supposedly backward and dirty ways, but it was middle-class young women who studied at these schools, which reinforced class and race stereotypes before sending students out to bring their message of scientific child rearing to women of less fortunate families.

At the same time, social workers found themselves truly caring for the women and families with whom they worked and going above the call of duty on their behalf. Social workers sometimes ran errands for poor mothers, helped them with confusing and intricate paperwork that needed to be filled out in order to gain access to useful public services, or intervened with errant fathers. In a 1993 interview with Karin Rosemblatt, retired Chilean social worker Tomy Romeo recalled how she helped to locate fathers who had abandoned their children. She described a typical conversation she might have with a father who did not acknowledge his child:

"Okay, sir, ahem, the señora so-and-so who has just had a baby says that you are the father of the baby."

"No, señorita. What hope! What a liar! Ehm, why, that woman is a public woman, señorita. She is involved with every Tom, Dick, and Harry. And, besides, she knew I was married, señorita. So why did she take up with me?"

"Ah," I would say, "she knew. But didn't you yourself know that you were married? Was she the only one who knew? Didn't you know?"

And we would cage him like that, let me tell you . . . In general the people had a lot of affection for us, but that little group of anonymous fathers didn't care for us at all.[31]

In this case, rather than simply standing in judgment of single mothers and lecturing them on how to raise children, Romeo and other social workers actively defended these women and sought justice for them by trying to hold men responsible for the children that they sired. This was rather different from official state discourses on child rearing, in which poor fathers were rarely mentioned unless it was to bemoan their pre-sumed alcoholism and its impact on families. Thus, while physicians often simplistically identified poor mothers as unfit and in need of super-vision in their homes, the social workers who actually interacted with poor mothers entered into multifaceted, contradictory relationships with them. Many, if not most, were sincere in their desire to help poor women overcome challenges and build better lives, and they worked hard to that end. At the same time, their work reinforced welfare and political systems determined to obfuscate the economic causes behind the familial prob-lems of the poor.

The Question of Motherhood, Women, and Work

Although many liberal or reformist governments supported middle-class women's right to work before marriage in certain professions – in fact they often needed them to do so due to the expansion of social welfare and health institutions – many conservative leaders and scholars remained skeptical about the appropriateness of women's work. In Brazil, the magazine *A Cigara*, the following image appeared with the caption "A Woman Can Do Whatever a Man Can Do," and although the text attached to it discussed how work increased women's independence, the image offered a very different, and less positive, message (Figure 5.2).

This image suggested that family life – and society more generally – would be threatened as never before if women began to go out into the workforce "like men." Every aspect of home life would change, and gender roles would be reversed. Images like this one were particularly powerful in suggesting not just the masculinization of women through work, but they also presented men as emasculated, staying at home and tending to children. The message in such texts and images was, overall, that if middle-class women worked, they not only had to make sure that it was in a gender-appropriate profession, but they also had to give up their careers for marriage and motherhood while they were still young enough to produce and raise healthy, strong children.[32] These notions

Figure 5.2   "A Woman Can Do Whatever a Man Can Do," *A Cigara* 14: 273 (March 1926).

were sometimes reinforced with medical policies: in both Brazil and Bolivia, for example, women that medical professionals deemed "overly ambitious" (such as those who had professional ambitions like men) ran the risk of being placed in a mental health asylum.[33]

With working-class women, the debates and dilemmas were different. As in other areas of the world, many women made up a large percentage of factory workers in the early phases of industrialization. Elite and middle-class men found this upsetting for a variety of reasons. First, factory work, unlike many aspects of women's work in Latin America before industrialization, had few clear links to the work that women did in the home. Furthermore, women factory workers often outcompeted men for jobs because they received lower wages than men. Finally, many political leaders were greatly concerned with the impact of the workplace on the health of women and their children. To deal with these perceived threats to social order and family (and therefore national) health, reformers drew up legislation to protect female wage workers and encourage them to stay in the home.

State officials, socialist leaders, and working-class men frequently identified working-class women with the home in their arguments for a family wage. If a working-class man's wage was high enough to provide for a wife and children, there would be no need for women to be involved in factory labor. Instead, they, like middle-class and elite women, could stay at home and tend to domestic and mothering tasks – with, of course, middle-class social workers and nurses available to teach them how to do this work properly. The family wage had clear benefits for male workers, who "gained political legitimacy, material benefits, and increased power over 'dependent' family members they supported and protected."[34] For employers and state officials, the family wage was attractive because it might be a useful way to control male workers: in return for higher wages, the responsibilities of providing for their families would (elites hoped) make the men less likely to agitate for further changes because they could not risk losing their only family income. Yet employers also disliked the idea of a family wage law because it would increase their labor costs. In some cases, such as in Chile, this could lead to quotas for married male workers in factories. In Brazil, however, factory owners used ideas about the family wage to justify paying women workers low wages, assuming (often wrongly) that their labor was simply supplementing household income.[35] As Chapter 4 discussed, this was often not the case, since many women workers in factories were the primary breadwinners for their households. In addition to earning low wages, working-class women were negatively impacted by the family wage system because it placed them clearly in a subordinate position to male breadwinners.

Trade union and socialist leaders often reinforced the identification of working-class women with the home and motherhood. When Chilean socialist leaders wrote their memoirs, they frequently noted the sacrifices that their own working mothers made for them (especially if they grew up in female-headed households), but they still advocated for a system in which men were the breadwinners and household heads. Such attitudes were not exclusive to the male socialist leadership; in 1947, during a coal miners' strike, Communist leader Eusebia Torres "touted the importance of the miners' labor and praised her women constituents for refusing to work outside the home."[36]

For those women who had no choice but to work in factories, central government officials sometimes provided protective legislation and maternity leave rights. The 1931 Chilean Labor Code guaranteed women workers a six-week maternity leave at a reduced salary, and employers with more than 25 women workers had to provide breast-feeding and child care facilities, allowing women to feed their infants periodically each day.[37] Brazil, Argentina, and Mexico had similar laws. Maternity laws provided benefits that could potentially help working-class mothers to raise healthier babies by mandating a period of rest after birth and time to nurse babies once they returned to work. However, the laws also identified women workers as being in greater need of protection than male workers, and many employers refrained from hiring women in order to avoid having to provide maternity benefits. In this case, the law backfired, and women lost income that could keep their families afloat, rather than gaining rights that would guarantee their infants' health.

Although there were many similarities in elite ideas about women and work in the late nineteenth and early twentieth centuries, the context and meaning of these issues had changed with the onset of industrialization and the growth of social welfare institutions. Middle-class women found more opportunities to work outside the home, particularly in professions where they supposedly taught poor women to do a better job of house-keeping and raising children. At the same time, they faced heightened criticisms and fears about their participation in the public, modern world of work. Working-class women did not simply continue to face the same obstacles as before either; instead, they were specifically disadvantaged by laws and practices that identified male workers as family breadwinners and heads of households. These dilemmas and conflictive changes regarding work and motherhood also had an impact on various forms of feminism in the early to mid twentieth century.

Feminisms and Motherhood in the Early to Mid Twentieth Century

Moderate feminists continued to emphasize their differences from men, particularly regarding their status as mothers, and this influenced the roles that they thought women could or should have in the public sphere. In Ecuador, for example, Zoila Rendón de Mosquera criticized men who wanted to deny women the right to take part in work and other public activities. However, she asserted that a woman should only involve herself in public matters "as long as she does not feel the movement of a child in her womb. That sensation, until then unknown to her . . . will make her think only about her home."[38] In short, according to Rendón de Mosquera, once a woman was pregnant, she should (and would naturally want to) retire to the private sphere. Moderate feminists often seemed caught in a paradox, seeking public influence while reinforcing women's identification with the home and femininity.[39] Paradoxically, some feminists identified the home as both the cause of women's oppression, *and* as the basis on which they contributed to the nation, thereby justifying an expansion of women's political rights.

The rise of leftist parties in Latin America by the 1920s provided new, more radical platforms for both working- and middle-class women who wanted to address class as well as gender inequalities. Socialists identified patriarchy as yet another form of subjugation created by capitalism, but in practice socialist leaders often gave priority to economic rather than gender issues, and they sometimes labeled women who pushed for gender equality as "bourgeois." This label suggested that the women had been too influenced by middle-class gender ideas and goals and abandoned their commitment to ending class differences. At other times, party leaders did not criticize socialist feminists, but quietly set aside gender issues in preference of class-based initiatives.

While many leftist feminists sought to change their party's attitudes and practices toward gender, some instead (or additionally) opted to act on class- and gender-based issues in different types of organizations. A good example of this strategy comes from the life of Ecuadorian communist and feminist Nela Martínez. Martínez was born to the hacienda-owning class, but in her early adulthood she committed herself to the newly formed Ecuadorian communist party, eventually becoming a party leader who was well-respected for her work with indigenous communities. However, although the communist party claimed commitment to women's equality, the reality was that the Ecuadorian communist party – like so many leftist parties in Latin America – rarely prioritized women's specific needs and issues. Perhaps for this reason, Nela Martínez helped to found the Alianza Femenina Ecuatoriana (the Ecuadorian Women's Alliance, or AFE) in 1938. As stated in an AFE announcement in *El Comercio* (one of the prominent dailies in Ecuador):

> [The] AFE will defend women's rights and social and political victories, but within a harmonious plan, very distant from any belligerence that could

cause disunity and jealousy. Because it aspires to create a society without privileges and to dignify the humble, the Ecuadorian woman is present in this hour of national reconstruction, with the intention of cooperating, from a position of struggle and spirit, in the arduous and hard labor of uplifting the Ecuadorian home from national ruins . . . We will fight untiringly for national unity and we will have our hands open in solidarity [so that] women of all the country, without distinction of class, race, or political party, [can] come together to form ranks in the crusade that we are initiating today for the wellbeing and benefit of the country.[40]

As this passage shows, Martínez and the other women who founded the AFE wanted to develop an organization that was open to all women, to advance women's rights and needs with dignity, and to transcend political differences in seeking justice and national wellbeing. The AFE members identified themselves with the cause of women's rights, but also with the needs of children within society, and its leadership often reinforced women's supposedly inherent maternalism.

This maternalism sometimes reflected the dominant, race- and class-based public health discourses of the day. Although the AFE welcomed women from all class and race backgrounds, and adhered to no official political ideology, most of its members were white, middle-class women, and the group tended to stay in a moderate political middle ground. Their roles in "mothering society" were evident in a number of their statements and activities. For example, one AFE announcement asserted that "All Ecuadorian women should feel themselves responsible with regard to the destiny of the poor child, of the ignorant campesino, of the women without assistance to fulfill her function as a mother. We need to raise funds to establish day care centers in order to avoid [the] national shame [of] childhood delinquency, to obtain food and clothing for all Ecuadorian children, to educate them and transform them into citizens. We should go to the humble home of the indigenous woman . . . to give her the possibility of improving her culture and progress."[41] Martínez, despite her record of working in close alliances with indigenous peoples, in this case often worked "for" rather than "with" poor and indigenous groups, as in the AFE's famous campaign to provide shoes for poor schoolchildren (Figure 5.3). Martínez herself advocated that the AFE should send teams to bring feminine sanitation to the countryside, and send cultural missions to the rural poor, and she supported the regulation of wet nurses.[42]

Nela Martínez was far from the only feminist to embrace practices that originally stemmed from eugenics and puericulture. Many moderate

Figure 5.3   Photograph of Nela Martínez. Courtesy of Archivo Martínez-Meriguet.

feminists openly supported and worked to advance the scientific child-rearing methods of puericulture, and many openly defended aspects of eugenics.[43] Regardless of political orientation, most early- to mid-twentieth-century feminists found it difficult to stray too far away from the dominant, eugenics-influenced medical notions of the day, or from strong associations with what they identified as traditional, home-bound notions of motherhood. It was not simply that feminists bought into these theories, though many did, but that it was virtually impossible to achieve any of their goals without using the language and platforms already established by governments and public health officials. Those women who attempted to break free of such discourses and advocate full equality for women were often marginalized, as is evident when one examines the life of Brazilian Maria Lacerda de Moura.

In the early part of her life, Lacerda de Moura was like many middle-class women: she was educated and worked as a teacher, and then she married. Unable to have children of her own, she adopted two children. In her late 20s, however, she left her family in search of the intellectual stimulation and political fulfillment that she could not find in prescribed middle-class marriage and motherhood. Strongly desiring to work on behalf of social justice, Lacerda de Moura searched for a political ideology that would fit her beliefs. She joined radical feminist and anarchist movements, but even these she often found wanting or, in her view, tied (hypocritically) to elite groups who were causing problems of oppression and suffering. In her many books, some of which had a wide audience, Lacerda de Moura promoted free love and voluntary motherhood. She found it ridiculous that men could have sex with whomever they wanted without repercussions, but women who did so were labeled whores. To her, domestication was but another form of servility and subordination, and the solution to this was "Love and Conscientious Maternity." She believed that children born out of love, rather than conventional marriage, would be healthier and loved better than those born within the bounds of marriage. She also believed that a woman was freer to live her life and seek full equality if she was not bound to a man who had power over her, and if she only had children when she wanted them. Even Lacerda de Moura, however, glorified motherhood and thought that women who did not have children of their own were only justified in doing so if they were going to devote themselves fully to social causes. In the long run, Maria Lacerda de Moura was too radical for even the feminist and anarchist groups that she joined. She spent the last years of her life isolated and disillusioned, and increasingly drawn to mysticism. She and other women who presented "extreme feminism" typically found themselves this way – marginalized and unable to effect change. Perhaps it was for this reason that most feminists chose a middle ground, reinforcing dominant ideas about maternity and women's roles in the home, rather than seeking radical change and full equality.[44]

Moving Forward While Staying Put?

Although early twentieth-century gender discourses continued to classify women as mothers, the purposes, context, and opportunities (or disadvantages) of this association for middle- and upper-class women were distinct from those of the late nineteenth century. Elite anxieties and social fears over industrialization and urbanization did not simply lead them to reinforce supposedly traditional notions of motherhood; rather, they deepened and extended these ideas. Because they believed that modern society threatened to seduce women away from their maternal destinies, political and intellectual elites deemed it necessary to defend domesticity and motherhood so that women could fortify national morality through their work in the home. Physicians and state officials simultaneously (perhaps paradoxically) sought to encourage modern, supposedly scientific techniques of motherhood via eugenics and hygiene. Even elite discourses themselves blended tradition and modernity around the theme of motherhood. Women picked up on this merger of old and new discourses in their actions, arguments, and relationships in the early to mid twentieth century.

Middle-class women, whether feminists or not, tended to reinforce dominant gender norms and thus limited the parameters of their possible engagement with modern, public life. Most of them still argued that women belonged in the home once married, especially after having children, and supported the medicalization – and thus masculinization – of authority over childbirth and child care. Those feminists who significantly challenged dominant gender norms typically found themselves on the margins of the movement. Instead, most middle-class women and feminists focused on expanding their gains and dignity within political, economic, and health care systems. By embracing femininity and maternity, feminists often succeeded in winning the right to vote in national elections, and sometimes to hold institutional or political positions – particularly those concerning children and childhood. They lay claim to puericulture methods in order to expand their roles in public, teaching other (poorer) women the latest hygienic child-rearing practices. Social workers and nurses, in particular, formed the front lines of work with poor families, and without their contributions the new welfare systems would not have functioned.

Yet even when women accepted limits and reinforced gender stereotypes, they were not simply passive recipients who consented to their own subjugation. Rather, they found ways within these systems to advance at least some of their interests, and they often interpreted or acted on political agendas in ways that were unanticipated by the state or physicians, such as when social workers identified more strongly with their poor clients than they were charged to do. Frustrated socialist feminists often challenged, or found ways around, male leaders' ambivalence and reluctance to move forward on issues of gender inequality. Thus, if association with motherhood and tradition restricted women's opportunities to engage directly with public concerns, middle-class women could also manipulate men's fears of modernity run amok in order to make some of their desired gains.

Where were working-class women in all of this? Generally, poor were caught between feminism, class-race identity, and motherhood. Many working-class women found it difficult to participate in socialist party activities on a regular basis due to their obligations at home with their children. Moreover, although middle-class feminists often expected their own gains to trickle down and benefit poor women, working-class women's concerns and priorities often differed from middle-class women's – even middle-class socialist women's. As in the nineteenth century, poor women's experiences did not match the feminine, motherly ideal that elites espoused. However, their experiences and strategies changed with the shift from agriculture to industry and from countryside to city.

Document: "Call to the Women of Mexico"[45]

Lázaro Cárdenas was president of Mexico from 1934 to 1940, during which time he undertook massive land redistribution and reforms aimed at improving the lives of Mexican workers. Though these laws did help the lives of the poor, at least in the short term, they also served to solidify working-class and peasant support for the state and the new central party, the *Partido Revolucionario Mexicano*, or PRM. While many new social institutions were created during the Cárdenas years, the government also sought the assistance of women volunteers to help with their social programs.

The document below is from one such voluntary women's movement, the Feminine League, charged with assisting social welfare institutions. As you read this document, consider: How do the claims here reflect ideas about womanhood and "social mothering" that appear in this chapter? In particular, how does the author of this document call upon motherhood without directly invoking it? How and why do we see womanhood or motherhood as an essential component of national strength here?

Sisters:

We, as a group of women, have met to form the Feminine League of Social Assistance, sponsored by the Public Welfare (Beneficencia Pública). Its goals are the alleviation of the suffering and misery of the handicapped, the incapable, the socially weak who need attention and help, and those for whom because of the misfortunes of existence, do not enjoy the most basic human conditions of life.

The Feminine League of Social Assistance is a generous, impartial group that is called to fill a vital function in the general task of social assistance that the government of General Cárdenas has so nobly begun.

Practically, one has seen that as much as Public Welfare tries, it could not alone materially meet through its beneficial action, all of those people, who, for one reason or another, have to beg for effective help in order to subsist and to reincorporate themselves into the productive layers of society.

The Feminine League comes precisely to complete, in this sense, the action of Public Welfare. It is this new organization that is charged with extending the social gesture throughout the country to the most needy classes; an efficient and decisive aid that compensates for the defects and injustices of a social body still full of imperfections.

So that this labor will be effective, and so that the realization would be free of the vanities that often accompany this type of work, the League has thought from the very beginning to make a heart to heart call to all the women of this country; to women who feel that noble goal of improving the condition of their unprotected sisters, who feel the need to group ourselves under one banner using it as a motto this great truth: he who understands human pain is better for it.

We want the collaboration of all women regardless of class or nationality. We propose to extend social action across the country; to even the most remote places, in order to create, in sum, a national institution.

We know that the women who covet taking a part in the creation of a better world, constructed on the most just bases, will have difficulty finding a more proper field of action. The most effective labor of Social Assistance is understood not only as the alleviation of misery as it has always been understood, but also as a just act full of love for the rehabilitation of the socially weak who, for the moment, have stopped being socially useful.

The league will have its seat in Mexico City and will create committees all over the republic, counting on the help that women who hear this call will surely loan us.

The field activity for this league is vast and difficult to succinctly describe. All we can say for now is that where social injustice or disaster has created a difficult situation that places the dignity and even existence of a family or individual in danger, the League should intervene and with their noble work help reestablish the lost equilibrium.

Any help that can be given would be invaluable. Time, money, something that is no longer useful to you, would be enthusiastically received as if it were the richest gift donated. All of your contributions are a must to help feed and cloth[e] the needy.

These lines are meant to be a warm vibrant call to all of the women of Mexico. Those who answer our call will be part of the Feminine League's organization, work, and goals.

Women of Mexico: Participate with us in the creation of a more fair and just existence and a better country!

The President
María J. Sierra de Barros

Notes

1 This quote appears in Licia Fiol-Matta, *Queer Mother for the Nation: The State and Gabriela Mistral* (Minneapolis: University of Minnesota Press, 2002), p. 74. Fiol-Matta's book is the basis for my short biography and interpretation of Mistral's life here.

2 Fiol-Matta, p. 39.

3 Ecuador was the first Latin American country to give women the right to vote in national elections in 1929, and Paraguay was the last in 1961, with most countries granting this right in either the 1940s or early 1950s. For a full list of when women got the right to vote in each country, see Francesca Miller, *Latin American Women and the Search for Social Justice* (Hanover, NH: University Press of New England, 1991), p. 96.

4 Susan K. Besse, *Restructuring Patriarchy: The Modernization of Gender Inequality in Brazil, 1914–1940* (Chapel Hill: University of North Carolina Press, 1996), p. 72.

5   Fiol-Matta has a particularly nice discussion of this with reference to Mistral on p. 92.

6   For an excellent discussion of women like this who joined the health service sector in Ecuador, see A. Kim Clark, *Gender, State, and Medicine in Highland Ecuador: Modernizing Women, Modernizing the State, 1895–1950* (Pittsburgh, PA: University of Pittsburgh Press, 2012).

7   For an important discussion of crime and spatial organization in Mexico during this period, see Pablo Piccato, *City of Suspects: Crime in Mexico City 1900–1931* (Durham, NC: Duke University Press, 2001).

8   Gustavo Atuesta, *La Mujer Moderna ante Diós, En la Sociedad, y Ante el Derecho* (Bucaramanga: M.A. Gómez, 1940), pp. 32–35. Atuesta did not elaborate on the kinds of books women were reading, let alone why he labeled them "pornographic."

9   Roberto Campolieti, *Conciencia Social de la mujer, su responsabilidad frente a la crisis moderna y al comunismo* (Buenos Aires: Editorial Tor, 1938), pp. 42–43, 117, 24–25; Atuesta, pp. 66–67.

10 This quote appears in Ann Zulawski, *Unequal Cures: Public Health and Political Change in Bolivia, 1900–1950* (Durham, NC: Duke University Press, 2007), p. 130.

11 For example, see Jadwiga E. Pieper Mooney, *The Politics of Motherhood: Maternity and Women's Rights in Twentieth-Century Chile* (Pittsburgh, PA: University of Pittsburgh Press, 2009), p. 16; also see Zulawski, pp. 124–125.

12 Campolieti, pp. 44 and 128, respectively.

13 Besse, pp. 101, 139.

14 Zulawski, p. 170.

15 Tomás Amadeo, *La función social* (Buenos Aires: Imprenta Oceana, 1929), p. 39.

16 For examples of such arguments, see José Vasconcelos, *The Cosmic Race/La raza cósmica* (Baltimore: Johns Hopkins University Press, 1989); or Gilberto Freyre, *The Masters and the Slaves: A Study in the Development of Brazilian Civilization*, 2nd English-language ed. Trans. Samuel Putnam (New York: Alfred A. Knopf, 1970), and *New World in the Tropics: The Culture of Modern Brazil* (New York: Alfred A. Knopf, 1959).

17 Nancy Leys Stepan, *The Hour of Eugenics: Race, Gender, and Nation in Latin America* (Ithaca, NY: Cornell University Press, 1991), p. 91.

18 Stepan, pp. 122–128; quote on p. 125.

19 Besse, p. 99.

20 Stepan, p. 50. For Mexico, also see Katherine Elaine Bliss, *Compromised Positions: Prostitution, Public Health, and Gender Politics in Revolutionary Mexico City* (University Park: Pennsylvania State University Press, 2002).

21 Besse, p. 3.

22 Asunción Lavrin, *Women, Feminism, and Social Change in Argentina, Chile, and Uruguay, 1890–1940* (Lincoln: University of Nebraska Press, 1995), pp. 163–164.

23 Departamento de Salubridad Pública, "Alforismos para la radio, durante la semana de hygiene: 'La Madre y el Niño'" (Mexico, 1940).

24 Besse, 99.

25 Zulawski, p. 132. Their suggestion that the "praying" (kneeling) position led to medical complications was false: in most cases, kneeling or squatting during labor allows gravity to facilitate the birthing process, whereas lying on her back could potentially slow a woman's labor.

26 Donna J. Guy, *Women Build the Welfare State: Performing Charity and Creating Rights in Argentina, 1880–1955* (Durham, NC: Duke University Press, 2009), p. 128.

27 Karin Alejandra Rosemblatt, *Gendered Compromises: Political Cultures and the State in Chile, 1920–1950* (Chapel Hill: University of North Carolina Press, 2000), pp. 130–131; also see Lavrin, p. 118, and Mooney, p. 39.

28 Besse, pp. 84–85.

29 Mooney, pp. 39–40.

30 Leticia Tuigueiros, Graduation Speech, *Escola de Puericultura* (November 24, 1941). This translated excerpt is from Okezi T. Otovo, "Rescuing the Sacred Mission of Motherhood: Brazil's Campaign for Healthy Babies and Educated Mothers," in Erin E. O'Connor and Leo J. Garofalo, eds, *Documenting Latin America, Volume II: Gender, Race, and Nation* (New York: Pearson/Prentice Hall, 2011), p. 161.

31 Rosemblatt, pp. 155–158, with the excerpt appearing on p. 156.

32 Excellent discussions of this for Brazil appear in Besse, pp. 7–8, 131–132, 160–161.

33 Besse, 159; Zulawski, 185. Zulawski also discusses how this worked similarly for indigenous people, where an Indian with "delusions of grandeur" – that is to say, ideas or aspirations not fitting with elite views of proper Indian behavior – could be institutionalized. Institutionalization was nothing to take lightly in the early to midtwentieth century, when primitive shock treatments were common, including ones in which nondiabetics were given massive doses of insulin in order to induce a hypoglycemic coma in patients identified with depression or manic depression (see Zulawski, p. 164). These treatments ran the risk of killing the patients that they were intended to cure.

34 Karin Rosemblatt provides one of the best analyzes of family wages in her *Gendered Compromises*, chapter 2. This chapter offers the foundation for many of my assertions here. The quote is from p. 59.

35 Barbara Weinstein, "Unskilled Worker, Skilled Housewife: Constructing the Working-Class Woman in São Paulo, Brazil," in John D. French and Daniel James, eds, *The Gendered Worlds of Latin American Women Workers: From*

       Household and Factory to the Union Hall and Ballot Box (Durham, NC: Duke University Press, 1997), pp. 72–99.

36   Rosemblatt, 209 and 72, respectively.

37   Mooney, p. 25.

38   Zoila Rendón de Mosquera, *La mujer en el hogar y en la sociedad*, 3ra ed. (Quito: Editorial Universitaria, 1961 [1923]), pp. 94–95.

39   Susan Besse has a good discussion of these issues in Brazil in chapter 7 of *Restructuring Patriarchy* and has several important references to this tension on pp. 188–189.

40   Julia B. de Reyes, "Llamamiento que Alianza Femenina Ecuatoriana dirige a las mujeres del pais," *El Comercio*, 8 de agosto de 1944.

41   "Llamamiento."

42   Archivo Martínez Meriguet, undated, unlabeled newspaper clipping obtained via Valeria Coronel. Also see article "Alianza Femenina inauguro nuevo curso de alfabetización" regarding work on literacy in women's prisons – where children also stayed with mothers. Also see Nela Martínez, *Yo siempre he sido Nela Martínez Espinosa: Una autobiografía hablada* (Quito: CONAMU-UNIFEM, 2006), p. 97.

43   See, for example, Lavrin pp. 111, 162; Stepan, pp. 56–57.

44   For Maria Lacerda de Moura's life, see Susan Besse's *Restructuring Patriarchy*, pp. 108–109, 157–158, 179–180. For a discussion of Lacerda de Moura that included excerpts from her written works, see Besse, "Maria Lacerda de Moura Advocates Women's Self-Realization through Free Love and Conscientious Maternity," in *Documenting Latin America*, pp. 166–174. For an excellent discussion of the shift in the Chilean feminist movement, the Movimiento pro Emancipación de la Mujer Chilena (the Chilean Women's Pro-Emancipation Movement), see Rosemblatt, especially chapters 3 and 7.

45   This document was translated and presented by Nichole Sanders in "Improving Mothers: Poverty, the Family, and 'Modern' Social Assistance in Mexico, 1937–1950," in Stephanie Mitchell and Patience A. Schell, eds, *The Women's Revolution in Mexico, 1910–1953* (New York: Rowman and Littlefield, 2007), pp. 194–195.

6

Poor Mothers and the Contradictions of Modernity, circa 1900–1950

Activism and Motherhood: Doña María Roldán in Argentina

Doña María Roldán was born in San Martín, Argentina, to an Argentine mother and an Italian immigrant father who, though intelligent, worked as a brick layer. She married a poor man and together they moved to the city of Berisso in 1931 so that he could search for work there. Berisso was a meat packing town, but there were often more workers than available jobs. Doña María stayed at home tending to cleaning and motherhood duties until one of her sons got sick. In need of money, she went to work in the meat packing industry. She later explained to historian Daniel James that she told her husband "Look, *querido* (darling), I'm going to work for a while." That "while" turned out to be over 10 years, even though her son died only a few years after she began work. She worked on the factory floor from six in the morning until noon, and then from one in the afternoon until seven or eight in the evening.

Working such long hours made it difficult for Doña María and other mothers to manage home life:

> There was little time to be with the children. It separated us a little from them because the parents had many hours of work to put food on the table and buy clothes. The children matured very quickly, working. Because I said to my son, Mario, "Look, little one, peel these potatoes, clean the squash, and cut the tomatoes, and when mama gets home she'll make the

Mothers Making Latin America: Gender, Households, and Politics Since 1825, First Edition. Erin E. O'Connor.

stew." My son helped me cook; he couldn't go and play while I was at work. Only someone who has worked, worked outside the home, the mother of the family who has worked outside knows what it was like.[1]

Doña María could not separate her identity as a worker from her identity as a mother, even though these two aspects of her personality and duties were often at odds with each other. Not only did women workers frequently have to have their children help out with household and cooking chores, but they lived bifurcated lives, with many of them literally running home and back on their lunch hours in order to see their children.[2] In addition to emphasizing that she began to work in order to buy medicine for her sickly son, Doña María also claimed to have left work at the plant in order to tend to her other children's needs, and particularly to keep an eye on her daughter, who was blossoming into a young woman.[3]

In addition to her work on the factory floor, Doña María also became a labor organizer and leader. She was among the Berisso meat workers who supported Juan Perón in his rise to power, and she continued her labor activism within Peronist organizations during his rule from 1946 to 1955. Though she had socialist labor origins, she strongly supported Perón and his policies, largely because they brought material benefits to the workers of Berisso, and to her family in particular. When discussing her labor organizing work with Daniel James, Doña María often called attention to the fact that in addition to decent wages and work conditions, the workers in Berisso sought respect from their employers. In the 1960s, some years after her husband's death, she became involved in local politics, becoming both a school delegate and a municipal delegate.

Despite many years of factory work, her role as a union leader, and her later political career, Doña María often reinforced dominant gender norms. When describing her life in Berisso, she claimed that "I always say that the woman who knows her place never lacks for respect. Nothing strange ever happened to me, but then it never happened because I never went around being cute, joking with men in the patio; I waited for my husband, gave him his food, cleaned, stayed with my children." Despite spending years in the factory, and becoming a labor union leader, she asserted that a woman was born to be at home with her children. Not only did she stress that she both started and ended her years working in the meatpacking industry for the good of her children, but she also identified strongly with wifely virtues. Her discussion of needing to leave work to tend to her daughter as she was approaching adulthood also suggested that Doña María considered it her motherly duty to make sure that her daughter maintained her own good moral reputation.

Doña María's life story highlights several important themes for poor women, particularly those of the urban working class, living through the transition into modernity. Unlike middle-class women who learned to "play" the contradictions of urbanization and modernity, poor and non-white women often found themselves at the margins formal institutions and systems, although some like Doña María were able to become leaders in leftist organizations. Working-class mothers typically juggled work and child rearing, and they faced challenges quite different from those of either middle-class women or working-class men. As seen in the last chapter, both socialist leaders' calls for the family wage and moderate feminists' trickle down approach did little to enable poor women to act on their own behalf. At the same time, medical and social work professionals viewed poor women as incapable mothers who could only be saved by having middle-class women teach and supervise them. Even women's relationships to work were problematic, because although women at first accounted for a large percentage of the industrial labor force, family wage policies and protective legislation often made factory owners less likely to hire women workers or to pay them decent wages. This left working-class women struggling to make ends meet, often in the informal sector – which was rarely protected by new labor legislation – or adrift at the margins of modern industrial cities.

Despite these struggles, poor mothers were hardly passive victims of modernizing processes. Government programs and policies required poor women's cooperation, which gave them some leverage in their relationships with social and medical workers. Whenever they ignored officials, made complaints, or reinterpreted policies, poor mothers made their voices heard and influenced how policies were put into effect. They often proved adept at such encounters, understanding far more about laws and policies than elites typically assumed. Other women, such as Andean mestiza women in urban markets, made a living and presided over their families while refusing to live according to elite-approved rules of conduct. Although their actions had roots in gendered market relations dating back to the colonial period, their status and conflicts with officials reflected the changing times just as much as the lives of women factory workers did. Finally, there were both urban and rural mothers who joined political organizations, particularly socialist or communist parties that – while imperfect and sometimes paternalistic – often offered more room for poor women to act than other parties did from 1900 to 1950. Whether negotiating with public officials, rejecting class-race-gender rules, or engaging in sociopolitical activism, poor mothers often provided important critiques of the changes that their societies were undergoing in the early to midtwentieth century. Sometimes, such appraisals were overt, but often one finds them by reading between the lines of women's actions and lives. After all – these women left behind far fewer sources for us than their middle-class and elite counterparts did, although more sources became available in poor women's voices as the twentieth century advanced.

Juggling Work and Motherhood

The nature of working mothers' struggles changed over the course of their children's lives. In the first years of a child's life, a working mother's challenges revolved around finding child care and being able to nurse (or find someone else to nurse) her child. Though on-site nurseries were occasionally available, many mothers had to hand their children over to relatives, or even pay another woman to tend to young children. A woman might be forced to have an older child tend to her infant, as was the case for Brazilian textile worker Dona Odette with her 13-month-old baby:

> I left the baby in a hammock, with a pan of *mingau* [cassava cereal] by his side. His older brother [aged nine years] fed him throughout the day. When I got home late at night, I fixed the baby's dinner. Many times I arrived to find the baby's bottle shattered in pieces on the floor. This was before we had plastic bottles. How he never fell on the glass, I'll never know. God must have watched over him.[4]

As children got older, the difficulties tending to and feeding them changed, but did not necessarily decrease. Older children might be able to help out around the house, and with younger siblings, but they were also more likely to get into trouble with other kids in the neighborhood, or to have conflicts with adults. Moreover, older children required more food to keep them healthy (let alone satisfied), putting further economic strain on already tight household budgets.

Although poor mothers had been coping with the dual – and sometimes dueling – challenges of working and child rearing for a very long time, industrialization and urbanization changed the nature of this struggle. Whereas preindustrial work often allowed poor mothers to keep babies and small children with them while working, the factory work system separated mother and child. Even laws that required companies to provide on-site nurseries, or time for women to go home to nurse their children, were usually very limited in alleviating the problem of mother–infant separation. Laws were often ineffective, forcing women to work long hours without nursing, and laws that allowed women to go home to nurse were often not practical because many women lived far from their workplaces.

Another new challenge that poor working mothers faced was the necessity of building a sense of community in urban environments. As in the late nineteenth century, many urban workers in the early to midtwentieth century were either migrants or immigrants; however, such migrations were occurring on a much larger scale in the twentieth century. Whether they moved from countryside to city or from another part of the world to a Latin American country, working women were torn away from the familial and social systems that they once would have relied on for mutual assistance in hard times. They felt this loss particularly keenly when they became mothers, missing the advice, support, and camaraderie that they would have had access to in their homes of origin. Some women were fortunate and moved into working-class urban neighborhoods that did provide a sense of community. Doña María, for example, described the city of Berisso as having a strong working-class support system:

> I didn't feel afraid when I first arrived, because when you arrive with your children and you find a neighbor who says, "Whatever you want, I'm here, if you need anything don't be shy, that's what we neighbors are for," then you feel encouraged. You leave your intimate family there in San Martín, but you have the other big family here, the one that isn't your blood but is also your family.[5]

Doña María's memory of Berisso provides an important reminder that those working-class women who found themselves alone in cities often reached out to each other and began to build new support networks. However, there are two reasons to be careful with Doña María's recollections of Berisso as a "big family." One is simply the limitations of oral history and memory. There may well have been an important network of women helping each other in Berisso during the 1940s, but it is possible that Doña María remembered it with rose-colored glasses, editing out conflicts and enmities.[6] Second, even when these urban support systems existed, they lacked the cultural and historical foundations that one would find in peasant communities (or in urban neighborhoods from one's home country) to sustain them through the most difficult times. The greater poverty, need, and desperation that urban workers experienced, the more likely it was that mutual assistance among neighbors would break down. This was nowhere more evident than in shanty towns that sprouted along the outskirts of large cities, such as São Paulo, Brazil. There, despite the similar problems that led them to shanty towns and plagued them while they lived there, dwellers often turned on each other in heated, and sometimes violent, arguments. The neighbor who lent you a bit of food one day could be your worst enemy the next.[7]

Poor women responded in a variety of ways to the problems and limitations of trying to raise their children in these modern, often insecure urban environments. In many cases, they had no choice but to send their own children to work in factories much earlier than they would have liked. Rent had to be paid, and food and clothing had to be purchased. Even a sickly child sometimes had to be sent to work at a young age in order to keep a family afloat. Given the great efforts required to secure life's necessities, many working-class women embraced the idea of the family wage. The rhetoric around the family wage put women in a subordinate and dependent position with regard to their husbands, and (as discussed in Chapter 5) it justified continuing to pay women workers very low wages. Nevertheless, many working-class women agreed that men should be wage earners for the family, making wages sufficient to support the needs of their wives and children. This did not necessarily mean that working-class women accepted a subordinate or passive position. Historian Karin Rosemblatt, for example, notes that working-class housewives in Chile protested vehemently about the company store's provisions, because the store sold rotten vegetables and often lacked meat. Thomas Klubock further noted that wives of Chilean copper miners sometimes demanded control over some of their husbands' wages based on their identities and responsibilities as mothers.[8]

Other women joined political organizations in order to address their problems, and they often saw them differently than middle-classes or elite women. For instance, women who joined the Bolivian Federation of Women Workers recognized that, despite elite discourses that pro-claimed the universal experiences of motherhood, "they did not share in any of the benefits or privileges that the mother of the upper classes enjoyed. Rather, motherhood was another source of oppression."[9] Far from indicating that these women did not love their children, such claims instead reveal that the women saw clearly how elite discourses about motherhood were being manipulated to maintain and justify poverty. Other women joined unions or leftist parties which, though often prob-lematic regarding women's concerns and needs, were at least more open to working-class women's and mothers' participation than most other organizations were at the time.

Though some poor women criticized elite-driven images of mother-hood, others embraced them. Yet just because some working women accepted certain dominant gender norms did not mean that they were complacent. Doña María, for example, often used motherhood imagery in her working-class activism, and she saw workers' rights and dignity and family needs as intertwined. She explained that a major strike had been necessary in order to increase workers' pay so that they could feed their children. Similarly, when she argued that workers had been fighting for dignity, she emphasized her point by proclaiming that "we want to send our children to school well dressed and with shoes . . .". When defending an older woman worker in her conflicts with the bosses, she professed to have scolded those bosses by saying "Why are you treating her this way, don't you see that she could be your mother?"[10] In Brazil, Dona Cinta recalled that her mother worked minor miracles to feed the family and, because she was such a good mother, her family gladly handed over the money they earned to her.[11] Members of the middle-class and elites may have considered it an "abomination" that poor mothers worked outside of the home, but working-class mothers devel-oped their own definitions of good motherhood and used these to advance their agendas.

Single Mothers Facing Modern Challenges

Elite and middle-class men and women who worked in government insti-tutions identified single mothers as "fallen" women. Although the wealthy hoped that single mothers would be redeemed by motherhood, they assumed that it fell upon the state or middle classes to take over in order to ensure that single mothers would not fall further into debauchery. Their concerns only deepened when urban growth dramatically increased the number of single mothers in many areas. Partly for this reason, state officials who intervened in the private sphere often focused their attention on single mothers. Sometimes, state actions were preemptive attempts to curb the number of single mothers, as when the Bolivian state provided housing for single women. The aim with this project was both to weaken female solidarity and activism while simultaneously instilling what elites deemed good morals in women who might otherwise be led astray. Women who lived in the state housing could not "commit acts contrary to good morals or conduct" or they would lose their spot.[12] Most programs, however, were geared toward women who had already fallen into single motherhood. In Chile, the *Caja de Seguro Obligatorio* (The Obligatory Insurance Fund, or CSO) provided various protections for single mothers, such as a home for single pregnant women, and day care and skills classes for working-class single mothers. The CSO also took in domestic servants who lost their jobs upon becoming pregnant. All of these benefits, of course, came with greater scrutiny from social services and other government organizations, and the goal was always to have these women marry so that a man could provide for them.[13]

In some cases, new social welfare services made life more manageable for poor mothers. Consider a case from Quito in 1948, when María Padilla sought asylum for her children in an orphanage. She had moved to Quito from her home city of Ibarra a few years earlier with her husband, but he had abandoned her and her two children (ages one and three) eight months before she sought assistance from social service workers. Padilla found work as a servant in a wealthy family's home, but they would not let her bring her young children to work. She tried but failed to find employment where she could bring her children with her, and she had no family in Quito to help out with her children. In this case social workers recommended placing her children in an orphanage, though only after trying and failing to reach the children's father to get support from him.[14] The outcome here was not ideal, since the Gordillo family was dispersed, but it did ensure their survival. In some other cases, social service workers were able to supplement a woman's or couple's income in order to make it possible to keep parents and children together rather than send the children to an orphanage.

Most poor single mothers, however, fell through the cracks of government assistance. An excellent and detailed account of the plight of single mothers can be found in Carolina Maria de Jesus's diary about life in a mid-century São Paulo *favela* (shanty town). De Jesus was originally from rural northeastern Brazil, but moved to São Paulo as a young woman where, with only a second-grade education, she worked as a domestic servant. Like so many maids, her employers fired her when they learned that she was pregnant. With nowhere else to go, she headed to the growing shanty town and built her own shack, just as other inhabitants had. No longer able to work because of her baby (in all she would have three children), de Jesus walked São Paulo's streets collecting paper and scrap metal that she could sell in order to feed her family.[15] Every day was a struggle for survival. One of her most difficult moments came when her youngest child, Vera, was born:

> I was alone in the *favela*. No woman showed up to wash my clothes or look after my children. My boys slept filthy. I stayed in bed thinking of my boys, afraid for them playing on the riverbank. After a birth a woman doesn't have strength to lift an arm. After the birth I stayed in an uncomfortable position until God gave me the strength to arrange myself.[16]

Although de Jesus struggled to birth, feed, and raise her children in the favela, she was wary – indeed often hostile toward the idea – of seeking social service assistance for her children. If anything, she feared that her children would be taken away from her and put in a government institution that was not adequately funded and in which poor children were treated badly.

Despite the trials she endured as a single mother, de Jesus did not envy her married counterparts. She explained:

> They [other women in the shanty town] gossip that I'm not married, but I'm happier than they are. They have husbands but they are forced to beg. They are supported by charity organizations. [. . .]
> I never got married and I'm not unhappy. Those who wanted to marry me were mean and the conditions they imposed on me were horrible.[17]

Throughout her diary entries, de Jesus referred to men of the shanty town as prone to drunkenness and disinclined to work in order to provide for their children. Thus, married women (or those with live-in partners) endured the same problems as a single mother like de Jesus herself. Worse, they had to feed their husbands as well as their children, and some of them suffered from domestic violence. Some married working-class women similarly noted that their husbands rarely (if ever) helped out around the house, and they often went out to bars or clubs – leaving their wives at home with children and housework.[18] Yet de Jesus's diary is often contradictory on the matter of her single mother-hood – while she sometimes expressed gratitude to be free of a burden-some mate, at other times she expressed loneliness and discussed how difficult it was to be a woman alone, raising children.

Whether being a single mother was an added disadvantage for a working-class woman was therefore dependent on context. If she married a man who made a good wage and treated her well, it was preferable for a woman to be married. However, if her husband beat her, had affairs, or abandoned her, then a married mother was some-times worse off than her single counterparts. Even if her husband was a good man who simply could not find adequate work, life might be more difficult married than single. Whether single or married, many poor mothers (unlike de Jesus) made use of newly available social serv-ices, entering into negotiations with state officials over the plight of their children and families.

State Intervention in Mothering: Conflicts and Benefits

State and medical officials might have viewed poor mothers as putty to be molded by their programs, but poor women found a variety of ways to assert their will in encounters with social workers, teachers, nurses, and other state officials. Their resistance, cooperation, or reinterpreta-tions of state goals often determined the relative success of new public assistance programs. Why and how did mothers sometimes ignore or reject the overtures of outsiders to help them? What convinced poor mothers to cooperate and advance state objectives in their communities and homes? How did they learn to work the systems in order to advance their own agendas? The answers to these questions are different accord-ing to the particular circumstances, regions, and communities in which women lived.

Rather than directly confront social workers, nurses, or teachers, poor women often simply ignored their advice. Consider the woman in Val-paraiso, Chile, who told a social worker that she did not need to practice bathing her child because "Since I am the mother of several children, I have enough practice."[19] The social worker in question was trying to teach proper hygiene, assuming that working-class mothers lacked sufficient knowledge or habits of cleanliness. It is easy to imagine her from a working-class mother's perspective: here was a young, childless woman claiming expertise on child rearing; what would she know about it? Probably, this woman thought that her own experience and the advice of other mothers were more valuable. Similarly, working-class women in São Paulo refused to enroll in home economics classes that were offered through government-backed education programs.[20]

When poor women and mothers took advantage of new social services and educational opportunities, for themselves or for their children, it was largely on their own terms. The same women who rejected home economics classes in São Paulo flocked to sewing classes, because learning to sew might help them to earn income even if they were bound to the home by children. Women in Argentina who were offered courses for "the agricultural home" also showed the most interest in sewing classes – probably for the same practical reasons.[21] Often, rather than entirely accepting or rejecting social workers' and other state officials' advice or ideas, poor mothers adopted only what appealed to them, often quite gradually.

Government workers frequently had to let go of their own preconceived urban and middle-class notions in order to get poor mothers to buy into their programs. When teachers and social workers in rural Mexico made the effort to cultivate ties with respected women in the communities they served, more women within the communities were likely to adopt new techniques and medical innovations, or to send their children to schools. Over time, some teachers and social workers learned to respect the logic of certain rural child-rearing practices, such as giving children pulque in small quantities when drinking water was unsafe. Pulque might have been mildly alcoholic, but it went through a distilling process that meant that it was sometimes safer than available water supplies. Mothers were also likely to accept new programs once they began so see positive effects for their children, as when they observed that children were much more likely to survive epidemics if they received vaccines beforehand.[22] In Argentina, the instructors for courses on rural homemaking not only had to provide classes that interested girls and their parents, but they also had to respect the dignity of the students. A report on the school in 1921 explained that although established rules had required students to wear a white apron at all times, the students themselves did not want wear them because they would then appear to be servants. The solution was for students to wear dusters rather than aprons, and for the teachers to wear them as well.[23]

State-appointed midwives in rural Ecuadorian provinces in the 1930s received a similar mixed reception. Members of the community of Pujilí regarded the state-appointed midwife as completely unnecessary because they preferred their own local midwives. In other areas, midwives were welcomed and maintained exceptionally busy schedules helping women give birth. Even in these cases, rural dwellers might complain the state-assigned midwife's charges were too high, or that she was not readily available when they needed her. Complaints like these, however, suggest that these communities viewed formally trained midwives as a benefit, since their complaints were aimed at making their services more wide-spread and affordable.[24] In some cases, poor mothers and social workers or nurses shared a similar and deep frustration. Although states initiated an established social service and health care offices, these were not necessarily sufficiently funded. Schools, clinics, and midwives all needed money and supplies, which were not always forthcoming from central state agencies.

Poor women were right to be wary of government programs, and not only because officials rarely funded them adequately. Many scholars have pointed out that state officials (especially the men in high government offices) were uninterested in challenging patriarchy. Instead, their programs and policies typically reinforced and *modernized* gender inequalities and reinforced male authority. Sometimes this took the form of orienting women's loyalties and obedience to (mostly male-run) state institutions rather than to their husbands. At other times, schools, social welfare reforms, and medical interventions encouraged a division of labor and authority that was even more extreme and male driven than previous customs had been.[25] If individual men's patriarchal authority was threatened in any way, it was always to the advantage of state officials or business owners, as when mechanized corn mills appeared in many areas of rural Mexico in the middle of the twentieth century. Grinding corn by hand had required hours of work each day, and it had reinforced women's association with the home and men's association as heads of households. Many rural husbands felt threatened when the mechanized mills liberated their wives from these hours of labor. Yet state and industrial elites encouraged the establishment of mechanized corn mills not to give rural women greater independence, but rather to gain access to cheap female labor in new factories.[26]

Poor mothers both reaped the benefits and suffered the consequences of modernization and its resulting proliferation of social, medical, and educational policies. Though state officials expected them to obey and appreciate all new forms of intervention in their homes, poor mothers decided for themselves which aspects of modernity and social services worked best for them. They weighed benefits and costs, argued for services that made the most difference in their own and their children's lives, and did what they could to maintain their dignity. They might not have initiated the policies of the welfare states that emerged in the early to midtwentieth century, but poor women's reactions often helped to shape and alter how policies developed "on the ground" in urban neighborhoods or rural communities.

Aberrant Motherhood?: Chola Market Women

In the Andean nations of Peru, Ecuador, and Bolivia, one particular type of woman stood out in strong contrast to the modernizing, scientific (yet traditionally deferential and home-bound) mother: the mixed-race market woman. According to members of the elite and middle classes, the market woman was traditional in all the wrong ways, maintaining indigenous forms of dress and refusing to adhere to modern standards. At the same time, she was too independent to fit the ideal of the mother who, by clinging to a traditional role in the home, would save the nation from modern debauchery. Who exactly was this mestiza market woman, and what was her role both in the urban arena and in nationalist discourses? How did market women understand and act on motherhood, female identity, and modernity?

In the Andes, the term cholo or chola refers to someone of mixed racial descent, particularly someone close to his or her indigenous past. It can also be a reference to an indigenous person living in an urban setting. It is a term typically used by wealthier people who do not associate themselves with indigenous identity, let alone with rural poverty that they assume goes along with "Indianness." The term is therefore caught up with racism, and it was (and is) often used to suggest the supposed inferiority of Indians or peoples of mixed racial descent, particularly if they maintain close ties to the countryside. Though one sometimes hears "cholito" or "cholita" as a term of endearment, the term is typically derogatory.

The feminine *chola* is often a specific reference to women vendors in urban, open-air markets who sell local produce or *chicha* (corn beer).

Their clothing and lives embody a mixture of the indigenous and European. They dress in *polleras* – multilayered skirts of indigenous origin, but that are far more expensive than rural indigenous peoples could afford to buy. With this, they blend more modern and European-based forms of clothing, combining polleras with European-style hats such as Panama hats worn by many women market vendors in southern Ecuador, or bowler hats in Bolivia. Chola market women often have connections with their rural roots and serve as go-betweens for market exchanges between city dwellers and indigenous peasants (Figure 6.1). They sell produce to urban whites, and provide manufactured and other necessary goods to Indian peasants. Yet in the early to mid-twentieth century, when elites officially glorified racial mixture (see Chapter 5), they viewed cholas as a dangerous, even deviant, symbols of cultural intermixing. Cholas engaged in mestizaje on their own terms, breaking out of racial and gender hierarchies. They also blended tradition and modernity, but in ways that were unintended by middle-class and elite authorities. Elites further suggested that cholas were loose women who did not marry and had several sexual partners throughout their lives. Suggesting that cholas were sexually loose was yet another way to categorize them as dirty and dangerous.

One of the main reasons that elites viewed cholas as problematic was that these women refused to be confined to the private sphere, or even to maintain the image of so-called proper domesticity despite working outside the home. Cholas worked not only in the public realm, but in an atmosphere that middle classes and elites thought of as most unbecoming for a woman: the open air market. These markets appeared disorderly and dirty to wealthy individuals, even though they (via their servants) depended on them for produce. Worse, in their view, was the fact that chola market women were bold and could be loud and aggressive. Rather than being dependent or obedient, they were in charge and knew how to haggle to defend their economic interests. Because chola market women were also sometimes women who had rejected elite men's sexual advances, outsiders occasionally labeled them *varonil*, or masculine.[28]

Marcia Stephenson keenly noted that chola market women may have been mestizas, but they did not live up to elite ideals regarding racial mixture. "The idealized, acculturated mestiza is represented as a woman readily taking up her assigned place inside the home as a housewife with the primary responsibility of reproducing the equally idealized nation."[29] Cholas refused to confine themselves to this private sphere, just as they

Figure 6.1 These images are of Bolivian cholas from the 1920s – the second one labeled as a "chola cook." Note how both women wore the pollera and shawl typical of cholas. The woman labeled a cook has a more demure look in the image taken of her (b), while the other chola (a) offers a more commanding presence. Frank and Frances Carpenter Collection, Library of Congress.[27]

refused to trade in their polleras for modern, nonindigenous skirts. It was not that they did not have families; most of them had children, and many had husbands or were in long-term relationships. What they did not necessarily do was defer to their male partners, which was an expectation of women in middle- and upper-class societies, and even among indigenous peasants.

Cholas, of course, did not see themselves as elites did. Although some saw marriage as another form of colonialism because it favored men's

Figure 6.1   (*Continued*)

power over women, others identified themselves as good wives and mothers. Lucrecia Carmandona was a market vendor and wife of union leader Agustín Mamami in Cuzco, Peru. Describing herself decades after her days of organizing vendors into a union, she said:

> I am a mestiza fighter, I have always worked along with my husband so that my children would never want for anything. I have stood up to anyone who disrespected me . . . I have insulted them and chased them out with knife in hand. I learned to talk to defend myself, and I have done it . . . I do not belong to the high society of Cuzco, those who despise us. They call us "those cholas," they insult us; they think that we are thieves and whores . . . I am only a worker and I have helped my husband all my life . . . [I]f I

have defended myself and insulted them, it is for my children. Because of that all my sons have been educated and now all of them, everyone is a professional . . . but my struggle continues because now I still have grand-children who have to grow up.[30]

Being a good wife and, especially, a good mother, was important to Carmondona and other cholas, but they defined this role differently than middle- and upper-class Peruvians did. Cholas saw their work in the marketplace as a means through which they could not only provide for their children's present needs, but also offer them with a better future than they might otherwise have. This maternal responsibility was more than simply economic; it also entailed actively and boldly defending their reputations and interests. Although outsiders – often negatively, sometimes with admiration – identified cholas as matriarchs in charge of homes where men were either absent or contributed little to household income, many cholas saw (and see) themselves as deeply religious and family oriented. They recognized that women earned greater respect if partnered with a man (whether in marriage or informally), but did not hold to the idea of chastity, nor did they see it as a problem if they broke ties with one man and later set up household with another.[31]

Cholas continued practices of mothering that harkened back centu-ries in Andean marketplaces, where women have always been active participants. Rather than stay at home with children, as middle-class women of the early twentieth-century did, or leave children in someone else's care as women factory workers were forced to do, cholas kept their young children with them throughout the workday. Like indigenous women of the countryside, cholas literally wore (and wear) their babies virtually all of the time. Their bodies were, for all intents and purposes, the universe to their children for many months. They thus refused to succumb to state pressures to modernize their child-rearing habits. Because many chola market women were financially stable, state officials had less sympathy for their insistence on raising children in traditional rather than modern ways than they did with women living in poverty.

Cholas might have refused to acquiesce to elite pressures regarding how to run their lives, but they did make demands of the modernizing states in which they lived. In Bolivia, for example, chola market women were often politically active. In the late 1930s, following the Chaco War (in which many Bolivians, mostly indigenous soldiers, lost their lives), chola women demanded relief and rights to help them during difficult economic times. They justified these demands "on the basis of their sacrifice to the nation as widows, mothers, daughters, or sisters of men killed in the frontline trenches." In 1938, when authorities removed many of the poorest women vendors from the streets, they protested: "Aren't we Bolivians? Didn't our sons and husbands burst like toads in the Chaco War, and now they want to take the bread out of our mouths? Down with the wealthy and privileged! We want the street, we need to take over the street . . .".[32] Cholas became increasingly politicized, demanding favorable labor legislation and licenses to sell goods in the streets. Though many of the cholas embraced radical politics, not all of their encounters with the state and nation were combative. In the 1940s, when Bolivian president Gualberto Villaroel made Mothers' Day a national holiday, he wanted to link it to patriotism, honor, and nation. Chola market women in Cochabamba, Bolivia used a mutual aid society to sponsor one of the most important parades on Mothers' Day (which also commemorated female heroines of the independence movement).[33] As with protests, this more peaceful engagement with the state intertwined motherhood, class, and politics.

In short, state authorities found cholas exceptionally difficult to control. Cholas blended the public and private on a daily basis. They clung to aspects of indigenous identity that most middle-sector and elite groups were trying to erase or play down. They defended their children's interests not by manipulating dominant motherhood ideals of suffering and sacrifice, but through loud and aggressive public actions demanding their rights. By the late twentieth century, some regional officials embraced cholas as symbols of their localities. This occurred in the Cuenca region of Ecuador, where tourist agencies and state officials formally idealize and celebrate (as well as stereotype) the "chola cuencana" with pride. At the same time, however, Cuenca elites continue to see cholas – the actual women, not the symbols – as dangerous, oversexed, and dirty matriarchs.[34]

Poor Mothers and the Limits of Modernity

Perhaps most obviously, an examination of poor women's work and motherhood experiences in the early to mid-twentieth century exposes the limitations, and sometimes outright failures, of modernization and social welfare policies based on middle-class and elite gender ideals.

Rather than addressing the core needs that poor mothers had – for reliable income, safe workplaces and housing, health care, and dignity – most government and charitable agencies continued to work on reforming poor mothers so that they reflected the middle-class ideal of womanhood, centered on motherhood. (As discussed in Chapter 5, even middle-class women often did not live up to these standards.)

Yet there important lessons of *historical agency*, below the surface level, that become apparent when one studies the poor women in Latin American from 1900 to 1950. Sometimes poor mothers asserted themselves by simply surviving, as did Carolina Maria de Jesus. Eventually, her literacy and diary (which was published and enjoyed a brief period of popularity in Brazil) got her out of the shanty town, though she ultimately died in poverty and isolation. Other poor shantytown and working-class women remain mostly nameless to us today, but they were the individuals who daily performed minor miracles in order to feed and clothe their children, and who did their best to keep them safe and healthy. They responded to their conditions, and to the employers and state officials who sought to change them, in a variety of ways. These variations are an important reminder that there was no single or authentic poor woman's encounter with modernity. Some resisted or ignored official outreach or demands, though more negotiated with new government, social service, and medical authorities. When authorities such as midwives or social workers treated poor mothers with dignity and respect, and when they tapped into preexisting networks and hierarchies, they had the greatest success at truly helping the women they claimed to serve. Therefore, the social workers noted in Chapter 5 who came to care a great deal about the poor women and families they encountered were motivated not only by their own internal sense of justice or affection, but also by the demands and priorities of poor women themselves. The relationship was, as historian Karin Rosemblatt aptly noted, a "two-way street" rather than merely a one-way encounter in which social workers and other authorities offered help or made demands of the poor.[35]

There was no unified poor women's experience or viewpoint of modernization and urbanization. Consider two of the women discussed in this chapter: Doña María Roldán of Berisso, Argentina and Carolina María de Jesus of São Paulo, Brazil. Roldán embraced dominant gender norms and glorified Peronism even though she worked in a factory and preferred socialism to Peronism. She also believed in and hoped for a better future through collective action. De Jesus was almost the complete opposite: she rejected most gender rules, held marriage in disdain, and mistrusted her fellow favelados. Her diary, unlike Roldán's testimony, contains no suggestion of hope for improvement through either state reforms or through favelados coming together to make demands. Their differing viewpoints emerged largely from the distinct situations in which they lived. Roldán had a committed marriage and regular work; she also had a strong sense of community in Berisso both in her neighborhood and her union. De Jesus was single, could not find formal employment, and often conflicted with her neighbors. Their contrasting lives and viewpoints serve as an important reminder that modernity meant many different things among poor women. Despite these differences, however, motherhood was at the center of both these women's lives, and it shaped how they interpreted events and circumstances in their lives. This was true not only of Roldán and de Jesus, but of the vast majority of poor women in twentieth-century Latin America.

Ideas about motherhood shaped how government officials engaged with poor women, and women's struggles to provide for their children patterned their actions and agendas. Moreover, women from a variety of class backgrounds learned how to "work" motherhood – how to blend it into their protests, demands, and descriptions of their lives. This was true of women regardless of their class or political leanings. Even women like cholas, whom elites identified as being at the margins of modern society and respectability, manipulated motherhood in their political activities and discussions of their lives. These relationships to motherhood patterned how women grew into (or failed to grow into) positions of political power or influence, how they experienced political revolutions or populist rule, and how they engaged with new medical technologies around reproduction.

Document: Dalia: A Black West Indian in Costa Rica[36]

Dalia was an Afro-Latin American woman from the English-speaking Caribbean who grew up and lived in Limón, along the Caribbean coast of Costa Rica. Though far from wealthy, these Afro-Caribbeans formed a kind of rural middle class, often better off than Spanish-speaking families around them, in part because foreign businessmen in the area were mostly English speakers who preferred to hire workers with English skills. It is difficult to learn much about this unusual class of workers in Costa Rica, especially about the women, who rarely worked in the formal economy. However, in the 1970s, the National University of Costa Rica collected a series of "peasant autobiographies" in which rural peoples were urged to write out and submit their life stories. Dalia was one of these women, and the excerpts of her story here highlight the many challenges that mothers faced, even in a group that generally experienced relative economic security. How does her life story compare and contrast to other women in this chapter? In what ways does it summarize main lessons from the chapter?

> One day one of my mother's brothers who managed an estate for a company offered to make my father an administrator of the estate. . . . At first everything went very well, he came back to the house every 15 or 21 days, at the weekends he took us to a matinee, out for a walk or something like that. Time passed and gradually he stopped coming by the house so often, and mama could not go to the estate herself because of us, my brothers and I were studying, so we could only go during the holidays, but then papa began to look for excuses for why we couldn't even come in the holidays, saying that there were not many comforts and that everything was in a mess. Since she knew something about this world, mama became suspicious that he had another woman, and so one day we went to surprise him on the estate, and her suspicions turned out to be true. He denied everything she accused him of, and then tried to excuse it by saying that he was not actually married to my mother. In view of the situation she decided not to go back again, and he for his part rarely came by the house, but he was very responsible in the maintenance of the house. [. . .]
>
> My father did not return to the house and almost never sent any money and so we wanted for many necessities, and the little he did send counted for almost nothing. We were seven children and mother made eight. One day out of the blue mother received a letter from my father in which he said

that he had gone to Panama in search of a better job in the canal zone, and that meanwhile we would have to see how things worked out. [. . .]

To cut a long story short, mother decided to return to the city. Our main anxiety was finding somewhere to live, because renting was so expensive. Poor mother worked so hard, day and night; in the day in a hotel as a chambermaid, in the night ironing close by. But not even this earned enough money to fill seven mouths with food, and with shoes to buy, uniforms, utilities, electric and the house to pay for . . . ay! And mother did not want me to leave secondary school, but I was already 15 years old, and I understood more about the hundreds of problems of my mother than any of my brothers. I remember one time that I looked longingly in a very beautiful shop window and pledged to buy myself a pair of shoes. My goodness, this was the last straw, and I decided to leave school and work, mother didn't want it but in spite of herself she put me in touch with an aunt she had in another city, and I went to the capital in search of work. [. . .]

I began to court various boys, I chose the one that seemed to me the most decent, but I was mistaken, and time has made this very clear . . . [With him] I had my first sexual relations. Goodness me, I couldn't decide how I felt afterwards, I believed that my mother would read what had happened on my face, and I couldn't look her in the eyes, I thought so many things, and I cried like never before, but everything passes in this life and I continued having sexual relations; and one day I realized in horror that I was pregnant. I didn't know how to say this to my mama, besides my boyfriend did not want to marry me, he told me that he was not prepared for this, besides he had another girlfriend whose parents had money, and if he had to choose between marrying her and me, he would pick her because he would not have to worry about how to buy things, whereas he would with me.

Between rows and problems over this issue after returning home to my mother my daughter was born. On her birth I registered her in my name. A little time afterwards he got a lawyer to change the name of the child to his. During all of this I had been offered a job in a supermarket, and because I could not risk losing the job, I went back to work only six days after giving birth. It was an experience that I will never forget, those pains that I felt below, of being stood up all day, of the fear that blood would pass through my clothes. I was so grateful to the owner of the business, who noticed my problem and told me that I could sit down when I didn't have anyone to attend to. For many months I was angry with the father of my child, but afterwards we made up. And, after three years my second child was born and then we got married. Then, two years after that my other daughter was born. But . . . what of all those years lived together? There are many things that I am determined to never tell, or at least not for a long time. The husband in question was a vain, crude, irresponsible man, a mindless womanizer, and the worst is that he was always playing cards. He always found the time for other things that were not his children or his home. He was out all hours of the night, playing cards, and the money that I earned had to work miracles in the house. I was always thinking perhaps he will change, tomorrow will be another day . . . but the truth was it went from bad to worse. Thus one fine day when I was three months pregnant I left the house. I left my children with my mother, and I went to live with my grandmother who was a widow. When my daughter was born I took her to see him, and he asked me to return to the house, but up to this day I never have. Now I understand that I was living under a personality that wasn't mine, because I had a job, I was working in the house and going to school. I left for work at 6 in the morning, got up at 5am to make breakfast and prepare my oldest daughter for school, and to start cooking the meat for the evening meal and make the beds. When I returned at 11:30 I would begin to make lunch, and to clean and wash. I would return at 2pm, and leave at 5:30 to get ready for school, and in this way I got my certificate of secondary studies and today I work in the Ministry of Government. I like my work, and most importantly I feel that I have realized myself fully as a woman.

Notes

1   Daniel James, *Doña María's Story: Life History, Memory, and Political Identity* (Durham, NC: Duke University Press, 2000), pp. 42–43.
2   James, p. 45.
3   James, p. 91.
4   Theresa R. Veccia, "'My Duty as a Woman': Gender Ideology, Work, and Working-Class Women's Lives in São Paulo, Brazil, 1900–1950," in John D. French and Daniel James, eds, *The Gendered Worlds of Latin American Women Workers: From Household and Factory to the Union Hall and Ballot Box* (Durham, NC: Duke University Press, 1997), pp. 133, 135–136.
5   James, *Doña María's Story*, p. 36.
6   James has two particularly good essays in *Doña María's Story* regarding use and analysis of oral histories. See "Listening in the Cold" and "The Case of María Roldán and the Señora with Money," pp. 119–212.
7   For a moving and detailed first-hand account of living in a shanty town (or *favela*) of São Paulo, see Carolina Maria de Jesus, *Child of the Dark: The Diary of Carolina Maria de Jesus*. Trans. David St. Clair (New York: Signet Classic, 2003 [1962]).
8   Karin Alejandra Rosemblatt, *Gendered Compromises: Political Cultures and the State in Chile, 1920–1950* (Chapel Hill: University of North Carolina Press, 2000), pp. 71–76; Thomas Miller Klubock, "Morality and Good Habits: The Construction of Gender and Class in the Chilean Copper Mines, 1904–1951," in *The Gendered World of Latin American Women Workers*, p. 244.
9   Marcia Stephenson, *Gender and Modernity in Andean Bolivia* (Austin: University of Texas Press, 1999), pp. 30–31.
10 James, *Doña María's Story*, pp. 37, 107, 65, 87 (respectively).
11 Veccia, pp. 116–117.
12 Ann Zulawski, *Unequal Cures: Public Health and Political Change in Bolivia, 1900–1950* (Durham, NC: Duke University Press, 2007), pp. 152–153.
13 Rosemblatt, pp. 169–171.
14 Archivo del Museo Nacional de Medicina (Quito): Junta Central de Asistencia Pública. Sección Servicios Sociales, Casos Sociales del Año de 1947, AP-1216. Cases are listed alphabetically, so this case appears under "Gordillo."
15 David St. Clair, "Translator's Preface," in Carolina Maria de Jesus, *Child of the Dark*, pp. viii–x.
16 De Jesus, p. 50.
17 De Jesus, p. 8.
18 For an example, see Veccia, p. 132.

19 Rosemblatt, p. 168.

20 Barbara Weinstein, "Unskilled Worker, Skilled Housewife: Constructing the Working-Class Woman in São Paulo, Brazil," in *The Gendered World of Latin American Women Workers*, p. 76.

21 Ministerio de Agricultura de la Nación, *Informe del Curso Temporario del Hogar Agrícola para Mujeres* (Buenos Aires: Talleres Gráficas del Ministerio de Agricultura de la Nación, 1921), p. 13.

22 Mary Kay Vaughan, "Modernizing Patriarchy: State Policies, Rural Households, and Women in Mexico, 1930–1940," in Elizabeth Dore and Maxine Molyneaux, eds, *Hidden Histories of Gender and the State in Latin America* (Durham, NC: Duke University Press, 2000), pp. 205–207.

23 *Informe del Curso Temporario del Hogar Agrícola*, p. 14.

24 A. Kim Clark, *Gender, State, and Medicine in Highland Ecuador: Modernizing Women, Modernizing the State, 1895–1950* (Pittsburgh, PA: University of Pittsburgh Press, 2012), pp. 129–132.

25 For particularly good and important discussions of state reinforcement of patriarchal relations, see Weinstein, and Vaughan ("Modernizing Patriarchy").

26 Jeffrey M. Pilcher, *Qué Vivan los Tamales! Food and the Making of Mexican Identity* (Albuquerque: University of New Mexico Press, 1998), pp. 100–107.

27 Both images are from the Library of Congress online collection, and both are from the Frank G. Carpenter collection. The first has a reproduction number: LC-USZ62-111676; the second is LC-USZ62-136385.

28 Mary Weismantel, *Cholas and Pishtacos: Stories of Race and Sex in the Andes* (Chicago: University of Chicago Press, 2001), pp. 46–47, 62–63.

29 Stephenson, p. 5.

30 Marisol de la Cadena, *Indigenous Mestizos: The Politics of Race and Culture in Cuzco, Peru, 1919–1991* (Durham, NC: Duke University Press, 2000), p. 217.

31 de la Cadena, pp. 239–240. Also see Weismantel, pp. 65–66.

32 Stephenson, pp. 24–25.

33 Laura Gotkowitz, "Commemorating the Heroínas: Gender and Civil Ritual in Early-Twentieth-Century Bolivia," in Dore and Molyneaux, pp. 215–237, and especially pp. 225–227.

34 Weismantel has a good discussion of this. See especially, pp. 25–29.

35 Rosemblatt, p. 14.

36 The Complete and unedited transcripts of the Peasant Autobiographies project is held in the library of the National University in Heredia, Costa Rica. Many thanks to Nicola Foote for allowing me to use this excerpt from her research.

7

Mothers and Revolution, circa 1910–1990

Mexico, Cuba, and Nicaragua

Tales of Gender and Revolution

Revolutionary conflict rocked Mexico from 1910 to 1920. Peasant armies faced each other in combat as several different revolutionary leaders strove to win control of the national government after Porfirio Díaz's fall from power. Amelio Robles was among those combatants. Recognized for his abilities and bravery during the war, Robles also earned entry later in life into the Confederation of Veterans of the Revolution,, and in 1974, the Ministry of National Defense decorated him as a veteran (*veterano*) of the revolution. Robles was a "macho among machos" who liked to drink, chase women, and fight violently. He was also born Amelia Robles in 1889 to a ranchero family and raised learning the domestic skills deemed appropriate for daughters. Other women fought in the Mexican revolution disguised as men, but all others on record returned to female identities after the conflict was over. Not so with Robles, who cultivated ties with powerful provincial politicians for rights as a man, and whose family and neighbors recognized and treated him as a man. At one point, Robles even adopted a daughter with his then-partner, Ángela Torres.

While it is tempting to take Robles's life experiences as evidence that the Mexican revolution challenged longstanding gender norms that identified women with the home and motherhood, in fact, the revolution did not lead to a radical or widespread change in social norms about sexuality, and its impact on women's roles in society was mixed at best. Robles

Mothers Making Latin America: Gender, Households, and Politics Since 1825,
First Edition. Erin E. O'Connor.
© 2014 John Wiley & Sons, Inc. Published 2014 by John Wiley & Sons, Inc.

gained acceptance because he reinforced a particular revolutionary masculine ideal of bravery. Revolutionary leaders and journalists were much less tolerant of men who transgressed gender norms to display what they deemed feminine qualities, and they especially scorned male homosexuality. Even Robles himself faced difficulties at times as the butt of his patrons' jokes. Moreover, after his death in 1984, many historians recognized Robles as a "symbol of the revolutionary woman" – an emphasis that does not seem in keeping with an individual who threatened physical harm to anyone who referred to him as a woman.[1]

In Cuba, when the revolutionary struggle was building in the 1950s, a young woman named Aleida March joined the urban underground that was working (along with guerrillas in the mountains) to overthrow Fulgencio Batista's regime. March was from a humble peasant background and had studied to become a teacher. While in the underground, she helped to relay messages and transport weapons. In 1958, one of her assignments was to carry money to the Escambray guerrilla camp. In her memoir, March noted that her presence surprised the guerrillas because "I hardly looked like a tough guerrilla fighter. I was quite a pretty young girl." According to her account, many guerrillas pestered her for attention or declared love for her – which she claimed to find annoying. She spent the rest of the war with the guerrillas, though she was not a combatant herself. During that time, she fell in love with and married one of the guerrilla leaders, eventually having four children with him. March was like many other women who supported the Cuban revolutionary cause, though there were also some who took up weapons alongside men.

Aleida March's particular story has always been overshadowed by the fact that the guerrilla she met and married was none other than Ernesto "Che" Guevara, the Argentine doctor and communist visionary who after his 1967 death in Bolivia became an icon of revolutionary commitment.[2] In fact, some Che biographers play down March's role in the revolution before she met Guevara, describing her only as Che's love interest, not as a woman committed to the revolution in her own right.[3] This happened even within the revolution itself, apparently, since March described how Fidel Castro and others referred to her (before her marriage) as "Che's girl," although she bristled at this reference and preferred to be identified as either his secretary or assistant. She indicated that after the victory, Raúl Castro (Fidel's brother) asked Guevara what rank she would receive to honor her contributions to the revolution. According to March, "Che bluntly replied, none, because I would be his wife." March appears to have accepted this shift from revolutionary supporter to wife and mother, and in her memoir, she emphasized that she was writing about her life with Che primarily for the benefit of their children.[4]

During the Nicaraguan revolutionary conflict of the 1970s, Leticia did not become directly involved in the fighting herself, but she supported and protected her siblings who joined the revolutionary struggle. Having grown up in poverty with a mother who was frequently beaten and abandoned by her male partners, Leticia went to cosmetology school and opened her own small hairdressing shop. She married Sergio, a university student studying business, and they had children together. Though her husband was not interested in politics, and Leticia herself did not do anything to advance the revolution directly, she hid her brother and sister in her home, risking not only her own life but those of her husband and children as well. After the revolution overthrew the Somoza regime in 1979, Leticia joined the national women's organization and continued to run her business. Though the revolutionary leaders vowed to overturn gender inequalities, Leticia's own marriage suffered. Her husband disliked her independence and sometimes beat her. She eventually left with her youngest daughter to live and work in the United States for a few months in 1985. While away, her husband began an affair with another woman and their marriage began to dissolve more rapidly, culminating in Sergio moving to Mexico with his girlfriend. Leticia was on her own, trying to resume her business under strained conditions. There was a war raging between the new revolutionary government and the conservative (US-backed) counterrevolutionary forces, the Contras. Supplies for her store were almost impossible to get because of the war, and even food was difficult, and expensive, to obtain.[5] Although Leticia continued to support the revolutionary government throughout the 1980s, it had provided neither the economic help nor the gender equality that she had hoped for.

For both Aleida March and Leticia, motherhood figured prominently in their experiences of the revolution. For Leticia, protecting and taking care of her children often took precedent over the revolutionary conflict and government that she supported. For March, the children she bore with Che Guevara were a culmination of her revolutionary experiences, while at the same time her marriage and motherhood marked her transition from revolutionary to domestic life. Amelio Robles's situation was significantly different. Though Robles adopted a child, he did so as a father rather than a mother. In this case, an individual born female rejected not only changed how she/he dressed, but also took on an entirely (and sometimes exaggerated) male persona, including a refusal to identify with motherhood or with domestic duties.

Though all three of the events examined in this chapter qualify as revolutions – because they all brought about enduring political, social, and economic change after a period of violent upheaval – they were not all the same. First, there were differences in the political ideologies behind these revolutions. The Mexican revolution has the distinction of having been the only pre-Bolshevik revolution of the twentieth century.[6] Though scholars sometimes discuss "socialistic" aspects of changes resulting from the Mexican revolution (particularly under the rule of Lázaro Cárdenas from 1934 to 1940), Mexico's revolution was not socialist overall. Instead, the revolution there focused mostly on land and labor reform combined with liberal constitutionalism. Even the 1930s reforms, which were fairly radical, were more corporatist than socialist. However, Cuba and Nicaragua's revolutions were socialist from very early stages, and the Cuban Revolution was strongly influenced by Marxist-Leninist doctrine. These political differences resulted from the timing and particular situations in each country. By the 1950s, when the Cuban revolution occurred, the Soviet Union had emerged as one of the two most powerful nations in the world, and the Cold War was well underway. This, in addition to long-standing tensions between Cuba and the United States, radicalized the revolution and drove it in a socialist direction. Nicaragua had a similarly difficult history with US intervention in the twentieth century, combined with a longer history of dictatorship than in Cuba. Though also a socialist movement, the Nicaraguan revolution was less focused on Marxist doctrine for a few reasons. One of the reasons for this was the fact that the Sandinista Front for National Liberation (FSLN) was an umbrella organization that included opponents of the Somoza regime from a variety of political perspectives. Another influence that made Nicaraguan socialism distinct from Cuban socialism was liberation theology, in which some members of the Catholic Church sought to address social and economic injustices, and many priests joined in the revolution itself. This led to a different understanding of socialism, particularly regarding church–state relations, than in Cuba or the Soviet Union.

The three revolutions were also different in their official stances toward women. In the Mexican revolution, many poor women picked up guns and fought alongside men, but after the fighting was over, their contributions were largely forgotten, or identified as merely supportive. Mexican women also did not gain the right to vote until 1953, long after the revolution was over. In Cuba, Fidel Castro formally recognized women's participation in the revolutionary conflict, and he proclaimed that he would put an end to gender inequalities. (The extent to which he succeeded will be explored later.) In Nicaragua, women both fought in the revolutionary conflict and were – in theory – supposed to benefit from the Sandinista takeover of the national government. Again, some of these differences resulted from the timing of these revolutions. The Mexican revolution was not only agrarian, but also more limited in its stance on women's rights partly because the revolutionary war occurred both before one sees women's suffrage granted anywhere in the world, and because most of the women who participated in the revolution did not have feminist goals (though some did). In contrast, women's suffrage was already a fact in Cuba and Nicaragua when their revolutionary wars occurred. Moreover, women's participation in these revolutions – especially in Nicaragua – was more formally militarized, and more difficult to overlook when the revolutionary leaders established new governments. Despite these differences, all three revolutions promised reforms and greater rights for women to one extent or another, and all three failed to live up to their promises. An examination of motherhood within these revolutionary processes helps to elucidate how and why women's relationships were fraught with contradictions.

Modernizing Patriarchy in the Mexican Revolution[7]

The revolutionary conflict years

In 1910, after decades of increasingly dictatorial rule under Porfirio Díaz, Francisco Madero took up arms against Díaz, after losing a presidential bid against the dictator in rigged elections. Madero unleashed unanticipated forces and demands among the majority of Mexico's peasants and workers. Mestizo and indigenous peasants, especially, had been losing land to large estate owners under Díaz's rule, and even those who had moved to work on large estates lacked security. Seeing the opportunity for change, they responded in huge numbers to Madero's call to arms. In the end, however, Madero was only in power for 15 months (1911–1913) before he was driven power and assassinated on his way to prison. From

1913 to 1915, Mexico was a virtual battlefield, with many different factions vying for power. On one extreme was Victoriano Huerta, who established a dictatorship that relied almost entirely on elite and foreign support. At the other extreme were leaders like Emiliano Zapata in Morelos or Pancho Villa in northern Mexico, who promised land redistribution. Although Villa and Zapata had tremendous popular support, they lacked any consistent elite and foreign backing, without which they could not win. In the end, it was Venustiano Carranza, a moderate Constitutionalist like Madero, who won the civil war and called for the drafting of the 1917 constitution. Regional battles decreased, but some areas remained in upheaval until almost 1920, with more sporadic violence breaking out until as late as 1929.

Although one hears most about the men who led the armies, it was ordinary people, usually the rural poor, who did most of the fighting, sacrificing and dying in revolutions. Poor mestiza and indigenous women had a strong presence in the revolutionary conflict: as in nineteenth-century military struggles, many poor Mexican women became camp followers, referred to in Mexico as *soldaderas* (Figure 7.1). These women

Figure 7.1 This image is of Mexican Soldaderas in Buenavista. Conacurta-Inah-SINAFO-FN-Mexico.

followed the army, usually when one of their male relatives joined or was conscripted. Soldaderas provided essential services: they cooked food, tended to wounded soldiers, and mended clothing; they retrieved useful objects from battlefields, and they buried the dead. They were as laden with bundles as men, if not more so, because they carried food, cooking supplies, and bedding. Although some of them were childless, there were many soldaderas with children. In 1914, a count of Pancho Villa's forces along the border with the United States included 4557 (male) soldiers, 1256 soldaderas, and 554 children, many of whom were babies or toddlers strapped to their mothers' backs. Historian Elizabeth Salas notes that soldaderas "transferred their traditional roles as wives, cooks, and nurturers to battlefield conditions."[8] Though some leaders such as Pancho Villa complained that these women were a distraction to his soldiers, the services that soldaderas provided were critical for armies' successes. At one point, when US general Pershing pursued Villa's forces into Mexico, his own supply lines lengthened so far that he had to give up his quest, whereas Villa's army had a ready supply of food thanks to the soldaderas. In fact, had they been men, they would have been counted among the active personnel; it was only their sex that officially identified them as noncombatants.

Other women took up arms and joined in combat. Often, this would happen when a male comrade (husband, brother) fell, and a soldadera would take up his rifle and continue the fight. It is difficult to gauge the numbers and impact of women soldiers in the Mexican revolution for several reasons. First, any count of the armies was unreliable because so many of them were spontaneously formed, and soldiers came and went on a regular basis. Second, a woman's role in the revolution might change over time, with her fighting in some instances and offering vital support in others. Finally, of course, is the fact that army leaders often discounted women fighters based on their sex. However, some women soldiers did earn reputations for their excellent fighting, and a few even entered the commanding ranks, though rarely any higher than captain. Robles was an exception to these rules, but he was rewarded and recognized for contributions to battle because he embraced a fully masculine identity.

Not all women who contributed to the revolution were poor indigenous or mestiza women, and not all poor women followed the armies. Middle-class school teacher and writer Dolores Jiménez y Muro, for example, was a radical (socialist) activist who supported Zapata and

helped to write the introduction to his "Plan of Ayala" in which he out-
lined his "land to the villagers" proposal. Other middle-class and elite
women provided funds, and women in Madero's family traveled to
camps in order to nurse the wounded in the aftermath of battles. They
did not, however, travel alongside the armies or participate in the fighting as poor women did.[9] Other poor and indigenous women in the
countryside did not join the battles, but they were nevertheless drawn
into the revolution. While men fought "for land and liberty," many of
their wives stayed behind with children to feed and farms to tend. They
lacked male protection from soldiers who, on all sides of the fighting,
came through their villages demanding that the women make them
tortillas – an hours-long process that took food out of families' mouths.
Moreover, women left behind were vulnerable to theft, sexual advances,
and rape from soldiers traveling through town.[10] Poor women sometimes had positive experiences with the military as well. In the Yucatán
peninsula of southeastern Mexico, Maya women flocked to military tribunals in order to address problems and to protect their children's needs.
Simona Cén used the courts to help her get medicine for the son she
had with her former employer, who had abandoned her. Widow Ber-
nadina Poot went before the court on behalf of her daughter, a 14-year-
old girl who had been raped. Many women petitioned for child support
from their husbands. These women did not always win their appeals,
but the military courts decided in their favor often enough to merit the
appeals.[11]

In Mexico City, women textile workers from the "La Sin" factory went
on strike just as Francisco Madero was coming to power after defeating
Díaz. Their actions were among those that forced the revolution in a
more radical direction than the moderate Madero had intended. Other
women textile workers also went on strike, and many women factory
workers joined emerging unions that struggled to gain better pay and
conditions. The results of their actions were, however, limited, in large
part because the ongoing war led to many factory shutdowns. Political
leaders were also lukewarm in their response to organized workers
and strikers, particularly women. Dictator Victoriano Huerta opened a
department for the protection of working women and children in
1914, but his other policies undermined the goals of working women.
Venustiano Carranza, the political moderate who won the quest for state
power, told women strikers that they "sold yourselves like a bunch of
whores."[12]

Poor urban women faced a variety of struggles on a daily basis: food was scarce in Mexico City during the wars, and businesses, including factories, often shut down leading to un- and underemployment. At the same time, many women and children were migrating from the countryside to the city, and the number of single mothers was on the rise. In this atmosphere, an increasing number of poor urban women had to bring their children to orphanages, unable to feed and care for them on their own. Other mothers became militant, demanding services and relief from hunger.[13] Such extreme actions on women's part, especially on the part of mothers, are not surprising. Partly because of their role in feeding families (and especially children), mothers have often been at the helm of protests and revolutionary violence.

In the long term, however, official recollections of the revolution remembered and honored only male soldiers. When women were recognized at all, it was for their supportive roles that fit more tidily with dominant notions of women's so-called traditional duties. Soldaderas, for example, were usually remembered as sources of inspiration and love interests for men. These "Adelitas" were recalled in *corridos* (ballads) for their beauty and the passion that they instilled in soldiers, not for the necessary food or medical care that they supplied to the troops, let alone for picking up weapons when soldiers fell. The erasure of women's significance to revolutionary conflict had policy repercussions: the new government rarely gave women military pensions except as surviving relatives of male soldiers, not for their own contributions to the wars.[14] The wrongs that soldiers committed against peasant women were left largely unaddressed as well, and in the Yucatán civilian courts rarely upheld poor women's interests in the way that the previous military tribunals had.[15] Similarly, factory women's contributions to labor agitation did not result in a strong position for them within emerging state-supported unions. By the 1930s, women were rarely among the leaders in textile and other industry unions.[16]

Motherhood, laws, and revolutionary state building in Mexico

Although Carranza won the civil war in 1916 and his government put a constitution into effect in 1917, Mexico's revolutionary process was not complete and it took until 1940 for a stable, enduring state to emerge. There were many reasons for this long process of revolutionary state building. The economic and political disruption of the 1910s required time to heal, and it took a great deal of time for central government leaders to bring regional political strongmen under control. The process of revolutionary state building was also a process of nationalist formation in which central state officials strove to construct a viable national identity that the majority of Mexicans, who did most of the fighting in the revolution, would accept. Both of these processes began with the 1917 constitution, but important promises in the constitution were not fulfilled until the 1930s under the populist rule of Lázaro Cárdenas. On the one hand, these changes altered women's as well as men's social and economic lives. On the other hand, political and economic changes primarily benefited men, and sometimes even worked to women's detriment.

Articles 27 and 123 of the 1917 constitution lay the groundwork for dramatic socioeconomic changes in Mexico. Article 27 asserted that all land was national territory that (a) the state could reclaim from foreign control as it deemed necessary to defend the nation, and (b) should undergo a process of land redistribution. This last aspect of Article 27 was crucial, because it was what the majority of men and women in the revolutionary conflict had fought for. Article 123 established workers' rights, including (which was unusual) the rights of domestic workers. This article set an eight-hour workday (seven hours for night work), and it established rights to healthy work conditions, minimum wages, and the right to strike. Article 123 also declared equal pay for equal work, regardless of sex, and addressed women workers' maternity rights:

> During the three months prior to childbirth, women shall not perform physical labor that requires excessive material effort. In the month following childbirth they shall necessarily enjoy the benefit of rest and shall receive their full wages and retain their employment and the rights acquired under their labor contract. During the nursing period they shall have two special rest periods each day, of a half hour each, for nursing their infants.[17]

The application of land and labor laws, however, was slow and uneven, and their impact on women – particularly mothers – was problematic. Although minimum wage laws technically protected women as well as men, state officials typically identified workers as male, and justified their gains through men's roles as heads of households. This tended to marginalize women in general, but especially women workers who were heads of households. New laws that kept women (and children) from night work in factories also put many women out of work.[18] As in other parts of Latin America, maternity rights were not always upheld in factory practices, and in fact often reinforced ideas that women were less than ideal workers. Factory inspectors who were concerned with hygienic and safety conditions for women were mainly worried about their possible impact on reproduction. Consider how Doctor Manuel Olea explained this position in 1922, when he explained in a talk to women textile workers:

> Women, due to the delicate nature of their sexual development, menstruation, pregnancy, and breast-feeding have a much weaker organism than that of men; and if we add to this the fact that before and after work they have to attend to housework and their children, it is easily understood that among them there are increasing reasons for their physical exhaustion, which also has a noxious influence on their children as well.[19]

While sympathetic to women, Dr. Olea and health inspectors implicitly suggested that women were not suited to factory work due to their physical needs and limitations resulting from maternity. Of course, the more stringent demands for labor conditions wherever women worked, in combination with women's maternity rights, meant that Mexican factory owners (like those elsewhere in Latin America) viewed women workers as too expensive to hire. Such distinctions continued with the 1931 Federal Labor Code, which – although it stipulated that a woman did not need her husband's permission to enter into a labor contract – prohibited women from working at night or doing "dangerous or unhealthy work." Further, worker compensation was tied to wages, and since women (despite Article 123) made less money than men, they got less in compensation as well.[20]

Land redistribution was equally problematic. In a 1920 law setting parameters for implementing the land redistribution called for in Article 27 of the constitution, heads of households were supposed to receive lands. There was no reference to gender here, though it is likely that the law assumed that most of the recipients would be men. Land was redistributed in a way that individuals within a community got a portion of an *ejido*, owned communally by the village. In 1927, the law proclaimed that to be included in the distribution of these communal lands, one had to be "Mexican nationals, males over the age of eighteen, or single women or widows supporting a family." This made it possible for childless men to get land before starting a family, but not childless women; only maternity without a proper patriarch in the household made women eligible. Further, if a woman with a portion of this communal land married a man who had a communal land share, she had to forfeit her own land portion. These gender inequalities were not changed until 1971, and even then practices continued to disadvantage women.[21]

If women's identification with motherhood and the home was subtle and uneven in the application of labor laws and land rights, their marginalization in politics was more blatant. Although feminist groups had advocated the vote for women throughout the long process of state building, they had little success, even though universal male suffrage was guaranteed in the 1917 constitution. Women did not win the right to vote in national elections until 1953, over a decade after the revolutionary state-building process was completed. At one point in the 1930s, it seemed that president Cárdenas was going to follow through with promises to support the vote for women, but he was sidetracked by a conflict between United States oil companies and Mexican oil workers that led to his famous 1938 nationalization of oil. In short: although revolutionary state builders did not necessarily resist women's right to vote outright, they continually made this a lower priority than purportedly gender neutral concerns that, in reality, often had a greater positive impact on men than on women. In fact, many revolutionary state leaders were wary of giving women the right to vote because they assumed that women would simply vote in defense of the Catholic Church (this was assumed in many other parts of Latin America as well), which might in turn weaken the state's position in its conflicts with the Church. Despite women's political marginalization from 1917 to 1953, however, images of motherhood were central to building the new revolutionary state, and to defining women's place within it.

Motherhood and the revolutionary nation in Mexico

Images of women and experiences of motherhood in Mexico from 1920 to 1950 were similar to those discussed in the last two chapters, because the state-building project in Mexico was a modernizing project, with urban areas and industries expanding rapidly. However, in Mexico, these shifts all occurred within a specific revolutionary context. Revolutionary motherhood images and practices had their roots in the 1920s: it was in 1922, for example, that Mexicans began to celebrate Mothers' Day. In the 1930s and 1940s, motherhood developed into a tactical tool for identifying women's place within and relevance to the revolution and its outcomes.

As in other Latin American countries, the image of the so-called modern woman was fraught with contradictions in Mexico. Historian Anne Rubenstein captures this well in her discussion of *pelonas* (women who bobbed their hair). Though the practice began with wealthy and middle-class white women, particularly those who followed the high fashions of the United States, it eventually spread to women of other classes and races by the mid 1920s. Pelonas represented modern fashion and athleticism, and they were (like the modern women discussed in Chapter 5) at the center of controversy over tradition versus modernity. In Mexico, this conflict took place within the context of revolutionary nationalism as well. Pelonas in Mexico were vulnerable not only to questions about their morality, but also to accusations that they were betraying Mexican national identity by cutting their hair short instead of wearing it in a so-called traditional or authentically Mexican long style. In 1924, this conflict even resulted in a few instances in which young men attacked pelonas and shaved their heads – an act aimed at shaming them publicly. However, Rubenstein points out that even the men who defended pelonas were more concerned with gendered notions of honor, and with keeping women in a subordinate position, than they were with the women's right to determine their own style preferences.[22]

It was during Lázaro Cárdenas's term of rule from 1934 to 1940 that motherhood began to develop as a symbol of the new revolutionary society. As in many other aspects of his rule – in which he brought great benefits to workers and peasants while simultaneously bringing them under the control of a single dominant party – Cárdenas's stances on and relationships to women's issues was paradoxical. Sometimes he suggested that women were equal to men, as seen in an argument he made in support of female suffrage:

CONSIDERING that the new organization of the family over bases of greater equality and the tendency to suppress injustice . . . have provided women with greater cultural, domestic, and citizenship oriented responsibilities [and] . . . recognizing . . . the plain civil, economic, and educational capabilities of women, the maintenance of their political incapacity is unjustified.[23]

Cárdenas was referring to laws that gave wives the ability to control money, provided women workers maternity rights, and upheld mothers' authority over their children. However, Cárdenas failed to follow through on promises to help women gain the right to vote, while he simultaneously identified women with motherhood in order to bring them under greater state control. He emphasized a secular, nationalist motherhood to challenge Catholics and conservatives who associated motherhood with religion. For example, Cárdenas's welfare secretary, Silvestre Guerrero, claimed that instead of sentimentalism, "The Mexican mother needs effective assistance to resolve her diverse problems and not empty words of praise with which she is often flattered."[24] The national government thus associated mothers' well-being with the social welfare policies and institutions that they were in the process of constructing – and controlling – in the 1930s.

At the same time, Cárdenas's state was also organizing *Ligas Femeniles de Lucha Social* (Women's Leagues for Social Struggle), in which women were to "smooth the path to collectivization [of landholdings] and modernized social relations by facilitating government campaigns favoring temperance, hygiene, and universal public education." Although the regime sought to use this space for its own purposes, women in the Leagues pushed the state to address their own needs as well, such as demanding state-subsidized child care and support for women's cooperatives. Dominant notions of femininity were at the heart of these leagues, and motherhood offered League members common ground on which to unite and discuss their missions. In the end, although Cárdenas made overtures to feminists regarding the vote, his government used these leagues to identify a "revolutionary femininity," via motherhood, that stood in opposition to feminists whom they identified as *marimacho*, or overly masculine. The revolutionary mother, they claimed, contributed to society without losing her essential domestic and maternal nature.[25]

By the 1940s and 1950s, the links between Mexican revolutionary womanhood and motherhood were more consistently developed. Presidents Miguel Alemán and Adolfo Ruiz Cortines claimed that women had a right to participate in politics not because they were equal to men, but rather because their motherhood-based tendencies would contribute a moral and stabilizing tendency in politics.[26] Motherhood, it would seem, provided a means through which to soften and eventually eliminate the danger that women – especially working-class and peasant women – would make radical demands or assert their equality if given the right to vote. Did this mean that Mexican women "experienced a revolution" or not? On the one hand, they benefited at least to a certain extent from labor and land redistribution policies, and learned to work the system of revolutionary motherhood to address their daily problems. On the other hand, although the revolutionary state manipulated all groups, it offered men formal means through which to participate in and make demands of the state – something which women did not get.

Gender in Cuba: A "Revolution within the Revolution"?

Gender and the Cuban revolutionary conflict

Although Fidel Castro's revolutionary struggle against the Batista regime lasted from 1956 to 1959, the Cuban revolution had its roots in the 1895–1898 war for independence. Cubans from a wide variety of backgrounds – from elite landowners to landless (often Afro-Cuban) workers – came together to fight for a *Cuba libre* (free Cuba). What that freedom meant, however, varied drastically among different groups. Elite landowners envisioned few changes beyond a constitution that they would control rather than answering to Spain. Middling classes sought more meaningful, if moderate, changes that would bring equality before the law and responsive government. Middle-sector Afro-Cubans, in particular, wanted to end racial practices that left them in a second-class status. Poor Cubans sought labor and land reforms. For almost all Cubans, the resulting 1901 constitution was a disappointment. Not only did the constitution deny women the right to vote, but its high literacy requirements for voting also kept most Cuban men disenfranchised. Making matters worse, the United States – which had helped the rebels win against Spain – required Cuban state officials to adopt the Platt Amendment, essentially making Cuba a protectorate of the United States rather than an independent nation. Over the decades, Cubans' frustrations mounted, as national leaders repeatedly promised to build responsive government, only to have economic problems and corruption dash Cubans' aspirations once again. There were brief moments of real hope, as when Fulgencio Batista's populist rule in the 1930s led to a new constitution in 1940, but that too failed.

When Batista returned to power in 1952, he was far more authoritarian than he had been in his previous era of rule. It was into this atmosphere that a young lawyer named Fidel Castro rose as an opposition leader, eventually building a guerrilla army that chipped away at Batista's power until the revolutionaries rode victoriously into the capital city of Havana on January 1, 1959.

It is difficult to piece together the extent of women's participation in the Cuban revolution. There were no women on the *Granma*, the boat in which Castro and a band of his followers sailed from Mexico to Cuba in July 1956 to begin their assault on the Batista regime.[27] However, there were some women who participated in the anti-Batista movement, mostly (like Aleida March) in supportive roles, working in the underground to provide supplies and information to the guerrillas, or to transport weapons to them. The most famous of these women was Vilma Espín, who supported the revolution in the 1950s and married Raúl Castro (Fidel's brother, who took over after Fidel stepped down from power in 2008). Espín was one of the few women who achieved high rank in the Cuban Communist Party.

Other women – though it is not clear how many – became guerrilla fighters. In a 1981 speech, Fidel Castro described what it was like when he put together a platoon of female fighters:

> I remember that when I organized the Mariana Grajales Platoon – in fact, I took part in the combat training of those comrades – some of the rebel fighters were furious, because they didn't like the idea of a platoon made up of women. We had some spare M-1s, and the M-1 was considered a good light weapon and, therefore, we thought it would be the right one for the women. Some of our fighters wanted to know why they had Springfields while the women were going to get M-1s. On more than one occasion I got so annoyed that I would answer, "Because they are better fighters than you are." And the truth is that they showed it . . . Near Holguín, a women's platoon engaged in a fierce battle with the army and the platoon leader was wounded. As a general rule, when a platoon leader was wounded the men had the habit of retreating – which is not correct but it had become practically a habit. The women's platoon had attacked a truck loaded with soldiers. When the platoon leader was wounded, they weren't discouraged. They went on fighting, wiped out the truckload and captured all the weapons. Their behavior was truly exceptional.[28]

Castro's description of the women fighters in this speech offers an interesting set of concepts for analysis. On one level, he was commemorating women's military contributions to the war; below the surface, however, many things were happening in this speech. Castro was claiming credit for organizing, training, and defending women soldiers, perhaps reinforcing that women should be loyal to him and his state. He also highlighted women's difference – needing lighter weapons due to their lesser physical strength, for example. His compliment of women who stayed and fought when their platoon leader was wounded is particularly telling: not only did Castro describe this in a way that would potentially shame men who retreated when platoon leaders were wounded, but his emphasis on women's collective coherence calls to mind dominant ideas about femininity and women's supposedly inherent cooperative nature. In essence, Castro indirectly referred to women's maternal tendency for self-sacrifice as something distinct from male self-sacrifice in wartime. In war, men were purported to sacrifice themselves for the nation, for the cause. Women were assumed to sacrifice themselves for the good of others, whether for the guerrillas in the mountains or for the others in their platoon. It is not surprising, then, that one of Vilma Espín's speeches referenced sacrificial motherhood by asking "How many mothers lost their sons and daughters? Twenty thousand martyrs gave their lives to make Cuba the first free territory in America!"[29]

Rather than erase the memory of women combatants in the revolutionary struggle as happened in Mexico, the Cuban revolutionary government at once remembered and downplayed women's direct military engagements. Often, the contradictions centered on ideas about feminine skills and home orientation. Ernesto "Che" Guevara, for example, at one point asserted that women were capable of fighting beside men, but most often he emphasized that women's role was primarily to "perform a relief role" for male combatants. He also claimed to have a "sincere appreciation for traditional female skills," explaining:

> The woman can also perform her habitual tasks of peacetime [during the war]; it is very pleasing to a soldier subjected to the extremely hard conditions of this life to be able to look forward to a seasoned meal which tastes like something. One of the great tortures of the [Cuban] war was eating a cold, sticky, tasteless mess. Furthermore, it is easier to keep her in these domestic tasks; one of the problems in guerrilla bands is that they [masculine] are constantly trying to get out of these tasks.[30]

Guevara seemed torn between viewing women soldiers as capable, if weaker, combatants versus comrades whose value came in "mothering" the troops with food. This fits with Guevara's assertion that Aleida March should not win any honors of her role in the revolution, but rather he assumed that her place would be in the home once he married her. Out of these rather contradictory beginnings came equally conflicted revolutionary gender policies.

Cuban laws: revolutionizing work and home?

Castro proclaimed that eliminating gender inequality would be the "revolution within the revolution," emphasizing that his regime would overcome prejudicial beliefs that all women could do was ". . . wash dishes, wash and iron clothes, cook, keep house, and bear children . . . age-old prejudices that placed women in an inferior position in society. In effect, [women] did not have a productive place in society." He further asserted that while all women were subject to these stereotypes, poor women were doubly oppressed by the class and gender systems. He concluded that the new socialist society would be a "double liberation" for women from both class and gender exploitation. Castro added that if women had been doubly exploited in the past, "then this simply means that women in a social revolution should be doubly revolutionary."[31] Castro clearly identified motherhood as being at the center of women's exploitation in the past. In order to liberate women so that they were free to enter economic and political spheres, the Cuban government established laws in the 1960s and 1970s to provide adequate support and child care for working mothers, and to change attitudes about gender and housework.

One of the key legislative features of this agenda to free women for entrance into the workforce was the Working Women's Maternity Law, first issued in 1963, and updated and expanded in 1974. This law gave women the right to six weeks prenatal leave from their jobs and 12 weeks postnatal leave, all paid. As of 1974, women could take an additional nine months of unpaid leave and still return to their positions afterwards. The law provided additional time off both during pregnancy and after childbirth for medical care and nursing (defined as an "extra hour of rest period").[32] The government also established day care centers to facilitate mothers' entry into the workforce, and began providing modern appliances for homes so that housework would be less time consuming. Why did the Cuban revolutionary government take these actions? The answers are multiple. First, the new government aimed at modernizing and diversifying the Cuban economy, which to that point had been agricultural and based mainly on sugar and (to a lesser extent) tobacco exports. To grow the economy, however, the government needed workers; it therefore behooved them to encourage women to enter the workforce. Second, addressing women's particular work needs was likely a tactic to win (or maintain) women's support for the revolutionary government. Finally, there was a precedent in Marxist ideology (particularly with the writings of Marx's partner, Friedrich Engels) that communist revolution should, in addition to ending economic inequalities, also put an end to men's exploitation of women.

In 1975, the Cuban government reinforced its commitment to gender equality with its Family Code. Chapter 2 of the Code, on "Relations Between Husband and Wife," indicated that marriage establishes "equal rights and duties for both partners," who are to live together in loyalty and mutual respect and assistance. To assure this equality, the law stated:

> Article 26. Both partners must care for the family they have created and must cooperate with the other in the education, upbringing, and guidance of the children according to the principles of socialist morality. They must participate, to the extent of their capacity or possibilities, in the running of the home, and cooperate so that it will develop in the best possible way.[33]

This article made shared domestic and child care duties a part of the legally binding marital contract. The Cuban Communist Party clarified the intentions of this law with a statement in December of 1975, highlighting women's rights in the Maternity Code and emphasizing "The view that child rearing is the exclusive responsibility of the mother must be rejected. The beautiful responsibility of caring for [children] . . . is a duty contracted equally by both father and mother."[34] Again, it is likely that Cuban government officials had reasons other than simply liberating women when the encouraged men to help tend to the home and children. If men helped out in the home, it would save the government costly investments in day care centers and other services that working women would otherwise require. Rather than have the state pay for formerly unremunerated work, state officials encouraged men to share in unpaid services in the home, alongside women.

In short, the Cuban revolutionary government did a great deal to put husbands and wives on a more equal footing, and to make work and motherhood easier for women to balance. Despite these commitments, and some considerable achievements for women in Cuban society, gender inequalities remained, particularly around assumptions that the home and children were primarily women's responsibility. How and why did disparities persist?

Motherhood in practice: the limits of Cuban policies

Practical considerations and limitations often got in the way of women's liberation in Cuba. Mothers who entered the work force had a right to maternity leaves, but other supports did not always materialize. Modern appliances that cut back on the time of household chores were often unavailable, and there were not enough day care centers built to keep up with the demand for them due in large part to insufficient government funding. Moreover, only full-time women workers were eligible to send their children to day care centers, making work an "all-or-nothing" proposal for them. Even when day care centers were available, women often found that facilities' hours of operation did not match their schedules. Day care centers themselves had problems: despite their increased training over the years, women working in day care centers continued to receive low pay, a pattern likely linked to ongoing devaluation of so-called women's work with small children (men did not work in day care centers based on the assumption that they were not patient enough to work with small children). Finally, as in other countries that underwent processes of industrialization and maternity protections, many employers found it too expensive to hire women workers who had children, due to the costs of their mandated leaves of absence.[35]

Cultural attitudes regarding gender roles were even more difficult to overcome. Previous to the revolution, wives were expected – regardless of whether they worked outside the home – to tend to their children's needs, keep house, and cook the family's food. Despite revolutionary laws and decrees to advance gender equality in the home, many Cuban men found little incentive to change their attitude toward marriage and parenthood. Men's resistance to the new laws and messages varied. Some men refused to make any changes, and their wives continued to do all of the housework and child care. Other couples claimed that they were embracing new ways, but in practice most domestic duties still fell upon women. Alternately, a husband who promised to take care of household chores for his wife might require an older child (most likely a daughter) to perform them in his stead. In short: laws can change overnight, but attitudes tend to change slowly. As is often the case with cultural change, the shift in Cuba was gradual, generational, and incomplete.[36] Younger generations tended to accept new ideas about marriage and parenting more readily than older generations. The Cuban government identified such resistance and slowness to change as signs of the vestiges of bourgeois society and policies, blaming capitalism and earlier regimes, rather than revolutionary policies, for the continuation of gender inequalities.

But practical problems and cultural attitudes (whether bourgeois or not) were not the only obstacles to gender equality in Cuba. The Communist Party leadership implicitly reinforced patriarchal ideas. The Family Code made no reference to men who abandoned their families being held accountable for child support. The Cuban state also left labor in the home invisible and unremunerated – housewives, for example, were ineligible to join the Cuban Workers' Union and thus had no means through which to address the conditions under which they labored. Even more telling is the fact that the only type of property that the Cuban Communist party allowed to families was the home.[37] If Cuban government officials formally indicated that family life needed to be equalized, they also sent mixed messages to women, and rewarded only those who did economic or political work that benefited the state.

The problem was not merely in the absence of strong state support for gender equality, but in state structures themselves. The *Federación de Mujeres Cubanas* (Federation of Cuban Women, or FMC) was charged with working to advocate women's rights and equality, but the organization lacked sufficient government support and funding to enact real change.[38] Fidel Castro himself took the role as the FMC's "guide" and ultimate authority (though his sister-in-law, Vilma Espín, was formally in charge of the FMC). Therefore, Fidel-the-father-figure presided over the organization meant to liberate women from centuries of gender domination. This paradox reflected the overall male dominance within the Cuban Communist Party and its failure to prioritize women's concerns. Moreover, the FMC has little power to influence the policies of the Cuban Workers' Union (CTC), whose own directives from the Party hierarchy are not always clear with regard to gender. Many women found the union indifferent toward their concerns.[39] Benefits to women, like so many other gains in the Cuban revolution, came at the price of authoritarian government power that made it virtually impossible for mothers to address their needs and concerns. In fact, one of the powerful political tools that other women in Latin America wielded – through their influence and symbolism as mothers – was unavailable to Cuban women, who were supposed to transcend their old and supposedly bourgeois domestic identities in favor of the socialist worker identities.

Nicaragua: Sandino's Daughters, Revolutionary Mothers

Motherhood and the revolutionary war

As with the Mexican and Cuban revolutions, the factors leading up to the Nicaraguan revolution were complex and decades-long. In 1936, Anastasio Somoza García, head of the United States-created Nicaraguan National Guard, took control of the country. For the next four decades he, and then his sons (Luís and Anastasio Somoza Debayle), ruled the country as dictators. Although Nicaragua's economy industrialized and expanded under the Somozas' rule, the benefits went mainly to Nicaraguan elites and to a small group of middle sectors. The vast majority of poor Nicaraguans struggled even more than they had in previous periods, and by the 1960s the government was increasingly repressive of the majority of its citizens. In the 1960s, the *Frente Sandininista para Liberación Nacional* (The Sandinista National Liberation Front, or FSLN) took shape. Resistance became more widespread in the 1970s, particularly in the aftermath of a terrible 1972 earthquake in the capital city of Managua when the Somoza regime did virtually nothing to rebuild the city. Because the FSLN was the longest-standing and best organized opposition group, it became the umbrella organization for a wide alliance of opponents to the Somoza dictatorship. After a final military thrust from 1977 to 1979, the FSLN (aka "Sandinistas") won, and they ruled in Nicaragua until the 1990 presidential elections, in which FSLN candidate Daniel Ortega lost to his opponent, Violeta Barrios de Chamorro.

Nicaraguan women were essential to the success of the revolutionary war, and their concerns and actions during the period of Sandinista rule helped both to define the regime's successes and bring about its downfall. The Nicaraguan revolutionary army included unprecedented numbers of women military combatants. They joined male comrades in the mountains to train and plan, and they partook in numerous procedures and battles. Although most women of the rank and file were from working-class or peasant background, many middle-class, educated women joined the military forces as well, sometimes rising into the officer ranks. Women who joined the revolutionary conflict beside male Sandinistas

often indicated that their male peers treated them as equals when training in the mountains. Sometimes, however, men chafed upon receiving
orders from a woman superior. Ana Juana, a former guerrilla fighter,
described such an encounter:

> I always gave order in as comradely a way as possible. I tried to make sure
> that people understood exactly what was required. [Once] I noticed that
> someone was sulking because a woman had given him an order. It was
> never direct, but I could sense it. When the situation arose I had to talk
> to the man about his attitude. It was necessary for him to realize that we
> women had earned out right to participate in the struggle. I had to explain
> to him that we deserved our rank and he'd have to understand that. There
> weren't too many of these problems though and the ones that did arise
> were not severe.[40]

Life in the guerrilla forces took all of the combatants, men and women
alike, outside of their normal experiences and they had to rely on each
other. It is possible that some of the women who fought recalled their
experiences with rose-colored glasses, but it is also possible that a certain
level of gender equality did exist in the mountains, where capability and
mission mattered more than status of any other kind. This was, after all,
the same kind of situation under which Amelio Robles gained acceptance
as a (male) comrade in the Mexican revolution. As a result, Nicaraguan
women could sometimes earn respect without taking on a masculine
identity altogether. The difference reflected changes in attitude over time
about gender roles as well as official leftist commitment to ending gender
as well as class discrimination.

Most of the women combatants were young and had few if any children.[41] For those women who already had children, the decision to join
the guerrillas had a huge and potentially painful impact on their private
lives. A former guerrilla identified as "Amparo" had a baby girl while
training to be a guerrilla, whom she had to send to her mother to raise.
Although Amparo dreamed of reuniting with her daughter, when the war
was over five years later her daughter wanted nothing to do with her,
causing Amparo great personal anguish.[42] Another female combatant,
whose wartime name was Yaosca, gave her daughter a name to symbolize
the revolution: Yaosca after her wartime identity, and Libertad, which
her husband chose because she was born in the year that he expected to
win freedom (it was indeed the year that the revolutionaries won).[43]
While Yaosca must have felt similar pain being away from her infant

daughter, she was reunited with her while her child was still young enough to bond with her.

For women with older children in their teens and twenties the mother–child relationship often encouraged increased political activism in one way or another. Sometimes, it was a mother's activism that encouraged her child's militancy. Emilia, who had been a guerrilla during the revolutionary war, explained that "My mom was the first to organize. Later she stared to integrate me."[44] Other mothers protested when not only repression, but high food prices that threatened their families' survival. More often, women's politicization occurred when their children were arrested or killed. Mothers' groups began to take shape, at first for mutual support, and then to speak out on behalf of their lost or fallen children. In March 1978, Albertina Serrano and other mothers went on a hunger strike to protest the torture of their children and other political prisoners. *La Prensa*, the main opposition newspaper, related their tale on Mothers' Day, highlighting Serrano's exemplary motherhood. The newspaper also printed a woman's letter to Anastasio Somoza's wife, Hope, which read:

> I appeal to your sensibility as a woman and your Christian spirit, and I hope that you can use a bit of your influence from your position as first lady . . . and also as wife of President Somoza.
>
> I cry out as a Nicaraguan mother and wife – you cannot ignore what is happening in the streets all over Nicaragua. They are massacring defenseless people, they are jailing, insulting, choking us in our homes, killing our children, our men, our bothers . . . and all this, you know, is ordered by your brave husband of the National Guard . . .
>
> It is time as a woman and a mother in Nicaragua to make your voice heard and intervene in some form. Well, I have some faith and think that you cannot remain indifferent forever in the face of the pain and disgrace of a whole people.[45]

Political scientist Lorraine Bayard de Volo identifies such actions as "combative motherhood" – taking radical action to protect one's children. The Sandinista leadership encouraged such maternally based activism during the revolutionary war. Women's contributions to the war, both direct and indirect, were instrumental in helping the Sandinistas win the war against Somoza as well as the hearts and minds of Nicaraguans.

Gender, motherhood, and Sandinista rule

In the first few years of Sandinista rule, from 1979 to 1983, the relation-ship between the rulers and Nicaraguan women was essentially positive. The new government recognized the contributions that women made to the victory over Somoza, and they proclaimed that their goal was to end all forms of oppression, including gender oppression. They named several women combatants to government posts (including some national posi-tions), they banned exploitative images of women in advertising, and they passed laws establishing equal pay for equal work. Similar to Cuban revolutionary leaders, the Sandinistas called on men to share in domestic chores.[46]

The formal relationship between the women's movement and the Sandinistas shifted once the Somoza regime was defeated. During the 1970s, the women's movement AMPRONAC (Association of Nicaraguan Women Confronting the Nation's Problems) had developed as part of the Sandinista movement, but it had at that time maintained a great deal of autonomy. After the revolutionary victory, it came under more formal control within the Sandinista structure, and its name was changed to the "Association of Nicaraguan Women, Luisa Amanda Espinosa" (AMNLAE), in remembrance of the first woman combatant to die in the war against Somoza. According to political scientist Katherine Isbester, this selection was telling: Espinosa had been "childless, autonomous, and above all a Sandinista." She was to represent a new female model, one that was not contained by the limits of the home and motherhood.[47] As with the Cuban revolution, this phase of Sandinista rule at once advanced women's interests and took away from them (or tried to take away from them) one of their main avenues for organizing to demand rights, via motherhood.

Around 1984, these dynamics began to change when counter revolu-tionaries (the "Contras") fought to bring down the revolutionary regime. Despite the Contras' strong US backing, the Sandinistas were able to maintain control of the state throughout the 1980s, but at the cost of many of their social and economic plans. Programs that the Sandinistas deemed unessential were dismantled or cut back, including gender ori-ented ones. Propaganda pertaining to motherhood was also part of the Sandinista-Contra war. Contras identified mothers with the home, tradi-tion, and domesticity, while Sandinistas presented images of an idealized socialist mother. Their message was that motherhood and national defense could blend seamlessly, and that the ideal mother upheld Sandinista principles without losing her nurturing qualities.[48] This stands in contrast to testimony from women guerrillas who fought against Somoza and found it painful to give up (or at least postpone) motherhood in order to fight in the war. Furthermore, the claim did not represent Sandinista gender practices in the war against the Contras. Although women were mobilized in the fight against the Contras, they were – over their own protests – relegated to supportive or backup roles, unlike how they had been treated in the revolutionary army before the Sandinistas came into power. At the same time, the Sandinista leadership was consolidating organizations and, as a part of this process, often taking women out of mid- and lower-tiered positions in favor of men.[49]

During the 1980s, AMNLAE (with state support) formed the Committee of Mothers of Heroes and Martyrs. The mothers, many of whom had been active on behalf of their children during the war against Somoza, were "the embodiment of the sacrifices made and the keepers of public memories." At the same time, the Contras were identifying mothers of counterrevolutionary prisoners in a similar campaign.[50] Women were not simply puppets of the two opposing sides, however. Although the Mothers Committees were organized by Sandinistas, they developed in ways that were not always under AMNLAE's control. The meaning that mothers derived from participating in the groups was personal as well as political, and it reinforced a motherhood identity that did not necessarily reflect the idealized mother of Sandinista propaganda. Many mothers also found themselves at odds with Sandinista rule based on their familial obligations, particularly because many essential products became expensive or difficult to obtain, and because they feared that their sons might be drafted into war.

The Mothers' Committees gradually found their own voices, neither playing by the Sandinistas' rules entirely, nor entirely rejecting association with AMNLAE or the state. They regularly published articles about problems that women faced in their daily lives, including their continuing experiences with the double workday despite the revolution and its supposed commitment to gender equality. Their criticisms were forthright, explaining how exhausted they were, and how it was not good for their children to be raised by mothers alone. This was not a message the Sandinistas particularly wanted advertised. At other times the Mothers' Committees and the Sandinista leadership came together seamlessly, as when the Mothers of the Heroes and Martyrs asserted that they were "proud to have . . . Sandinista children and prouder to have given my children to this Revolution."[51]

In 1990, the Sandinistas were shocked when, in a free and open election, their candidate (Daniel Ortega) lost the presidency to Violeta Barrios de Chamorro, candidate for the conservative opposition party. Chamorro's victory was due in large part because many women voted for her against Ortega – not because she was a woman, but because of the economic strain of the war and US economic sanctions against Nicaragua (which the United States promised to lift if the Sandinistas stepped down from power), and because the Sandinista leadership had failed to establish a strong record around the changes that mattered most to women. Chamorro's victory did not mark a victory for womankind, let alone feminism. Chamorro identified herself strongly with motherhood and domesticity (for more details, see Chapter 8), and her government reversed many of the social reforms that the Sandinistas had managed to put in place to address women's needs and concerns. The women's movements did not, however, fade away during Chamorro's rule. Instead, a wider variety of women's organizations developed autonomously, many of which are still functioning today. Nor did the Sandinistas disappear from national politics: they continued to hold some seats in Congress, and in 2007, Daniel Ortega was reelected as president. Ortega, however, continued to fight abortion during this term (see Chapter 9).

Mothers and Revolution: An "Unhappy Marriage"?

In 1979, economist Heidi Hartmann wrote an article about the "Unhappy Marriage of Marxism and Feminism," in which she discussed how, although Marxist theory and leadership often claimed to uphold women's rights and gender equality, in practice, economic concerns always took precedent over gender issues.[52] Hartmann's article was not limited to Latin America, and it did not consider non-Marxist revolutionary movements like Mexico's, but her insight holds true for the revolutions examined in this chapter. Although women fought in all of these revolutions, their contributions were often downplayed or relegated to appropriately female domain as supporters rather than combatants. Only in Nicaragua was female combat fully recognized and officially glorified, but even there, rhetoric was often at odds with practices that increasingly margin-alized female soldiers. The impact of the revolutions on women was also complex. This was most obvious in Mexico, where women only gained the right to vote in national elections long after the revolutionary process was complete. But even in Cuba and Nicaragua, where socialist govern-ments officially stood behind gender equality, policies and practices were limited and contradictory.

Revolution and motherhood may indeed make strange bedfellows, but they are often intertwined. The same broad socioeconomic problems that led men to revolt also affected mothers when they struggled to feed their families, and they often joined in protests and wars. However, it is not simply that women's concerns were sidelined for supposedly gender neutral agendas, but rather that revolutionary memories and outcomes have consistently been gendered male. Advancements for men often widened the gap between men and women, rather than narrowing the gap or even leaving it unchanged. One sees this in Mexico in particular, when land reform gave men access to the most important resource in peasants' lives, thus deepening women's dependence on men. In Cuba, women were constrained in that they had to downplay their identities as mothers even though the revolution did not resolve the strains of their double burden of work and motherhood. In Nicaragua, women's rights were treated as distinct from, and subordinate to, other economic agendas or the war against the Contras.

But revolutions are not simply stories of conflict and loss for women. Instead, in all of these examples, one finds stories of women who found ways to make the system work for them and their families. In Mexico, Yucatán women went before the military tribunals to get child support from husbands who abandoned their families. In Cuba, women worked to hold the system accountable for their rights, and many of them raised their children (sons as well as daughters) to think of gender relations in new and more equitable ways. In Nicaragua, mothers who had lost chil-dren to war found comfort in organizing with other mothers, and they learned how to shape movements to advance their own agendas.

Attention to gender and family in these three revolutions highlights both similarities and discrepancies in men's and women's experiences of revolutionary changes. It was not simply that revolutions were gendered male, but also that their impact was felt differently, and often at different times, by men and women. In Mexico, women did not gain the right to vote in 1953, and they only gained greater access to communal lands in the 1970s. Their experiences do not fit well with historians' references (including my own, made in several classrooms over the years) that revolutionary change occurred in Mexico from 1910 to 1940, after which the state became more conservative and distanced from social reform. In Cuba, women did gain many rights alongside men, perhaps partly because of the heavy hand of the Cuban state in the economy and society, as well as in political matters. Yet women and men's interpretations of and encounters with socialist reforms were quite different. In Nicaragua, although the Sandinista government initially made some changes, government officials (including President Daniel Ortega) never stood firmly behind gender reforms, making them largely ineffective. Therefore, changes for women in Nicaragua were often evolutionary rather than revolutionary, with women's movements and achievements developing over time, and unevenly – often despite rather than because of central state officials' actions.

What one does not often find in these revolutionary histories are evidence of women in the highest positions of political power. Certainly, women helped to determine the outcome of revolutionary wars and the success of subsequent revolutionary governments. Some women even achieved high rank in armies or governments – but most were kept out of the highest echelons of these movements. Revolutionary leaders' rhetorical (and sometimes practical) commitments to gender equality did not often translate into political power for women at the national level. Instead of rising in political power and influence by emphasizing gender equality, Latin American women often achieved political power and influence, at least before the 1990s, by reinforcing (and reinventing) their maternal identities.

Document: Castro on "The Revolution within the Revolution"[53]

Below is an excerpt of a speech that Fidel Castro gave on December 9, 1966 and that appeared in the *Granma Weekly Review* on December 18, 1966. In it, he famously called for a "revolution" in gender rights to go along with the revolution in politics and the economy in Cuba. When reading it, consider: How and why did Castro call for gender equality? How did motherhood fit into the broader message in Castro's speech? How did his proposed changes serve to justify socialism and advance Castro's own political and economic agendas? Look back over the section on the Cuban revolution in this chapter: did Castro keep his promises?

Arriving here this evening, I commented to a comrade that this phenomenon of women's participation in the revolution was a revolution within a revolution. [Applause] And if we were asked what is the most revolutionary thing is that the revolution is doing, we would answer that it is precisely this- the revolution that is occurring among the women of our country! [Applause]

If we were asked what things in the revolution have been most instructive for us, we would answer that one of the most interesting lessons for revolutionaries is that being offered by our women. [Applause]

You all know perfectly well that, in saying this, we are not uttering given words with intent to please the compañeras who are here tonight, but that we say it because it is what we firmly believe and feel.

[. . .]

[P]rejudices . . . have existed, not for decades or centuries but for thousands of years. We refer to the belief that all a woman could do was wash dishhes, wash and iron clothes, cook, keep house, and bear children – [Applause and exclamations] age-old prejudices that placed women in an inferior position in society. In effect, she did not have a productive place in society.

[. . .] Naturally, a considerable amount of prejudice still persists. If women were to believe that they have totally fulfilled their role as revolutionariese in society, they would be making a mistake. It seems to us that women must still fight and exert great efforts to attain the place that they should really hold in society.

If women in our country were doubly exploited, doubly humiliated in the past, then this simply means that women in a social revolution should be doubly revolutionary. [Applause]

[. . .]

There are two sectors in this country, two sectors of society which, aside from economic reasons, have had other motives for sympathizing and feeling enthusiasm for the revolution. These two sectors are the Black population of Cuba and the female population.

[. . .]

In a class society, which is to say, a society of exploiters and exploited, there was no way of eliminating discrimination for reasons of race or sex. Now the problem of such discrimination has disappeared from our country, because the basis for these two types of discrimination which is, quite simply the exploitation of man by man, has disappeared.

[. . .]

I described before the opinion held by many men concerning the functions of women, and I said that among the functions considered to belong to women was – almost exclusively – that of having children. Naturally, reproduction is one of the most important of women's functions in human society, in any kind of human society.

But it is precisely this function, relegated by nature to women, which has enslaved them to a series of chores within the home.

There is a sign here in front of us, for example, which says "One million women working in production by 1970." Unfortunately, it will not be possible to have one million working in production by 1970. We feel that this goal may be reached, perhaps, within ten years but not within four.

We could propose it as a goal to be reached by 1975. Why can't this goal be reached in four years? Because in order to have one million women working in production, we must have thousands of children's day nurseries, thousands of primary boarding schools, thousands of school dining halls, thousands of workers' dining halls; thousands of centers of social services of this type must be set up, because if not, who is going to cook for the second- or third-grade child when he comes home for lunch?

Who is going to care for the unweaned infants, or babies of two, three, and four years of age? Who is going to prepare dinner for the man when he comes home from work? Who is going to wash, clean, all of those things? [Applause]

In other words, in order to reach the social goal of liberating women from all these activities that enslave her and impede her from full incorporation into work outside the home and all these activities she can engage in society, it is necessary to create the necessary material base, to attain the necessary social development.

It is impossible to construct the required thousands of children's day nurseries, school dining halls, laundries, workers' dining halls, boarding schools, in four years. In fact, merely to meet present needs, great effort is necessary on all fronts.

Everywhere women are working it has been necessary to make a special effort to establish day nurseries, to set up boarding schools and all of the necessary institutions so that these women could be free to work.

[. . .]

Many of the plans that the revolution is today drawing up and beginning to carry out could not have been conceived until the great reservoir of human resources that our society possesses in its women was clearly seen for what it was.

These plans, which stand for extraordinary contributions to the economic development of our country, to the increased well-being of our people, could not have been conceived without the mass incorporation of women into the work force.

Notes

1   Gabriela Cano, "Unconcealable Realities of Desire: Amelio Robles's (Trans-gender) Masculinity in the Mexican Revolution," in Jocelyn Olcott, Mary Kay Vaughan, and Gabriela Cano, eds, *Sex in Revolution: Gender, Politics, and Power in Modern Mexico* (Durham, NC: Duke University Press, 2006), pp. 35–56.

2   Aleida March, *Remembering Che: My Life with Che Guevara* (Minneapolis, MN: Ocean Press, 2012).

3   See, for example, Jon Lee Anderson, *Che Guevara: A Revolutionary Life*, revised ed. (New York: Grove Press, 2010).

4   March, on kindle, 38–43% regarding how she became wife and mother, and 4% regarding her purpose in writing her memoir primarily for her children's benefit.

5   Diane Walta Hart, "Leticia: A Nicaraguan Woman's Struggle," in William H. Beezley and Judith Ewell, eds, *The Human Tradition in Latin America: The Twentieth Century* (Wilmington, DE: SR Books, 1987), pp. 259–273.

6   In fact, by the time that the Russian revolution began in 1917, the Mexican revolutionary conflict was coming to a close, and the revolutionary victors had written a new constitution.

7   This phrase for the Mexican revolution was made famous by Mary Kay Vaughan's "Modernizing Patriarchy: State Policies, Rural Households, and Women in Mexico, 1930–1940," in Elizabeth Dore and Maxine Molyneaux, eds, *Hidden Histories of Gender and the State in Latin America* (Durham, NC: Duke University Press, 2000), pp. 194–214.

8   Elizabeth Salas, "Soldaderas in the Mexican Revolution: War and Men's Illusions," in Heather Fowler-Salamini and Mary Kay Vaughan, eds, *Women of the Mexican Countryside, 1850–1990* (Tucson: University of Arizona Press, 1994), p. 96.

9   Shirlene Soto, *Emergence of the Modern Mexican Woman: Her Participation in Revolution and Struggle for Equality, 1910–1940* (Denver, CO: Arden Press, 1990), pp. 47–48, 36 (respectively).

10 For a wonderful and detailed first-person account, see Oscar Lewis's famous ethnography, based on interviews with peasants who lived through the revolution, titled *Pedro Martínez: A Mexican Peasant and his Family* (New York: Random House, 1964), in which Lewis interviewed not only the peasant Pedro, but also his wife Esperanza, whose experiences of the revolution differed dramatically.

11 Stephanie J. Smith, *Gender and the Mexican Revolution: Yucatán Women and the Realities of Patriarchy* (Chapel Hill: University of North Carolina Press, 2009), pp. 54–73.

12 Susie S. Porter, *Working Women in Mexico City: Public Discourses and Material Conditions, 1879–1931* (Tucson: University of Arizona Press, 2003), pp. 100–108, 169.

13 Ann S. Blum, *Domestic Economies: Family, Work, and Welfare in Mexico City, 1884–1943* (Lincoln: University of Nebraska Press, 2009), pp. 118–123.

14 Salas, p. 101.

15 Smith, pp. 75–77.

16 Porter, pp. 109–117.

17 An English translation of the 1917 Mexican constitution can be found online at http://www.latinamericanstudies.org/mexico/1917-Constitution .htm (last accessed November 13, 2013).

18 Porter, pp. 174–176.

19 Porter, p. 178.

20 Porter, pp. 184–185.

21 Carmen Diana Deere and Magdalena León, "Women and Land in the Latin American Neo-Liberal Counter-Reforms," Working Paper No. 264, MSU, 1997. Available online at: http://gencen.isp.msu.edu/documents/Working _Papers/WP264.pdf (last accessed November 13, 2013).

22 Anne Rubenstein, "The War on *Las Pelonas*: Modern Women and Their Enemies in Mexico City, 1924," in *Sex in Revolution*, pp. 57–80.

23 Sarah A. Buck, "The Meaning of the Women's Vote in Mexico, 1917–1953," in Stephanie Mitchell and Patience A. Schell, eds, *The Women's Revolution in Mexico 1910–1953* (New York: Rowman and Littlefield, 2007), p. 74.

24 Blum, pp. 171–174.

25 Jocelyn Olcott, "'Worthy Wives and Mothers': State-Sponsored Women's Organizing in Postrevolutionary Mexico," *Journal of Women's History* 13:4 (Winter 2002), pp. 106–131.

26 Buck, pp. 73–74.

27 Lois M. Smith and Alfred Padula, *Sex and Revolution: Women in Socialist Cuba* (New York: Oxford University Press, 1996), p. 26.

28 Elizabeth Stone, ed., *Women and the Cuban Revolution: Speeches and Documents by Fidel Castro, Vilma Espin, and Others* (New York: Pathfinder Press, 1981), "Introduction," p. 8.

29 Espín, in Stone, p. 40. "America" here is used in reference to the entire hemisphere, in order to suggest that only socialist revolution and government brought true freedom from oppression.

30 These passages from Guerrilla warfare appear in Francesca Miller, *Latin American Women and the Search for Social Justice* (Hanover, NH: University of New England Press, 1991), pp. 146–147.

31 Fidel Castro, "The Revolution within the Revolution," in Stone, pp. 50–51.

32 The full text of this law can be found in Stone, pp. 133–139.

33 Stone, p. 146. The Entire Family Code appears in this volume.

34 Stone, p. 86.

35 Smith and Padula, pp. 112–113, 119, and 132–138.

36 Two very interesting sources that highlight these gradual and contradictory processes are Margaret Randall, *Cuban Women Now* (Toronto: Dumon Press, 1974) and Cuban films. Cuban films offer interesting sources for analyzing gender relations. In particular, see "Retrato de Teresa" (Portrait of Teresa), directed by Pastor Vega, a classic film that engages one in exploring

the pressures that a married woman might feel in the "New Cuba" following the Revolution. Director Tomás Gutierrez Alea has made several important films on Cuban society under the Revolution, including "Hasta Cierto Punto" (Up to a Certain Point), which follows the life of a woman factory worker.

37   Smith and Padula, pp. 146, 150–151, 158, 161.

38   An excellent analysis of the FMC is Maxine Molyneaux's "State, Gender, and Institutional Change: The Federación de Mujeres Cubanas," in Elizabeth Dore and Maxine Molyneaux, eds, *Hidden Histories of Gender and the State in Latin America* (Durham, NC: Duke University Press, 2000), pp. 291–321.

39   Smith and Padula, pp. 112–114. Porter noted a similar trend with the government-sponsored union in Mexico, p. 109.

40   Margaret Randall, ed., *Sandino's Daughters* (Toronto: New Start Books, 1981), pp. 132–133.

41   Karen Kampwirth, "Women in the Armed Struggles in Nicaragua: Sandinistas and Contras Compared," in Victoria González and Karen Kampwirth, eds, *Radical Women in Latin America, Left and Right* (University Park: Pennsylvania State University Press, 2001), p. 98.

42   Katerine Isbester, *Still Fighting: The Nicaraguan Women's Movement, 1977–2000* (Pittsburgh, PA: University of Pittsburgh Press, 2001), pp. 3 and 7.

43   Randall, p. 137.

44   Kampwirth, p. 86.

45   Lorraine Bayard de Volo, *Mothers of Heroes and Martyrs: Gender Identity Politics in Nicaragua, 1979–1999* (Baltimore, MD: Johns Hopkins University Press, 2001), pp. 28–31 (quote on p. 31).

46   Bayard de Volo, p. 35.

47   Isbester, p. 48.

48   Baynard de Volo, p. 40.

49   Isbester, pp. 55, 61.

50   Baynard de Volo, pp. 45–48.

51   Bayard de Volo, pp. 86, 96.

52   Heidi I. Hartmann, "The Unhappy Marriage of Marxism and Feminism: Towards a More Progressive Union," *Capital and Class* 3:2 (Summer 1979), pp. 1–33.

53   This speech, in translation, appears in Stone, pp. 48–54.

8

Maternalizing Politics, Politicizing Motherhood
Women and Politics, circa 1950–1990s

Women and Politics in the Late Twentieth Century: To Be or Not to Be (a Mother)?

Rigoberta Menchú Tum is a Quiché indigenous woman from Guatemala who grew up in poverty. Her youth was dominated by the struggle for survival and by the brutality of the Guatemalan government toward the rural poor, especially the indigenous peasantry. Her father was an important peasant leader, and she and her other family members became activists as well. By the time that Menchú met anthropologist Elisabeth Burgos-Debray at the age of 23, the Guatemalan military had killed many of her family members, and she had fled Guatemala in order to save her own life. Menchú's encounter with Burgos-Debray in France proved pivotal in bringing international attention to the plight of indigenous peoples in her country. Burgos-Debray taped interviews with her that served as the basis for Menchú's book-length testimony about growing up indigenous in Guatemala and about the horrors that the government was committing against the poor there. This book made Menchú the most famous indigenous woman in Latin America, and it brought international attention to the Guatemalan civil war and its many indigenous victims. In 1992, Menchú won the Nobel Peace Prize for her struggle to win attention for the cause of the poor in Guatemala, and her work helped to create the atmosphere that made the 1996 Guatemalan Peace Accord possible.

Mothers Making Latin America: Gender, Households, and Politics Since 1825,
First Edition. Erin E. O'Connor.
© 2014 John Wiley & Sons, Inc. Published 2014 by John Wiley & Sons, Inc.

Menchú had given over her life to politics and to the Guatemalan poor. One of her decisions as she grew into this role was that, at least while the struggle was still going on, she would not marry or to have children. Menchú often explained in her testimony that indigenous women in Guatemala typically married and started having children while quite young. To explain her decision not to marry or have children she told Burgos-Debray:

> But the time came when I saw clearly – it was actually when I'd begun my life as a revolutionary – that I was fighting for a people and for many children who hadn't anything to eat. I could see how sad it would be for a revolutionary not to leave a seed, because the seed which was left behind would enjoy the fruit of this work in the future. But I thought of the risks of having a child. It would be much easier for me to die, at any time or place, if I weren't leaving anyone behind to suffer. That would be sad, because although my community would take care of my child, of my seed, no other person can give a child the love his mother can, however much that other person looks after and cares for the child.[1]

Many years later, after helping to achieve peace accords between revolutionaries and the Guatemalan government, Menchú returned to Guatemala, married, and gave birth to a son.

While Menchú was growing up and coming of age in Guatemala, Elena Larraín Valdés of Chile engaged in conservative political activism. The daughter of wealthy landowners and wife to a medical doctor with whom she had several children, Larraín had never worked for money, although she had done volunteer work. In the 1960s, her motherly identity and interest in politics merged when she helped to found the group *Acción Mujeres de Chile* (Women's Action of Chile). Acción Mujeres de Chile's membership was made up almost entirely of elite women, and they did not question dominant gender ideologies. Larraín's view was that men and women were inherently different. Because men were politically ambitious, they did not work well together and in political parties, even in conservative parties whose policies she favored, therefore they rarely achieved their goals. She thought that women could be more effective because they were willing to work together for outcomes rather than for their own status. Though Larraín broke with the idea that women belonged only in the home, she identified strongly as a mother with her new activism. In her opposition to socialist Salvador Allende (through the scare campaign, discussed later), she used her motherly status to suggest thatAllende would, if given the chance, break apart Chilean families.[2]

Chilean conservatives continued to cultivate idealized notions of motherhood in their quest to gain women's votes and favor. In the 1960s, moderate conservative president Eduardo Frei of the Christian Democratic Party sought to incorporate women into his movement by establishing Mothers' Centers in various towns, city neighborhoods, and remote villages throughout Chile. In addition to providing women a place to gather, discuss their lives, and receive benefits from the state (such as sewing or knitting materials), Mothers' Centers also served to glorify a conservative vision of female identity centered on motherhood. This emphasis was clear when Doña Doralisa Marambio Catalán, a member of the Talagante Mothers' Center and mother of seven, was voted "Mother of the Year." An article describing Doña Doralisa and this award listed her profession as "mother and wife." It also emphasized that her dedication to home is what made it possible for her children to succeed in their own professional lives. The article listed her children's professions, which included programming, architecture, and journalism. One daughter was listed as a *matrona* (matron), suggesting that she had continued her mother's legacy of dedicating her life to her home. This was the ideal mother: the one who had a large brood of children and devoted her life to their success rather than her own.[3] Though Marambio was not terribly political, she represented the conservative association of womanhood with motherhood, and her participation in the Mothers' Center also bolstered conservative politicians who established the centers.

This chapter examines case studies in which motherhood and politics overlapped in particularly compelling ways in the mid- to late twentieth century. It opens with one of the earliest and most famous combinations of motherhood imagery and national politics via a discussion of Eva Perón's influence on Argentine populism in the 1940s and early 1950s. Perón successfully presented herself as the "mother of Argentines." Decades later, Violeta Chamorro used a similar argument in her bid for the presidency in Nicaragua. Together, these two women's stories reveal a great deal about both continuities and changes in the ways that motherhood imagery offered a stepping stone to political power. Maternalism also affected indigenous women's politicization in the late twentieth century. Since the 1980s indigenous activist organizations have become increasingly influential in national and international politics. An examination of indigenous women and political activism explores how motherhood made women central to the politics of ethnic activism in the late twentieth century, while it simultaneously made it difficult for many women to participate in ethnic-based movements. Finally, motherhood itself was often a direct route to politicization under authoritarian regimes. Many women in Argentina and El Salvador sprang into action when their (adult) children disappeared due to state violence. Though many of them had no previous political experience, they often had great impact as critics of authoritarianism. In Chile, however, one can also find evidence of women who opted to use the authority of motherhood in order to bolster conservative regimes rather than to protest against them.

An examination of the various ways that motherhood shaped women's political actions and achievements in mid- to late twentieth-century Latin America shows that the relationship between motherhood and women's political advancement is multifaceted. Although in some circumstances, women's association with motherhood blocked women from power in others it provided them with the means to effect change. Moreover, evidence from Latin America complicates ideas that emphasis on motherhood belongs naturally to either the conservative or radical end of the political spectrum. Having a woman in political power, for example, does not necessarily mean that she will work to advance women's rights or challenge double standards. Similarly, having a woman define herself through motherhood does not necessarily mean that she is unconcerned with gender equality. Instead, experiences and ideologies of motherhood offered rich (and sometimes dangerous) terrain on which women worked through contradictory relationships to home and nation, class or race and gender, power and justice.

Mothering the Nation: From Evita Perón to Violeta Chamorro

Evita and Peronism

María Eva Duarte de Perón (better known as Eva Perón, or just as "Evita") was born in 1919 in a small town near the Argentine capital of Buenos Aires. She moved to Buenos Aires in her teens, eventually building a career as a radio actress. In 1943, she met and began an affair with Juan

Perón, a military officer who was then serving as Secretary of Labor. As Perón rose to power based on the benefits and favors he granted to the workers (whom he called the *descamisados* or "shirtless ones"), Evita gradually became one of his important political collaborators. They were married by the time Juan Perón won the presidency in 1946, and she became the direct link between him and the workers. From that point until her death (by cancer) in 1952 Evita was essential to Perón's success, and her death was a considerable blow to his regime. Her influence and prominence in his administration led historian June Hahner to refer to her as "The Most Powerful Woman in Latin America."[4]

Eva Perón's power and influence was considerable, but she consistently identified herself within the bounds of traditional womanhood and motherhood. Yet she did not adhere to traditional gender norms in her own life: she was an actress, a profession that led many in elite and middle-class society to suspect her of loose behavior and morals. Such assumptions would have been reinforced by her open love affair with Perón before they married. Moreover, she had no children of her own, and she could be exceptionally demanding, even authoritarian, in her political dealings.[5] How did such a woman claim, successfully, to be a defendant for traditional family values and motherhood? In part, Peronism itself made this possible. Juan Perón's rule in Argentina during the late 1940s and early 1950s was a classic populist regime: he appealed to the popular sectors through nationalist rhetoric, and he advanced himself as a paternal figure who would work on behalf of the poor (without alienating the industrial elite). The paternalism inherent in populism made it relatively easy for Eva Perón to identify herself as *mother to Argentines*. Consider how she described her role in one of her ghost written autobiographies:

> I feel, like [other Argentine women], that I am the head of a home, much larger, it is true, than those they have made, but in the final outcome a home: the prosperous home of this country of mine which Perón is leading toward its very highest destinies . . . Like all [women] I get up early thinking of my husband and of my children . . . and thinking of them when I go about all day and a good deal of the night . . . Like them I always like to appear smiling and attractive to my husband and children, always serene and strong so as to inspire them with faith and hope . . .
>
> Like all women of all the homes of my people, my joyful days are those when all the children, happy and affectionate, are gathered around the head of the house."[6]

Eva Perón may have exercised considerable political influence and power, but she very carefully identified herself with a conservative model of womanhood, focused on women's inherent destiny to mother. In this case, her "children" were Argentines, and in particular the descamisados. She was a mother figure leading alongside and in support of Perón's father figure. More than that, she constantly used her speeches and writings to build up Juan Perón's persona as the savior of Argentina and its workers, and to highlight her husband's superiority and rightful authority. In short, she played the role of the humble homemaker, obeying and fulfilling her husband's will.

Eva Perón repeatedly highlighted the maternal nature of her work in her interactions with the Argentine people, particularly the Argentine poor. For example, in the image below, she spoke to a crowd of women, many of whom wore kerchiefs and appear to have been housewives and mothers. This photograph had a twofold image: first, it was one of many that showed Evita "mothering" Argentines through her work for the Peronist government. Moreover, the image showed the childless Eva Perón identifying herself and her cause with that of all women, and of mothers in particular (Figure 8.1).

Figure 8.1   Eva Peron addressing women. Getty Images/Hulton Archive.

Eva Perón took social mothering to a new political level, nurturing the sick and downtrodden by visiting them in hospitals and even in prisons. This helped to build her image as a concerned mother figure, and it reinforced her popularity as a beloved patroness of the poor. Argentine meatpacking worker Doña María Roldán, discussed at length in Chapter 5, recalled Evita as "a perfect human being, who loves the other" and asserted that "there was one moment in the Argentine nation when she almost, almost surpassed Perón. People were forgetting their leader, because she was leading such splendid humanitarian campaigns."[7]

Yet for all her appeal, Eva Perón's political power was limited. True, she was Perón's connection to the descamisados, without whom he could not maintain power, and she was an important voice extolling his virtues as a leader. She also headed the women's section of the Peronist party and the Eva Perón Foundation (a charitable organization meant to absorb all existing private charities). She did not, however, hold any government office. When Perón ran for reelection in 1952, he initially proposed having his wife be his running mate. However, when the military leadership resisted he backed down and kept Evita in her more informal, if influential, party positions.

Nor did Evita use her political power and influence to propose drastic changes to women's roles in society or politics. In fact, she often reinforced gender norms that identified women with the home and motherhood, frequently accusing women who chose to work for wages of abandoning their true duty to society. To balance this, Eva Perón at one point suggested that housewives should receive a government stipend in order for them to fulfill their duties without becoming completely economically dependent on their husbands.[8] Her position on female suffrage was similarly paradoxical: when the proposal came up for a legislative vote in 1947, Evita supported the passage of the law, but she did so based on an argument that allowing women to vote in national elections would enable their inherently emotional maternal natures to balance men's more rational interests. She was particularly critical of Argentine feminists, whom she described as ugly and bitter women whose only goal was to become like men. She claimed that Juan Perón once explained to her: "Don't you see that [feminists] have missed the way? They want to be men . . . Don't you see that this class of 'feminists' detests womanhood? . . . And if what the world requires is a woman's political and social movement . . . how little will the world gain if the women want to save it by imitating men!"[9]

Not all women's issues under Peronism focused on women exclusively as mothers, but they almost always identified women with the home, as when the regime encouraged women to help the economy by being responsible consumers of Argentine products.[10] Yet the strong association that Peronism made between women and the home shows that motherhood could be a powerful tool for populist political agendas. It helped to keep workers in line under Evita's maternal care, discouraged women from challenging the gender status quo, and identified Juan Perón as the savior of Argentine families. Eva Perón's ability to present herself as a symbol of motherhood bolstered Juan Perón's social control. It is perhaps because of this that Peronism is remembered as one of the most powerful and (for a short time at least) successful populist movements in Latin America. Other populist father figures in the region identified with similar family and social values, but they did not have figureheads like Evita to "mother" the nation.

Doña Violeta and the Nicaraguan family

Decades after Eva Perón submitted herself as mother of Argentines, Violeta Barrios de Chamorro (typically referred to as Violeta Chamorro, sometimes as "Doña Violeta") ran for president in Nicaragua. Her opponent was none other than Daniel Ortega, the Sandinista leader who had held the presidency since 1985. Her victory over Ortega was a true upset, since the Sandinistas had expected an easy victory for Ortega. Chamorro also became only the second woman president in Latin American history, following Isabel Perón in Argentina (1974–76). How had she done it? In part, the answer lies in the contentious internal and international politics of Nicaragua in the late 1980s (see Chapter 7). In particular, Nicaraguans feared that the war with the Contras would continue, and that perhaps the United States would intervene directly if the Sandinistas remained in power. Also, her late husband, Pedro Joaquín Chamorro, was a famous newspaper editor and martyr to the revolution, and her connection to him was a great political advantage. Finally, Violeta Chamorro successfully manipulated the symbolism of womanhood when she campaigned for president.

In contrast to Daniel Ortega's macho image in which he alternately posed as a cowboy and caring father, Chamorro highlighted her gendered purity with regard to politics. She often wore white, conjuring up images of the Virgin Mary – a meaningful image in a nation with so many devout Catholics – and emphasized her *lack* of political experience. Rather than engage directly in politics, Chamorro presented herself as having risen above the fray of partisanship, suggesting that she was in a much better position than the politically entrenched and overly macho Ortega to heal the divided nation which, after suffering dictatorship for decades, had most recently endured a civil war between the Sandinista leadership and the Contra movement supported by the United States. Chamorro's emphasis on her supposedly apolitical nature centered on her womanhood and especially her motherhood.[11] Both during and after the campaign, Chamorro used her control of the newspaper *La Prensa* to cultivate her image as a good and traditional woman. The newspaper claimed that she was "without vanity, without pride, without ambition, a home-loving woman . . . she is not a feminist nor does she aspire to be one. She is a woman determined to support the valor of our Nicaraguan men."[12] It was Violeta Chamorro's personal experiences as a mother, however, that provided her strongest argument for allowing a supposedly apolitical woman to take over the presidency in Nicaragua. Of her four children, two of them supported the Sandinista regime and two opposed it. Yet rather than have this lead to a hopelessly divided family, Violeta Chamorro brought her children together and maintained good family relations among them all. She promised that she would unite the divided and war-torn Nicaraguan people just as she had healed her own family, a pledge that appealed to many Nicaraguans. One woman described her support for Chamorro by saying that Chamorro was "not a political woman, better yet she's the symbol of the woman that the country needs . . . She's the figure of a frail woman but at the same time [one] with the decision to maintain the unity of her family in spite of multiple problems and who even wants to maintain the unity of her people . . . They say she is the Mom of all Nicaraguans."[13] Chamorro's motherly promises to end the civil war and heal the "Nicaraguan family" also appealed to many Nicaraguan mothers who opposed the draft that endangered and all too often took the lives of their young adult children.[14]

Once in power, Violeta Chamorro was able to promote conservative womanhood through policies, not just rhetoric. Chamorro helped to reverse many Sandinista reforms, including some related to health care, education, and social welfare. In their place, the new conservative government cut spending, encouraged members of the state bureaucracy to leave office, and promoted Catholic moral values. Most of these policies had a negative impact on Nicaraguan women, either directly or indirectly. Economic austerity policies that cut social spending tended to hit poor women, particularly poor single mothers, especially hard. At the same time, policies encouraging bureaucrats to give up their jobs in return for a one-time payment led mostly to women state officials leaving the public sphere to tend to their homes. Even new textbooks reinforced gender traditionalism, in which "Happy mothers are pictured cooking or scrubbing their middle-class kitchens; happy fathers are pictured sitting in overstuffed chairs or engaged in paid employment."[15] Antifeminist groups enjoyed special access to the state during Chamorro's presidency and that of her conservative follower, Arnoldo Alemán, and some even held powerful positions within state agencies. Many of these antifeminist women's groups claimed that they sought "to benefit women . . . so that they have access to education, to protect them in all that pertains to women . . . not just our organs but our psychology, which is based on motherhood."[16]

Not all mothers bought into this conservative view of traditional womanhood. Many of them thought that Chamorro's elite status meant that she could not understand what motherhood meant to ordinary women in Nicaragua. The Mothers of Heroes and Martyrs of Estelí, Nicaragua, petitioned Chamorro in a 1991 letter:

> We come representing the calls of thousands of mothers all over the country who, the same as us, are suffering a difficult situation in their homes . . . Currently, the pension we receive does not even cover the costs of food for a week, not including the other costs that come up . . . We believe that your good sense, sincerity, and spirit of justice will lead you to understand that our request is not a response to a whim or a political position because we are also asking that you help the mothers of the dead children who were in the Resistance [meaning the Contras]. Even though their struggle was wrong and they were clearly manipulated, these mothers also suffered the same pain that we experienced in losing our children.[17]

By petitioning the new president in this way, the Mothers of Estelí used Chamorro's own symbolism and language against her. The petitioners sought government assistance based on their identities as mothers, with a careful avoidance of partisan politics. Although they saw the Contras as "wrong" and "clearly manipulated," they argued that their mothers and families deserved rights and assistance just as much as mothers of fallen Sandinista soldiers did.

If Chamorro's conservatism benefitted antifeminist women's groups, it also helped to spur feminist organizations into action. No longer under the control of the Sandinistas who had fallen from power (see Chapter 7), women's rights organizations grew in numbers and autonomy during the 1990s even though they faced presidents who were opposed to their goals of equality, social reforms, and reproductive rights.

Eva Perón and Violeta Chamorro offer examples of women who strongly influenced national politics in their respective countries, and as such reveal that women started making political advancements quite early in some parts of Latin America. Yet both of them supported traditional notions of womanhood and motherhood even as they stepped into new public and political roles that had previously been closed to women. They are clear reminders that political ideology and class–race identity, not just one's sex, play a role in determining an individual's gender politics. Even among radical indigenous activists, however, gender issues are often quite sensitive, sometimes contentious, and women's identification with motherhood remains strong.

Poor Mothers, Identity Politics, and Political Activism

Poor women, particularly from indigenous communities, have had an important but paradoxical role in political activism since the 1970s and 1980s. During the late twentieth century, new forms of sociopolitical protest emerged to challenge elite-run states. In Brazil, favela dwellers, and particularly women, began to organize to get more reliable utilities, schooling, and other government support for their communities. In Bolivia, miners' wives formed a cooperative in order to get better pay and work conditions for their husbands, and better living conditions for their families. In some countries – notably in Bolivia, Guatemala, and Ecuador – indigenous peoples began to organize politically. Though many of their demands have focused on economic concerns about land tenure, access to water, and incentives for businesses, indigenous activists have also pursued cultural concerns, such as bilingual education and respect for their particular ethnic laws within the broader nation.[18] Women have been strong supporters, and sometimes leaders, of many of these grassroots activist movements.

Poor women's politicization developed out of their long history with resistance movements. Latin American history offers evidence of indigenous women participants and leaders in court cases, protests, and rebellions going far back into the colonial period. Their engagement with resistance to elite rule varied: in court cases, women were usually relegated to supportive roles, because both colonial and nineteenth-century laws made the court system a male domain in which women could often only voice concerns directly if their male family members were absent. Rebellions, however, were extralegal acts – violent acts, outside of the constraints of the law – in which women not only participated but often took on leadership roles. Until the twentieth century, however, these movements were not political per se, but rather were aimed at addressing specific grievances and needs of poor communities. By the twentieth century, however, the rise of socialist and communist parties in many Latin American countries opened new possibilities for poor indigenous (and mestizo) communities to take part in formal political protest. Although men ran leftist movements in most cases, women were sometimes also important leaders, such as Dolores Cacuango, an Ecuadorian indigenous woman who became one of the great heroic figures in ethnic activism in the country.

Dolores Cacuango was born to an indebted hacienda worker in 1881. After marrying another indigenous hacienda worker and having children, she sent her only surviving son, Luís Catacuamba, to school; however, she had to pay her son's mestizo teacher to educate him rather than treat him like a servant. These experiences left her determined to establish bilingual programs for indigenous children, where they would benefit from learning Spanish while also maintaining the Quichua language and Indian customs that were central to their identity.[19] Cacuango's dream became a reality when she formed a friendship and partnership with Luisa Gómez de la Torre, who helped to finance a bilingual school for indigenous children. Meanwhile, Cacuango emerged as a leader in struggles against the hacienda system in Cayambe, the region of Ecuador in which she lived. She joined the recently established Communist Party in Ecuador, where she had strong alliances with its leaders.[20] She was also cofounder, along with fellow hacienda worker Jesús Gualavisí, of the Federation of Ecuadorian Indians (FEI), the first national-level indigenous organization in Ecuador.

Many themes in Cacuango's life story can be connected to the prevalence of motherhood in her political involvements. Cacuango – and many of those who later wrote about her – focused on her commitment to Indian children's education, which in turn was closely connected to her own motherhood experiences. She was clearly publicly and politically active, but she never blatantly discarded the idea that her primary role in life was as a mother; instead, she reinforced this preconception. Cacuango, in fact, came to become the symbolic mother of the modern indigenous movement in Ecuador and was often referred to as "Mamá Dolores" among indigenous activists. Cacuango's extension of her motherhood experiences into the public sphere took the notion that women belonged to the domestic sphere and turned it into a source of political strength.[21]

Another woman who took her housewife and mother identity and put it to work for her political goals was Bolivian tin miner's wife Domitila Barrios de Chungara. One of the founding members of the Siglo XX tin mine's Housewives' Committee, Barrios de Chungara recalled how difficult it was for the founders to organize and gain acceptance among the men who worked in the mines. Yet it was not simply the men's resistance that stood in the housewives' way, but their own uncertainty of their abilities as well. Barrios de Chungara reflected upon this:

> At the beginning, we had the mentality they'd taught us, that women are made for the home, to take care of the children and to cook, and that they aren't capable of assimilating other things, of a social, union, or political nature, for example. But necessity made us organize. We suffered a lot doing it, but today the miners have one more ally, a pretty strong one, an ally who's sacrificed a lot: the Housewives' Committee, the organization that arose first in Siglo XX [mine] and now exists in other nationalized mines.[22]

The housewives' association with the domestic sphere was at once their source of strength and their weakness. Though others might mock housewives becoming political, it was their identities as mothers and wives that was the source of the women's deep commitment to their cause and their willingness to take risks. Motherhood would continue to be the source of both strength and suffering for Domitila Barrios de Chungara as her political involvement deepened. In order to fight for a better future for her children, she also had to put them in danger. At one point, she was imprisoned and threatened when she was late into her pregnancy; she went into labor while in prison and gave birth to a baby who died. The event haunted Barrios de Chungara, but she continued her political struggle.[23]

Women continued to contribute to political movements, particularly indigenous movements in which women are symbolically important and yet often marginalized. Indian women, much more consistently than Indian men, embody authentic ethnic identity through dress, language, food preparation, and child rearing. Their roles as mothers, in particular, make them central to the identity on which these movements are based. Ironically, motherhood is also what often marginalizes them within the movements. Despite the rise of some women to prominent leadership positions, many indigenous women find themselves too busy with responsibilities in the home to attend meetings on a regular basis. Others have encountered resistance from male activists who express concern that if Indian women become too involved with politics, they will abandon the home – and thus their role in maintaining cultural identity.[24]

Given that motherhood simultaneously made indigenous women central to indigenous movements *and* marginal within them, it is not terribly surprising that some of the most famous indigenous women activists chose to remain single and childless for much of their lives. Nina Pacari of Ecuador, for example, was the first indigenous woman in the country to obtain a law degree, and who served briefly as Foreign Minister during Lucio Gutiérrez's presidency in 2003. Like Rigoberta Menchú, Pacari chose to remain childless in favor of committing herself to political causes.

None of the women mentioned here were fighting for women's rights per se, though that does not necessarily mean that they were *against* equality for women. Rather, it was that most poor and indigenous women saw feminism or women's movements as either the domain of middle-class and elite women who did not prioritize the needs of poor women, or as a struggle that pitted women against men. Most poor women have chosen instead to put their efforts into class or ethnic based movements through which they can work on the goals that they share with male peers. This, plus the association of women with motherhood, often makes it difficult for movements like indigenous organizations to address gender inequalities and problems, though many groups are making efforts to do so. In fact, many of them see all forms of exploitation and division as intertwined problems that must be solved together. As Menchú put it: "[W]e have to erase barriers which exist between ethnic groups, between Indians and *ladinos* [non Indians], between men and women, between intellectuals and non-intellectuals."[25]

Mothers and Military Governments

The Mothers of the Plaza de Mayo in Argentina

Military authoritarian governments ruled much of Latin America from the 1960s through the 1980s, and they were particularly prominent in the South American nations of Brazil, Argentina, Chile, and Uruguay. Claiming that only military institutions could restore social order and get national economies back on track, military regimes upheld so-called traditional social order focused on Catholic morality and the nuclear family, and they embraced neoliberal policies that deregulated and privatized industries and cut social spending. They were also exceptionally brutal against their own citizens. Individuals were routinely captured, tortured, and imprisoned, and many of them died. Few of the victims of state terrorism ever had formal charges brought against them, let alone trials by jury. In Argentina, the military regime killed somewhere between 10,000 and 30,000 people in what the government referred to as the *Proceso* (Process), and which many now refer to as the Dirty War, between 1976 and 1983. In Chile, General Augusto Pinochet's regime of the 1970s and 1980s resulted in the death of approximately 3,000 Chilean citizens and the torture of another 29,000.

In Central America, military rule also reigned supreme in countries such as Guatemala, El Salvador, and Nicaragua, but these military regimes were less bureaucratically organized. Nevertheless, the Central American military governments also brutalized their own populations, especially the rural poor. In Guatemala, Civil War and military governments led to the death of almost 100,000 people from 1961 to 1992, and 80% of the victims were indigenous peoples (this was the context in which most members of Rigoberta Menchú's family members died). In El Salvador, the military government worked on behalf of the interests of the tiny group of elite families in the nation, targeting the poor as subversives regardless of whether or not they joined leftist resistance forces. Even priests and nuns were regularly tortured and killed.

It was in this atmosphere of state-generated terrorism that groups of mothers – many of them housewives without any previous political experience – organized to protest the violence that robbed them of their loved ones. Argentine women were among the first to organize. As stated in Chapter 1, the first 14 Mothers were mostly middle-aged housewives with no previous political experience.[26] When they could not find answers about what happened to their missing adult children, but instead found each other and discovered that they all had the same problem, they decided to act. But how could one make demands of a government that was terrorizing its own citizens? The first 14 mothers marched silently around the Plaza de Mayo because they did not know what else to do, what else to try, in order to get information on their missing children. Even when the movement began to grow, the Mothers had no clear political plan.

At first, their lack of experience bought them time: the Argentine military regime initially ridiculed or ignored the women, calling them *las locas de la Plaza de Mayo* (the crazy women of the Plaza de Mayo). They assumed that such politically naïve, middle-aged housewives would be completely ineffective. When this proved wrong, and the Mothers began to draw national and international attention to the disappearances, the military often arrested them. However, it was more difficult for the military to disappear the mothers as they had done with virtually all other protestors. First, the Mothers had become well known, and any mass disappearances of them would bring international consternation and closer scrutiny of government actions against the citizens of Argentina. Second, the Mothers represented the very traditional family values that the regime claimed to be upholding. They identified strongly with motherhood, had stayed out of politics, and were often deeply religious. It was almost impossible to label them as subversives. Although many of the mothers were arrested, some of them several times, threats and jailing did not scare them off. These women were not only torn apart by losing their adult children, but they defined themselves through their identities as mothers. Once their children were gone, there was nothing left to lose and they were beyond being able to be intimidated.

If the Mothers of the Plaza de Mayo at first lacked political experience, they proved to be adept at learning and utilizing their advantages relative to the regime. They began to wear white head scarves and to carry pictures of their disappeared children (and grandchildren – many grandmothers joined the group). These practices reinforced the power of their identities as traditional, moral mothers. They also did not allow conventional politics or party affiliations to play any part in their association. Matilde Mellibovsky wrote that "Preaching any ideology was something we did not allow. The only thing that moved us, always, has been the search for our children."[27] Although most of the first Mothers were working-class Catholic housewives, their members became more diverse as the association grew and included women from different class and religious backgrounds as well as from different political viewpoints. What they shared in common was the loss of their adult children to the military regime. The rest, they said, did not matter – and in the end it was a wise move to reject any standard political affiliation, because such a link would have targeted them for worse military harassment. The Mothers also refused to let men join their ranks, because that would make the association more vulnerable to violence and therefore less effective. Moreover, if the fathers were not formally involved, they could phone lawyers whenever the Mothers were arrested, facilitating their release.

The Mothers of the Plaza de Mayo continued to march in search of answers even after the military regime left power and democracy returned to Argentina.[28] They criticized President Raúl Alfonsín (1983–1989) for maintaining military and judicial officials in his government who had been involved in the Dirty War. The Mothers further rejected Alfonsín's heavy-handed rule, in which he often rushed bills through congress or ruled by decree. Alfonsín's government responded by going on the attack, maligning the Mothers for purportedly standing in the way of national unity and interests, and claiming they were puppets of leftist political forces. The Mothers' confrontations with the government were most intense regarding the trials of military officers who had been involved in carrying out the Dirty War. Although it was unprecedented in Latin America to hold the military accountable for such actions, the trials also marked a series of compromises between the military and Alfonsín's government, resulting in relatively light sentences for the accused. In December 1986, the government passed a law that would suspend trials of those who participated in the so-called war against subversion. Courts also took a stance of "no bodies, no homicide," requesting that the Mothers provide dental records of their children so that bodies could be identified before any trial was held.

The Alfonsín government both prolonged the Mothers' pain over the loss of their children and deepened their political commitment. Alfonsín's lenience, along with judges' refusal to hear cases, meant that the Mothers were unlikely to get the closure that they sought. They had already lost their children as well as any hope of ever having them back – even if just as bodies to bury. Alfonsín's actions left them convinced that they would also be denied justice for what was done to their children. Carmen Aguiar de Lapaco explained their tenacity by saying "Maybe the person who killed my daughter won't be judged in my daughter's case, but it's possible that he'll be judged in others'. And this, I believe, was worth our fight."[29] But the Mothers' criticisms and ongoing protests in the 1980s (and beyond) were more than an extension of their previous protests. With democratization, many Mothers began to think in terms of the legacy of their children's sacrificed lives. Gladys Castro de Lepiscopo captured this when she remarked that "I want to express my wish that my son, like so many others who have vanished, may have created an opening for a more just, more reflective, and more participatory society."[30] Though the Mothers began their quest out of the pain of losing their individual children, their experiences during and after the Dirty War broadened their understanding of their political task. Now they saw themselves as not only seeking answers about their individual children, but charged with the task of acting as mothers to all oppressed groups. To do so, they allied with a variety of grass roots movements and called for a more truly participatory and responsive democratic state.[31]

CoMadres in El Salvador

El Salvador was caught in the middle of a bloody civil war between leftist guerrillas and a government that backed elite interests. As in Argentina, state violence against citizens ran rampant and individuals were often targeted for their poverty or desire for social justice rather than any suspicion that they were leftist subversives. Although this situation brought Salvadoran mothers together to try to find their missing adult children, they had support and guidance from religious officials (at least initially) that the Argentine mothers did not. Central American civil wars and revolutionary struggles were greatly influenced by Liberation Theology, which emphasized that the Catholic Church had the responsibility to address problems of poverty and exploitation and act on behalf of the needs and dignity of the oppressed. Many priests and nuns in El Salvador became involved in poor urban and rural communities, trying to help them in a variety of ways and to defend them from government violence. Some priests even joined the guerrilla forces. Until 1977, however, the Church hierarchy in El Salvador remained closely allied with the elite and the state. When Oscar Romero became archbishop many Salvadorans expected that he would remain out of politics, but instead he used his position to try to help and protect ordinary Salvadorans.[32] In fact, Archbishop Oscar Romero was the one who helped to establish CoMadres (the Committee of Mothers and Relatives of the Prisoners, the Disappeared, and the Politically Assassinated of El Salvador, Monsignor Oscar Arnulfo Romero) as a group dedicated to a larger social struggle. Even after Romero's death by assassination in 1980, his legacy continued in this and other organizations.

In addition to external guidance in forming their group, CoMadres also differed from the Argentine Mothers in the makeup of their organization. Although most members and leaders were mothers, the group welcomed men as well as women, and it did not distinguish between those who had lost children versus those who had missing spouses, siblings, or other relatives. In 1984, CoMadres even began including mothers of fallen soldiers, particularly because so many soldiers were poor young men of the working or peasant classes who were forcibly recruited by the government. CoMadres leaders therefore saw these young men as "merely instruments of war, and when it is useful, they are assassinated."[33]

CoMadres members, similar to the Mothers in Argentina, expanded their sociopolitical roles over time. They not only sought justice for the disappeared, but they also brought food and clothing to men and women in prison, and they sought justice for the poor. One interesting difference in this expansion between the Argentine and Salvadoran groups is that, in El Salvador, many of the CoMadres willingly associate with feminism. As María Teresa Tula put it:

> "[W]e don't run around calling ourselves feminists, but we are feminists because we are fighting for our rights. The difference for us in El Salvador is that our struggle as women comes together with our struggle for change in El Salvador. Our feminism doesn't just involve fighting for ourselves, but for a change for all of us . . . We see all women as feminists, whether they are workers, peasants, or professionals. In El Salvador and other Latin American countries, there are big differences between bourgeois women who call themselves feminists, and other women. Sometimes we meet with these feminists, but all they do is talk, roaring like lions, but not doing anything."[34]

Instead of identifying feminism as opposed to or distinct from their goals, some of the CoMadres women redefined feminism, understanding it as the quest for all forms of equality and justice, and requiring specific social action rather than rhetoric or legal pressure only. It is not clear whether this difference from the Mothers of the Disappeared in Argentina stems from how the Salvadoran group defines itself with justice outside of a motherhood identity, or out of broader sociopolitical differences between the two countries. Both groups, however, began when women were transformed by losses that touched upon their most personal and supposedly traditional gender identities. It was because of their motherhood, rather than in spite of it, that Salvadoran and Argentine women found the strength and will to stand up politically to violent regimes.

Conservative women and the military in Chile

Not all women politicized by motherhood struggled against military regimes. Some women, particularly from middle and upper classes, politicized their motherhood in support of conservative military governments. One of the most important works on this subject is historian Margaret Power's study on right-wing women in Chile.[35] Conservative women's tactics focused around their identities as mothers and housewives, and they had a significant impact on politics in the 1960s and 1970s.

Chilean physician and leftist politician Salvador Allende seemed to have a good chance of winning the presidency in the 1964 elections. His opponent, Eduardo Frei of the moderate conservative Christian Democratic Party, sought to defeat Allende by focusing his campaign in two ways. First, he highlighted the positive aspects of what his own conservative agenda would bring to Chile; and second, his campaign suggested that voting for Allende would destroy democracy in Chile. Women in Frei campaign advertisements appeared consistently as mothers who warned that an Allende victory would threaten their children and undermine the foundations of their homes and families. One advertisement told Chilean women that "Today you have a great responsibility. Have you thought of the unity of your home? The future of your children? Your children's happiness? Remember that what you value most in life is in danger. And remember that the choice is Democracy or Marxism!"[36] Other ads suggested that Allende would destroy femininity and life as women and home makers knew it. Frei won the presidential election in 1964, and women's votes were essential to his victory – even 59% of working-class women voted for him. The Scare Campaign's manipulation of family, home, and motherhood was a contributing factor to Frei's success at winning women's votes, but was not the only reason. Perhaps just was important was the fact that Allende's own sexism tended to turn women voters away from him. Still, what one sees with the scare campaign, and with the rise of conservative women activists such as Elena Larraín Valdés earlier in the chapter, was an opening for conservatives – including those much more conservative than Frei – to manipulate traditional notions of motherhood to their political purposes.

Over the course of the 1960s, however, the Vatican's emphasis on social justice, combined with an upsurge in urban activism, meant that political right was losing popularity. Additionally, deeply conservative Chileans (like Larraín) were displeased with Frei's moderate and reformist policies. This paved the way for Allende's election to the presidency in 1970 as head of the Popular Unity party, a coalition of Socialists, Communists, Radicals, and Social Democrats. However, conservative women once again played an important role in opposing Allende once he rose to the presidency. The Popular Unity coalition sought to establish a mixed economy, and once in power they nationalized many resources, redistributed land, and expanded social services. Though popular with many Chileans, these reforms met with resistance from the Chilean elite and the US government, and many Chilean industrial owners resisted government measures, even when that meant a drop in their own profits. Additionally, government policies led to inflation that made rising wages less effective.

In this atmosphere – and in fact *before* the shortages of food and goods became widespread – a group of (mostly elite) conservative women organized the "March of the Empty Pots and Pans" in December 1971. Thousands of women demonstrated in the streets of Santiago, the nation's capital. They carried pots and pans to symbolize the supposed lack of food for their families under the Popular Unity government, and they claimed to be concerned primarily with the well-being of their families, especially their children. Like the Mothers who fought against military regimes elsewhere, the women demonstrators emphasized that they were apolitical and merely concerned with their children's health and futures. They effectively manipulated motherhood to give voice to the conservative opposition. The success of the march resulted not only from the demonstrators' actions and symbolic motherhood, but also from the government responses to the marchers. Oscar Weiss, director of the pro-government newspaper *La Nación* described the women demonstrators as a "parade of old women who can barely move and who brayed hysterically against the [poor]," and he suggested that the government should "send the old ladies with the pots and pans back to their houses with their tails between their legs."[37] Such insults did little to appease Chilean women, particularly because not long thereafter prices for food did indeed begin to rise rapidly.

Although the March of the Empty Pots and Pans did not bring down the Allende regime, it was certainly an important event that damaged the image of the Popular Unity government. Not all women joined the protest – even though the organizers claimed that women were there from all walks of life, the majority of protestors were women of considerable wealth. Their claims to represent the needs and views Chilean women more generally were, at best, greatly exaggerated. But the protest convinced conservative women that they could have a voice and an impact in the political sphere, even if they were housewives without much public experience. Many of these wealthy women who opposed Allende were also strong supporters of Pinochet's regime, even though it was one that led to the arrest of tens of thousands of Chileans and the deaths of a few thousand. They bought into the notion that Pinochet had to protect Chileans from communist subversion in order to establish order and prosperity – and to uphold traditional Catholic and family values.

Women, Motherhood, and Politics in the Shift to the Twenty-First Century

In some parts of the world women have had to shed their identification with motherhood and the home in order to enter politics at the national level. In Latin America motherhood has sometimes been a stepping stone to political activism, sometimes even to political power. Eva Perón and Violeta Chamorro used motherhood images to fuel their political ambitions and agendas. Similarly, the Mothers of the Disappeared in Argentina or Chilean opponents to Allende used their identities as mothers, and the symbolic power of motherhood, to impact politics, albeit in very different ways.For other women, the association between womanhood and motherhood has been a challenge to their political aspirations or commitments. In addition to indigenous women like Rigoberta Menchú or Nina Pacari who chose to forego (or postpone) motherhood in order to focus on political struggles, other women have also experienced motherhood as a barrier to political aspirations. Most Latin American women who achieve national political power – as presidents, or legislators, or cabinet ministers – are typically either childless or old enough that their children are grown and out of the house. The association of women with motherhood and the home can also make women politicians vulnerable to criticism – in addition to being judged for their clothes and hairstyles, women politicians also face opponents who think they should "go back to the kitchen" where they belong.[38]

There was no single, definitive connection between motherhood and political power in Latin America during the mid- to late twentieth century. Nor did women in Latin America necessarily see their interests as being best represented by middle-class feminisms, even if they shared feminists' desire to eradicate gender inequalities. For both better and worse, motherhood remained tightly interwoven into the politics of gender and the gendering of politics in late twentieth-century Latin America.

Document: Matilde Saidler de Mellibovsky Remembers Her Daughter, Graciela Mellibovsky, Abducted September 25, 1976 (29 Years Old)[39]

In the excerpt below, Matilde Mellibovsky described her daughter, Graciela (whom she often refers to as "Gra"). Graciela had become an active political opponent of the political regime, and worked on behalf of the poor. Her mother was one of the early members of the Mothers of the Plaza de Mayo. Mellibovsky is also author of *Circle of Love Over Death*, in which she discussed the history of the Mothers of the Plaza de Mayo in Argentina, and collected Mothers' remembrances of their children. Her own recollection of her daughter is the last to appear in the book. Though Mellibovsky described her daughter's disappearance and the impact this had on her, the selection here is her description of her daughter and what she remembers about her. What does such a description, that does not mention the horrors of the Dirty War directly, show about how and why state terrorism politicized mothers in Argentina?

Remembering Gra

What is Graciela like? What is Graciela like physically, what was her character like? In my dreams, in my frequent dreams, I reexperience Graciela, but it is remarkable, it's not always the same face, nor is she the same age, nor is her frame of mind always the same. I reexperience Graciela's numerous faces, sometimes the very distinctive smile she had when she agreed to something, another time her smile of amusement, another her face of disgust. Graciela had many aspects, like everybody. She had many moods, and she passed rapidly from a happy to a sad mood. Some moments spent together were really so amusing that I will never forget them. We didn't have to invent games during our short moments together, because, anyway, we couldn't spend much time together.

But Graciela also had some moments of great impatience. We would start chatting in a very lively way, and all of a sudden Gra would look at her watch and become impatient, hysterical, and bam – the conversation was over, but just like that! – with a slam of the door, "Bye" . . . and we both would dash off.

I don't want to idealize Gra as if she were a perfect human being. I want to remember her with all her faults and weaknesses, because that's the way we loved her. She was totally obsessive about her work, really obsessive. When she was studying she was obsessive, not for the grade, but for the fulfillment of her task. And when she committed herself to something, it was exactly the same.

And there were other quite negative things about her, but in general, Gra was fun. I remember that she was very jealous, and that she suffered because of that. Maybe she was excessively jealous of the people she loved, of her friends. She deeply loved her grandmothers: I would go as far as to say they were her weakness. If I complained about my mother, she would become annoyed and say: "Careful, don't speak ill of my grandmother." And if I made a comment about my mother-in-law, she would say: "She's your mother-in-law, but don't forget, she's my grandmother." She adored them. I think it's curious how many things they passed on to her. Well, she liked children a lot, babies, the children she never managed to have. She used to play with them, playing as if she were one of them, having a lot of fun, enjoying herself in their company.

[. . .]

When Gra came into the house, everything would light up. Each wall and each object took on meaning. The whole house would seem to sway as if it were a house of cards. Everything acquired energy, life, and noise. Noise above all: "I've lost a notebook! Mom, help me with the curler for my hair! Just leave the phone alone, it's for me! Turn on the oven, I've learnt to make the cheapest dessert! Look at the shirt I bought for my brother! Are you going by the post office?"

Because she was always in such a hurry, she drew two large ears with a black marker on the side of the electric intercom to the building's entryway . . . why? "So that you can hear it faster!" From this I acquired the mania of writing on the walls . . . drawing . . . I drew her image, and now I write things, things that only I can understand. It is one of my ways of being with Gra . . . And toward the end when she was going out, when we would start quarreling. Ah, if I only could quarrel a little bit with her now, just a little bit!

"Where's my beige coat?" I asked her, making fun of her before she had the chance, because I knew her answer beforehand: "I needed it. Look mom, you have three coats, you won't be any colder outside because you are missing one . . ." I'd complain: "Then why didn't you take the oldest one?" "Well, I the one I took was the nicest and looks better on the person I gave it to. She needs to be presentable for the new job she got . . ."

I've never managed to do it – never managed to remember the horrible night of the abduction without evoking Graciela within myself, her personality – without ceasing to hear her voice. It doesn't matter how much time goes by, when I remember that day's events, I inevitably hear Graciela speaking. The two of us have told this story together. And what's more; even now we continue to disregard and interrupt each other . . .

Notes

1   Elisabeth Burgos-Debray and Rigoberta Menchú, *I . . . Rigoberta Menchu: An Indian Woman in Guatemala*. Trans. Ann Wright (London: Verso, 1984), p. 224.

2   Margaret Power, *Right Wing Women in Chile: Feminine Power and the Struggle Against Allende, 1964–1973* (University Park: Pennsylvania State Press, 2002), pp. 75–81.

3   "Doña Doralisa, una mujer fecunda," *Perfil* (n.d.). Thanks to Margaret Power for sharing this document with me.

4   See June E. Hahner, *Women in Latin American History: Their Lives and Views* (Los Angeles: UCLA Latin American Center Publications, 1976), p. 90.

5   For biographical information on Eva Perón, see Nicholas Frasier and Marysa Navarro, *Evita: The Real Life of Eva Perón* (New York: W.W. Norton, 1996). For a shorter piece that focuses on Eva Perón's importance within Peronism, see Marysa Navarro, "Juan and Eva Perón: A Family Portrait," in John Charles Chasteen and Joseph S. Tulchin, eds, *Problems of Modern Latin American History: A Reader* (Wilmington: SR Books, 1994), pp. 103–113.

6   Eva Perón, *My Mission in Life* (New York: Vantage Press, 1953), pp. 211–212.

7   Daniel James, *Doña María's Story: Life, History, Memory, and Political Identity* (Durham, NC: Duke University Press, 2000), pp. 76–77.

8   See *My Mission in Life*, pp. 191–194.

9   *My Mission in Life*, pp. 185–186.

10 Natalia Milanesio, "'The Guardian Angels of the Domestic Economy': Housewives' Responsible Consumption in Peronist Argentina," *Journal of Women's History* 18:3 (2006): 91–117.

11 My discussion here of Violeta Chamorro is influenced greatly by the work of Karen Kampwirth and, in particular, her essays: "The Mother of the Nicaraguans: Doña Violeta and the UNO's Gender Agenda," in Jennifer Abbassi and Sheryl L. Lutjens, eds, *Rereading Women in Latin America and the Caribbean: the Political Economy of Gender* (New York: Rowman & Littlefield Publishers, 2002), pp. 179–196; and "Gender Politics in Nicaragua: Feminism, Antifeminism, and the Return of Daniel Ortega," in Elizabeth Maier and Nathalie Lebon, eds, *Women's Activism in Latin America and the Caribbean: Engendering Social Justice, Democratizing Citizenship* (New Brunswick, NH: Rutgers University Press, 2010), pp. 111–126.

12 This quote was cited in Lorraine Bayard de Volo, *Mothers of Heroes and Martyrs: Gender Identity and Politics in Nicaragua, 1979–1999* (Baltimore, MD: Johns Hopkins University Press, 2001), p. 1.

13 Ninoska Robles de Jarquín, Nicaraguan Institute for Research on Women, quoted in Karen Kampwirth, "The Mother of the Nicaraguans," p. 179.

14 Bayard de Volo, pp. 157–158.

15 Kampwirth, "The Mothers of the Nicaraguans," pp. 184–185.

16 Kampwirth, "Gender Politics in Nicaragua," p. 121.

17 Bayard de Volo, pp. 175–176.

18 The particular nature of indigenous activists' political, economic, and cultural demands is complex, and the scholarship on these movements is vast. Anyone interested in such topics could start by consulting a few of the interesting comparative books on the topic, such as Kay B. Warren and Jean E. Jackson, eds, *Indigenous Movements, Self-Representation, and the State in Latin America* (Austin: University of Texas Press, 2002); A. Kim Clark and Marc Becker, eds, *Highland Indians and the State in Modern Ecuador* (Pittsburgh, PA: University of Pittsburgh Press, 2007); Deborah Yashar, *Contesting Citizenship in Latin America: The Rise of Indigenous Movements and the Postliberal Challenge* (New York: Cambridge University Press, 2005); Nancy Grey Postero and Leon Zamosc, eds, *The Struggle for Indigenous Rights in Latin America* (Brighton: Sussex Academic Press, 2004).

19 Biographical information for Dolores Cacuango is, as of this writing, available only in Spanish. See books by Raquel Rodas Morales, in particular: *Crónica de un sueño: Las escuelas indígenas de Dolores Cacuango* (Quito: Proyecto EBI-GTZ, 1998); *Dolores Cacuango* (Quito: Proyecto EBI-GTZ, 1998); and *Dolores Cacuango: Gran líder del pueblo indio* (Quito: Banco Central del Ecuador, 2005).

20 For information on the alliances between indigenous activists and the Ecuadorian Communist Party, see Marc Becker, *Indians and Leftists in the Making of Ecuador's Modern Indigenous Movements* (Durham, NC: Duke University Press, 2008).

21 I have discussed Cacuango in these terms previously in Erin O'Connor, *Gender, Indian, Nation: The Contradictions of Making Ecuador, 1830–1925* (Tucson: University of Arizona Press, 2007), pp. 195–199.

22 Domitila Barrios de Chungara with Moema Viezzer. Trans. Victoria Ortiz, *Let Me Speak! Testimony of Domitila, a Woman of the Bolivian Mines* (New York: Monthly Review Press, 1978), p. 71.

23 Barrios de Chungara, pp. 147–157. Barrios de Chungara was not certain if her baby was stillborn or died shortly after birth, because she was traumatized and fainted several times.

24 For examples from Ecuador, see Mujeres de CONAIE, *Memorias de las jornadas del foro de la mujer indígena del Ecuador* (Quito: CONAIE-UNFPA, 1994), pp. 2–4, 95, 103; and Emma Cervone, "Engendering Leadership: Indigenous Women Leaders in the Ecuadorian Andes," in Rosario Montoya, Lessie Jo Frazier, and Janise Hurtig, eds, *Gender's Place: Feminist*

Anthropologies of Latin America (New York: Palgrave MacMillan, 2002), pp. 179–196. I have described this issue previously in *Gender, Indian, Nation*, pp. xi–xv.

25 Burgos-Debray and Menchú Tum, p. 223.

26 There are many good books and articles on the Mothers of the Disappeared in Argentina. Among those that I found the most useful for this chapter were: Marguerite Guzmán Bouvard, *Revolutionizing Motherhood: The Mothers of the Plaza de Mayo* (Wilmington, DE: SR Books, 1994); Matilde Mellibovsky, ed., *Circle of Love Over Death: Testimonies of the Mothers of the Plaza de Mayo* (Willimantic, CT: Curbstone Press, 1997); Jo Fisher, *Mothers of the Disappeared* (Boston: South End Press, 1989); Marysa Navarro, "The Personal is Political: Las Madres de Plaza de Mayo," in Susan Eckstein, ed., *Power and Popular Protest: Latin American Social Movements* (Berkeley: University of California Press, 2001), pp. 241–258; Graciela Di Marco, "The Mothers and Grandmothers of the Plaza de Mayo Speak," in Elizabeth Maier and Nathalie Lebon, eds, *Women's Activism in Latin America and the Caribbean: Engendering Social Justice, Democratizing Citizenship*,(New Brunswick, NJ: Rutgers University Press, 2010), pp. 95–110.

27 Mellibovsky, p. 101.

28 My discussion of the conflicts between the Mothers and the Alfonsín government comes from Guzmán Bouvard, pp. 154–166.

29 Mellibovsky, p. 151.

30 Mellibovsky, p. 157.

31 Guzmán Bouvard, pp. 185, 199.

32 The literature on Liberation Theology is extensive. For some classic sources, see Gustavo Gutiérrez, *A Theology of Liberation: History, Politics, and Salvation* (Maryknoll, NY: Orbis Books, 1988), or Phillip Berryman, *Liberation Theology* (Philadelphia: Temple University Press, 1987). For some of Romero's sermons and ideas, see Oscar Romero, *The Violence of Love*. Trans. James R. Brockman (Maryknoll, NY: Orbis Books, 2004).

33 María Teresa Tula, *Hear My Testimony: Maria Teresa Tula, Human Rights Activist of El Salvador*. Ed. and trans. Lynn Stephen (Boston: South End Press, 1994), p. 35.

34 Tula, p. 125.

35 See Power, *Right Wing Women in Chile*. My discussion of Chile here is also influence by her essay "Defending Dictatorship: Conservative Women in Pinochet's Chile and the 1988 Plebiscite," and by Lisa Baldez, "Nonpartisanship as a Political Strategy: women Left, Right, and Center in Chile," both in Victoria González and Karen Kampwirth, eds, *Radical Women in Latin America, Left and Right*, (University Park: Pennsylvania State University Press, 2001), pp. 299–324 and 273–298, respectively.

36 Power, *Right Wing Women*, p. 81.

37   Power, *Right Wing Women*, pp. 159–160.
38   A good example of this appears in Karin Rosemblatt, "Verónica Michelle Bachelet Jeria: A Woman President," in Erin E. O'Connor and Leo J. Garofalo, eds, *Documenting Latin America, Volume 2: Gender, Race, and Nation* (New York: Pearson, 2011), particularly p. 263.
39   Mellibovsky, pp. 238–241.

9

Bodies, Policies, and Globalization

Contraception and Abortion in Latin America

Gabriela's Story

"Gabriela" a 37-year-old divorced woman living in Quito, Ecuador, had two children, ages 18 and 9. When she was raped, she decided not to report the crime to the police, because gossip got around her neighborhood spread fast and her neighbors were skeptical about the reputation of women who claimed they were raped. Shortly thereafter, Gabriela realized that she was pregnant, and she did not think that she could manage to raise a third child on her own. She obtained pills to insert in her vagina to induce abortion, but the pills did not complete the process, and she had to go to a local hospital for treatment. When Gabriela arrived at the hospital, the staff were quick to point out to her that she had committed an illegal act for which she could go to jail. Then she was made to wait a long time without any explanation, visitors, or telephone before doctors treated her. Once the procedure was completed, doctors forced her to look at the expelled fetus. She was then put in a recovery room along with women who had just given birth – women who had somehow found out that she had chosen to abort a fetus and literally turned their backs on her. When the ordeal was over, Gabriela kept the fact of her abortion to herself, afraid that others would judge her harshly if she told them about it.[1]

Mothers Making Latin America: Gender, Households, and Politics Since 1825,
First Edition. Erin E. O'Connor.
© 2014 John Wiley & Sons, Inc. Published 2014 by John Wiley & Sons, Inc.

Gabriela's experience was not unique in Quito, and probably not different from the experience of many women like her throughout most of Latin America. During her fieldwork at a Quito hospital, María Rosa Cevallos found that women who had attempted to abort pregnancies were consistently shamed. Cevallos describes hospital staff as both complicit with and punishing of women who came to the hospital because of incomplete or botched abortions. On the one hand, the staff saw it as their job to attend to the health of all patients, including women whom they suspected of inducing abortions (the women in question never admitted to having gotten or tried to cause an abortion). Moreover, they did not report their suspicions to the authorities, even though abortion is illegal in Ecuador except in cases when a pregnancy threatens the mother's life, or when an insane or retarded woman becomes pregnant after being raped. On the other hand, staff made sure that women who tried to abort knew that they disapproved of this choice, and that they thought of them as bad women. One doctor told Cevallos that women suspected of aborting were given low doses of pain medication "because it's another form of punishment, so that she hurts, so that she hurts physically and in her soul, and won't do it again."[2] Although unwilling to report women suspected of intentionally aborting to the police authorities, Ecuadorian obstetrical staffs had other ways to ensure that women who aborted paid for their actions, specifically for their rejection of motherhood.

Like Gabriela, other Ecuadorian women who attempted to abort experienced shame, silencing, and fear at every turn. Cevallos notes that the treatment of these women has to do not just with Ecuadorian law, but also with the medical staff's own social (and sometimes religious) views. Even with dropping fertility rates in recent years, motherhood is still highly valued in Ecuadorian society, and many people continue to associate it as the most important part of a woman's identity and responsibility in life. Hospital staff, in fact, ignore two aspects of Ecuadorian law in their reactions to women who enter the hospital after attempting (or being suspected of attempting) abortions. As already stated, the staff treat women without reporting them to police authorities, thus ignoring Ecuadorian law making abortion illegal. Yet at the same time, staff usually use methods to extract the fetus that are both more invasive and more painful than those called for by the Ecuadorian Minister of Public

Health for circumstances in which a woman is in the process of losing a pregnancy.[3] Their choice of more invasive methods is made for moral rather than medical reasons.

Gabriela's story is from 2010, but similar practices and contradictions have been occurring for decades in Ecuador. Nor is Ecuador unique in Latin America, where abortion is illegal in virtually the entire region (except in Cuba, and in some individual regions such as Mexico City). At the same time, abortion rates are higher in Latin America than in any other part of the world (approximately 32 per thousand), and it is the fourth most common birth control method in the region. Abortion has, in the words of one scholarly study, become a "clandestine epidemic" among Latin American women.[4] The policies, contradictions, and dangers surrounding abortion are intricately intertwined with broader debates and concerns over reproduction and motherhood more generally. In Latin America, as in the United States and Europe, reproductive issues – particularly abortion – are sometimes quite controversial. Political scientist Mala Htun points out that abortion is an "absolutist" issue on which all members of the population have an opinion and feel able to speak, making it a tremendously volatile political issue, difficult to resolve.[5]

This chapter aims to historicize reproductive debates in Latin America, identifying historical events and problems that have shaped social, medical, and religious discourses and policies over family planning. Contradictions abound in the history of reproductive rights. Though one might expect left-leaning politicians, because of their claims to advance gender equality, to support family planning wholeheartedly, leftist leaders sometimes banned contraception or abortion for women in their countries. Similarly, although the Catholic Church hierarchy has taken a clear stand against contraception and abortion, it has not always been able to influence laws, and some Latin American Catholics are advocates of contraception. Moreover, although both supporters and opponents of family planning and abortion rights discuss "women" as a unified category, in fact, class-based factors have played a significant role in determining individual women's access to reproductive technologies. The debates and problems surrounding family planning and abortion issues are interwoven with other social, economic, and political histories in Latin America. They engage not only broad-based or abstract gender discourses, but they also intersect with how individual men and women "live gender" in their daily lives.

Contraceptives and abortion issues were not simply concerns that remained local, or even national. International Catholic and feminist organizations had (and have) an interest in how these play out in Latin America, and pharmaceutical companies often profit from contraceptive experiments performed on Latin American women (and sometimes men). Since the 1970s, organizations, such as the United Nations (UN) and the World Health Organization (WHO), have played roles in tracking and making suggestions regarding reproductive rights throughout the world. Despite the influence of powerful national and international concerns, however, reproductive rights issues remain tense and unresolved throughout most of Latin America. In many countries, laws criminalizing abortion were made even stricter around the close of the twentieth century.

Historical and Technical Foundations for Reproductive Politics in Latin America

The first important phase of birth control modernization in Latin America occurred in the 1920s–1940s. As industrialization and urbanization changed patterns of life and work, it became particularly difficult for working-class women to handle large families. Not only did they often lack the economic resources to care for many children, but most of them had jobs where they could not bring children to work with them. Unless relatives were available (and many migrant women were without strong family support in cities), poor mothers either had to leave babies in the care of older children or spend much-needed household money to have someone else tend to young children (See Chapter 6). But it was not only working-class women who were increasingly interested in limiting family size. Historian Susan Besse notes that "In practice . . . the new urban style of life and the high standards of child rearing made it impractical for women to continue to raise large families."[6] New emphasis on quality mothering thus led women to concern themselves with limiting the number of children they raised. In Chile, working-class women often sought to limit family size in order to create more free time for them to participate in political matters. Yet because few reliable birth control methods were available before the 1950s, and men habitually refused to wear condoms, controlling family size often meant secretly getting an abortion, which Chilean working-class women often alluded to as "going to the butcher's."[7]

Responses to rising use of birth control and abortion were mixed in the early to mid-twentieth century. Given that they were already vulnerable to criticisms that they were immoral or unfeminine, feminists did not typically address sex or birth control issues directly. They did, however, sometimes discuss the extensive burdens that large families placed on women, thus indirectly critiquing the dominant gender norms that identified good motherhood with a large brood.[8] Medical doctors were divided on how they interpreted the changing fertility practices, and the policies they proposed also varied. Although some doctors viewed women who used birth control or got abortions as unnatural women who should be punished, others were more nuanced in their approach. Some had sympathy for working-class women's dilemma of either aborting a pregnancy or losing their jobs, and advocated better support and birth control to help them manage their families and work. Many doctors were increasingly concerned with the rising number of health complications (and deaths) for women who had illegal abortions; for them, the problem was a public health concern.[9] Most politicians of the time were critical of women who got abortions, and continued to promote *natalism* – identifying women primarily as mothers and encouraging them to have children – rather than controlled family growth. Even socialist leaders had a split reaction to birth control and abortion, with some advocating birth control and abortion as a means to liberate working-class women from the double burden of work and family responsibilities, while others were staunch opponents to all forms of family planning.

Abortion had been illegal since the first law codes of the nineteenth-century republics, though it was rarely punished in practice. In the 1920s and 1930s, many criminal codes were amended to tighten laws and increase penalties. The 1922 Argentine criminal code, for example, identified abortion as a "crime against life," and stated that women who had abortions, and anyone who performed them, could be punished with one to four years imprisonment. Any practitioner who performed an abortion against a woman's consent faced 3–10 years in prison. Abortions in cases where the pregnancy endangered the life or health of the mother, or resulted from rape, were made legal. Similar codes passed in Brazil, Mexico, Uruguay, and Cuba based on the Argentine model. Legalization of so-called therapeutic abortions to protect the life and health of the mother were quite forward-thinking in this period, putting Latin America on the cutting edge of reproductive rights at the time.[10]

Further complicating matters was the modernization of birth control and abortion techniques, a process which began in the nineteenth century and culminated with the availability of a reliable birth control pill in the 1960s. The discovery of rubber in the nineteenth century made some long-standing birth control devices, like the condom and diaphragm, more effective. Scientists also experimented with new versions of spermicidal jellies and foams, though these were not very effective, and there was up to a 70% rate of pregnancy for women who used them. In the twentieth century, new and more reliable birth control methods became available in the form of intrauterine devices (IUDs) and birth control pills. The IUD, invented in Germany in the 1930s, was further developed and regularly used in the United States by the 1950s. At the same time that IUDs first appeared, scientists seeking hormonal treatments to alleviate menstrual disorders and treat menopausal or infertile women found that the hormones often had the effect of inhibiting ovulation.[11] For a variety of reasons, some of which are explored later in the chapter, this discovery led to the development of birth control pills in the 1950s, with their availability becoming widespread in the United States and western Europe in the 1960s.

Forms of induced abortion (versus spontaneous abortion, or miscarriage) have been available since ancient times, but often these were ineffective or dangerous. By the nineteenth century, more reliable methods were available, but social and religious resistance to abortion meant that the doctors who were able perform the procedure safely typically refused to do so. This gradually changed, and by the mid- to late twentieth century, many western countries began to legalize abortion. However, abortion remained illegal in most or all cases in many parts of the world, including Latin America. Abortions performed in hospitals and clinics have typically proven safe for women, whereas clandestine abortions often are not. Even in countries where it is legal, abortion is often a deeply divisive social and religious issue. In Latin America, the conflicts and problems have been made even more intense by the high rate of illegal and unsafe abortions that take place.

A Problem of Population?

On the surface, population statistics often appear straightforward. However, interpretations of population counts are fraught with class, race, political, and international agendas. In some Latin American countries, notably Bolivia and Chile, government officials in the 1920s and 1930s were deeply concerned with what they viewed as a problem of under-population in their countries. They developed public health policies and institutions in order to lower infant mortality rates and to promote healthy pregnancies. They worried that low birth rates – particularly among middle-class women whom they saw as ideal mothers – would leave their nations weak and backwards. Between the 1930s and 1960s, international attitudes about population shifted, and in particular officials in the United States became increasingly troubled by supposed overpopulation in poor areas of the world, including Latin America.

What led to this shift in thinking? Why did international officials consider Latin America overpopulated rather than underpopulated? In Puerto Rico, the concern emerged early, largely because Puerto Rico had (and as of this writing still has) the distinction of being a commonwealth of the United States. Commonwealth status means that Puerto Ricans are US citizens and have the right to vote and move freely in all US territory, but they have no voting representatives in congress. Maintaining Puerto Rico in this secondary status relative to US states posed a challenge for US government officials who wanted to uphold the myth that the United States was anti-imperialist. To smooth over the seeming contradictions between US democratic rhetoric and imperialist practice, US officials emphasized that whenever they intervened in other world regions, they aimed to improve and democratize conditions they found. As historian Laura Briggs notes, "The U.S. has understood itself as bringing public health, science, technology, and improvements to the status of women on the island." US officials first claimed that industrialization would eradicate poverty in Puerto Rico. When that did not work, they decided that overpopulation was the cause of poverty. It was not the inequalities of colonialism or global capitalism that lay at the root of the problem, US experts claimed, but rather Puerto Ricans' inability to limit the size of their families. This claim was erroneous. It could not explain wide-spread hunger in Puerto Rico in the 1920s, and it did not take into account that Puerto Ricans' per capita income was rising faster than population growth in the 1940s. In addition to the flawed logic in declar-ing Puerto Rico overpopulated, US policy in Puerto Rico did little to advance family planning in any reliable way. When Puerto Ricans opened clinics in the 1930s, they quickly closed for lack of funding, and when US mainlanders provided birth control, it was typically in the form of cheaper (and mostly ineffective) spermicidal jellies and creams rather than the more effective diaphragm.[12]

If US overpopulation arguments about Puerto Rico did not reflect realities on the island, they did dovetail neatly with US eugenics ideas of the early to mid twentieth century. Eugenicists' goal was to encourage middle- and upper-class whites to have more children in order to improve the race and to discourage the poor, nonwhites, or the disabled (or diseased) from reproducing. Given that many US officials saw Puerto Rico as "colored," it was not a far stretch to suggest that their rates of reproduction needed to be reduced; after all, eugenics was widely accepted good science at the time. This was clear when Puerto Rico's governor, (mainlander) James Beverly claimed in 1933 that:

> I have always believed that some method of restricting the birth rate among the lower and more ignorant elements of the population is the only salvation for the island. The tragedy of the situation is that the more intelligent classes voluntarily restrict their birth rate, while the most vicious, most ignorant, and most helpless and hopeless part of the population multiplies with tremendous rapidity.

While Beverly's statements here were made in terms of class, he and other mainland US officials' discussions of class were bound inextricably with race, particularly because miscegenation, abhorrent to eugenics advocates in the mainland United States, was common on the island.[13]

This tendency to blame poverty on overpopulation continued to spread in the 1950s and 1960s in response to Cold War fears and goals. During the Cold War, US government officials feared the spread of Communism, particularly in areas of the world with large, poor populations whom they thought could be easily swayed to act violently in order to overthrow their rulers. Historian Heidi Tinsman noted that the fear was not just of a worldwide Soviet takeover, but also that poor people in the so-called Third World would succumb to violent revolution. US officials convinced themselves that the answer to the threat of violence from the poor lay not in addressing the structural problems of poverty, but rather in reducing the population of poor, politically volatile groups.[14]

In some cases US-sponsored projects to curb population growth in poor countries coincided with Latin American governments' own agendas. A good example came from Chile, where central state politicians collaborated with US organizations (especially the Rockefeller Foundation) to reverse population growth. Some Chilean officials shared

US views that slowing population growth would alleviate poverty, likely because they, like US officials, were disinclined to address the structural problems that were the root causes of widespread poverty in Chile. Other Chilean officials were not convinced that population control was the answer to poverty, but the US family planning agenda included prenatal and postnatal care for mothers and babies that promised to address high infant and maternal mortality rates, which greatly concerned them. It was during Eduardo Frei Montalvo's conservative presidency from 1964 to 1970 that family planning and birth control expanded in Chile, marking the first time that the Chilean poor had birth control readily available to them. For many Chilean women, the fact that family planning derived from Cold War fears was perhaps less relevant than the cheap and ready supply of birth control options when they wanted them. Although Chile was (and remains) a deeply Catholic country, religion did not appear to determine whether or not a woman sought birth control.

In Puerto Rico, where the discourse on overpopulation dated back to the 1920s and 1930s, the emphasis shifted from overtly eugenic claims to Cold War emphases on population and political stability. There were, however, few effective and affordable forms of birth control, and as a result many poor women chose sterilization as a means of controlling the size of their families. Although mainland-based feminists argued that there was a policy of forced sterilization between the 1940s and 1970s in Puerto Rico, historian Laura Briggs argues that despite very high rates of sterilization, she could find little evidence of consistent or effective force over the decades. She did acknowledge that some hospital staff pressured women into sterilization. This was the case at Presbyterian Hospital in San Juan, which in 1947 developed a policy refusing to let women who were having a fourth baby to deliver there unless they agreed to sterilization. She also noted that there were a number of US mainland officials who were interested in spreading sterilization policies. However, few women delivered babies in hospitals, and funding for sterilization was limited. Therefore, while she did find evidence that women factory workers faced pressure to get sterilized in order to keep their jobs in the late 1960s and early 1970s, Briggs did not find sufficient proof of widespread, long-term pressure or forced sterilizations. What, then, fueled mainland feminist claims about sterilization in Puerto Rico? The answer is twofold. First, mainland feminists picked up on how some Puerto Rican (mostly male) nationalists identified sterilization as a virtually genocidal policy that was forced on Puerto Rican women from the mainland. Second, feminists were particularly sensitive to issues such as sterilization and forced birth control due to their experiences on the US mainland, where there were state officials who tried to force women on welfare to go on birth control, and there was a history of forced sterilization for peoples deemed "unfit."[15]

Rather than being a private concern for a woman about how and when to have a family, reproduction became a national and global concern. Although both advocates and adversaries of birth control and sterilization often meant well, most (though not all) of them were disinclined to let Latin American women decide for themselves about what was in their best interests with regard to reproduction. Instead, their reproductive destinies were in the hands of national or international government officials and doctors, and it was outsiders who debated their well-being. Moreover, while government and international officials touted that birth control would solve problems of poverty, more middle-class than poor women benefited from family planning clinics.[16] Thus, not only did discourses and policies on overpopulation fail to take poor women's own experiences and viewpoints into account, but they often fell short of making a significant difference in the lives of the women who were the target groups for these policies.

Population and Reproduction as International and Class Conflicts

If one finds a consistent message on Latin American overpopulation emanating from the United States and western Europe in the mid- to late twentieth century, reactions to birth control and population issues within Latin America were more mixed. As with international discourses, reproductive debates and practices within Latin America were fraught with class and race contradictions. In particular, many Latin American government and intellectual leaders claimed to speak for the poor with regard to reproduction, just as international authorities did.

Catholic Church officials were often split in their reactions to birth control initiatives. Although most members of the Church hierarchy ardently opposed birth control, some priests who worked in poor urban neighborhoods were less certain that birth control was a bad thing altogether, because they saw how difficult it was for poor parents to provide for large families. Furthermore, not only have many deeply Catholic women chosen to go on birth control in Latin America, but there is also a group of Latin American Catholics for the Right to Decide (*Católicas por el Derecho a Decidir en América Latina*, or CDD). This group, while inspired by a US Catholic feminist pro-choice group, seeks to address the particular problems and challenges women in Latin America encounter with regards to family planning. Through their journal *Conciencia Latinoamericana*, as well as through campaigns, the CDD has sought to make birth control available, as well as working to decriminalize abortion.[17]

Some leftist and nationalist leaders of the 1960s and 1970s opposed birth control as an imperialist plot aimed at weakening Latin American peoples. Groups of Puerto Rican nationalists, along with the Roman Catholic hierarchy on the island, argued that widespread sterilization was a genocidal policy instigated on the mainland. In Chile, leftist leader Salvador Allende staunchly opposed US-funded birth control. He framed this as a defense of the Chilean people when he became president in 1970, writing to US population council that "I am a medical doctor, I know the problem of large families, and believe that to decide about the size of the family is a human right, and being the President of a poor country I need to help make it a reality."[18] Although Allende identified himself as working on behalf of poor women, in practice, his administration typically reinforced traditional gender norms.

Similarly, when Bolivian leftist activist Domitila Barrios de Chungara went to the 1975 International Women's Year Tribunal in Mexico City, she was critical of western- and middle-class style feminist ideas:

> the women who defended prostitution, birth control, and all those things, wanted to impose their ideas as basic problems to be discussed in the Tribunal. For us [poor Latin American women attending the Tribunal] they were real problems, but not the main ones.
>
> For example, when they spoke of birth control, they said that we shouldn't have so many children living in such poverty, because we didn't have enough to feed them. And they wanted to see birth control as something which would solve all the problems of humanity and malnutrition.
>
> But, in reality, birth control, as those women presented it, can't be applied in my country. There are so few Bolivians by now that if we limited birth even more, Bolivia would end up without people. And then the wealth of our country would remain as a gift for those who want to control us completely, no? It's not that we ought to be living like we are, in miserable conditions. All that could be different, because Bolivia's a country

with lots of natural resources. But our government prefers to see things their way, to justify the low level of life of the Bolivian people and the very low wages it pays the workers. And so they resort to indiscriminate birth control.[19]

Barrios de Chungara's views were shared by many poor, especially indigenous, women in Latin America. Due to the histories of negative consequences from outside intervention – from losing land in the nineteenth century through problems with pesticides in the Green Revolution to general policies of oppression – indigenous peoples in the countryside are often wary of outsiders. Making matters worse, most staff members who provide birth control to indigenous peoples of the countryside are non-Indians who often fail to listen to indigenous voices in the decision-making processes regarding the establishment of family planning clinics. The result is at best indigenous ambivalence, and at worst open resistance, toward family planning initiatives. It is not that all indigenous women are disinterested in birth control. Many of them would like to space their children a few years apart, and they recognize the difficulties of raising large families. However, there are many rumors and myths that they first need to work through with health care workers, and many of them have understandable concerns about possible side effects of birth control. The challenge for many well-intentioned health care workers will be to do a better job of working with, rather than simply for, indigenous dwellers in the countryside with regard to family planning.[20]

Over time, fertility rates in Latin American have gone down, mostly in urban rather than rural areas. Yet this process has occurred differently in Latin America than in many other world regions, most notably with regard to the United States and western Europe. For one thing, although fertility rates are down, Latin American women's desire for birth control still surpasses the availability of contraception. More significantly, Latin American women choose different ways to limit family size than their US or European counterparts. First, whereas many women in the United States or Europe limit family size by postponing marriage or childbirth, Latin American women have often tended to have children relatively young (between 20 and 24 years), and adopt methods later to keep their families from getting any larger. What might at first glance look like Latin Americans "don't use birth control as often as US or European women do" looks rather different if one pays attention to global variations with birth control. For example, IUD use is lower in Latin America than in Europe, but higher than in the United States, and use of the pill is almost as high in Latin America as in the United States. There is also a higher use of so-called traditional methods, such as the rhythm or withdrawal methods, in *Europe* than in Latin America.[21] Moving beyond grand claims about birth control and examining particular practices breaks the myth that "Latin American women don't care about family planning" and helps one to understand the choices that Latin American women make among a spectrum of birth control options, particularly since some of the more expensive hormonal options are not affordable for the majority of women in the region.

It remains a worldwide challenge to establish family planning organizations that respond to the needs and views of the women that initiatives are designed to help. In Latin America, the challenges sometimes have to do either with women's religious beliefs or, at least, with pressure that they feel from the Catholic Church hierarchy. At other times, the cost of birth control, or miscommunication between outsiders who staff clinics and the women whom they are intended to serve, are the obstacles to effective family planning. Finally, men's cultural attitudes about birth control can get in the way of women's desires to limit family size. In some regions of Latin America, for example, men identify their virility through their ability to father numerous children, and they resist or resent the idea of birth control and attempt to stop their wives or partners from using it. Despite obstacles, it is clear that Latin American women are using what methods they can to decide for themselves how many children they want to have.

Latin America and the Development of the Pill

History is often presented as the study of the past in which "the facts speak for themselves." Yet the historian's interests and agenda always shape the historical narrative, and in most cases one can only aspire for a good but incomplete discussion and analysis of past events. Mexicans across a wide spectrum of regions and classes, for example, have been struck from the historical record of how the birth control pill was developed, even though their contributions were critical in this process. Research and product development for the Pill were heavily dependent on the discovery of barbasco, a wild yam that contains diosgenin, which enabled chemists to make progesterone – from which all other hormones can be manufactured. Barbasco flourished in tropical rainforests of southeastern Mexico, where peasants generally considered it a weed that threatened production of marketable food products. Traditional healers, however, had long recognized that barbasco could be used to ease pain in wounds. One could also use it to induce a miscarriage, though it was rarely used that way because it was so potent that it might kill the pregnant woman as well as expel the fetus.[22]

Though there had long been interest in progesterone sources to develop lucrative hormonal treatments of various kinds, few chemists or pharmaceutical manufacturers had turned their attention to Mexico as a source of innovation in the field. Why? Drug companies claimed that "Mexico had neither the scientists nor technicians capable of running a hormone processing plant."[23] US businessmen viewed Mexico and Mexicans as backwards, incapable, and volatile. US and European views of Mexico as backwards enabled pharmaceutical company owners to pay barbasco collectors little, and to bring in foreign chemists to supervise Mexican scientists in laboratories despite the fact that it was Mexican chemists who often understood barbasco and its possibilities better than their foreign supervisors. Even so, in the 1950s and 1960s, harvesting and research with barbasco provided many Mexicans with jobs, from urban professionals to peasants seeking extra income to make ends meet. Though peasants were not paid a great deal, collecting barbasco was at first worth it to them, because they rarely had to travel far to find a plentiful supply of it.

By the 1970s, the situation had changed. Readily available barbasco supplies were already harvested, and peasants had to travel further into dense tropical forests to get the product. Making matters worse was the fact by this time, there were alternative sources for making progesterone, so demand for barbasco declined by the mid-1970s. At the same time, the Mexican population was expanding dramatically. In 1970, the national population was 48.3 million; by 1976, it was 70 million. Mexico City alone had more than doubled in size during the same period, from 6 million to 13 million residents. While contraceptive pills derived from barbasco helped women in the United States and Europe to curtail their fertility, Mexican women were seemingly having more babies than ever.

Once they had a viable basis for creating a birth control pill, scientists and pharmaceutical manufacturers had no way to know if it would have serious negative side effects. To find out would require human testing, which most pharmaceutical leaders deemed unethical due to the high risks involved. However, one company, Searle, came up with a solution: test the pill in Puerto Rico. The island had been the site for testing new birth control methods since the 1930s, becoming a virtual laboratory in which pharmaceutical companies could assess the benefits and problems with different products. Beginning in the 1940s, Puerto Rican working-class women became the primary test subjects to assess the effectiveness and safety of the pill and IUD. Not only did these experiments take significant risks with Puerto Rican women's lives, but they were not always well conducted and results were sometimes disappointing. In a 1956 study of women from two sites (a Puerto Rican housing project and a hospital), half of the trial participants dropped out due to side effects such as severe headaches, nausea, vomiting, and mid-cycle bleeding. Seventy-nine percent of the women who dropped out of the test were pregnant within four months of when they stopped taking the pill (this is what is known as a "rebound effect," in which women had an even greater chance of getting pregnant once they stopped taking the pill than they would have if they had never used it).[24]

Researchers decided it was ethical to conduct these experiments in Puerto Rico because of their perception that overpopulation was the cause of poverty in Puerto Rico. Therefore, unlike in the mainland United States, they believed that the potential benefits of a reliable and easy form of birth control outweighed the risks involved in testing it on human subjects. They blamed Puerto Rican women for overpopulation, alleging that the women "refused to be bothered" to use other birth control techniques and required something simple and doctor supervised like the pill. As usual with overpopulation discourses, the emphasis was on the women's backwardness. Yet these claims did not match reality in Puerto Rico, where the birth rate was actually down in the 1950s.[25]

Politicians, doctors, and feminists within Latin America also supported birth control tests, mainly on working-class women, due to their own concerns about overpopulation and ideas about class and race. In Puerto Rico, many middle-class feminists collaborated with pharmaceutical companies regarding birth control tests, though feminists tended to be more concerned with side effects than researchers were.[26] In Chile, Jaime Zipper created and tested an intrauterine device (the "Zipper Ring") on hundreds of women *without* their informed consent. Zipper justified his actions to himself and his colleagues by emphasizing that the risks with his tests were minimal compared with the dangers to women who got clandestine abortions. Chilean doctors rarely recommended other available birth control methods, such as condoms, which required "individual incentive rather than MD control" to ensure effectiveness.[27] Many Chilean doctors, like international pharmaceutical company owners, thought that working-class women were incapable of seeing to their own best interests.

The availability of a birth control pill transformed the lives of countless women in the U.S. and western Europe: no longer did they have to fear pregnancies that would interrupt their professional or personal plans. These benefits, however, only came to them because of the Mexican scientists and peasants who discovered the usefulness of barbasco for making synthetic progesterone, and because of the risks that Puerto Rican women took when they tested the drug. These stories often go unrecorded in feminist histories of the United States and Europe that evaluate the benefits of the pill. Unfortunately for poor Latin American women, the pill has not provided the answer to their birth control needs. Instead, they turn to a variety of other methods to control the size of their families, including abortion.

Abortion in Latin America: The "Clandestine Epidemic"?

Over the course of the twentieth century, Latin American governments gradually increased women's rights and reformed family laws to achieve greater gender equality in the home. Women have not only won the right to vote in national elections, but they have greater control over property within marriage and decision-making power in raising children. Most countries also allow couples to divorce by mutual consent.[28] Why has abortion not followed suit, and with what consequences?

Some countries do allow what they term "therapeutic" abortions, which are those cases where a woman's life is in danger and in a few cases where her health is in danger. Most of the countries that allow therapeutic abortions have done so since the 1930s or 1940s, but the way that a mother's health is defined has often changed over time. For instance, Chilean doctors included a wide array of health or emotional conditions as sufficient reason to allow a pregnant woman to have a legal abortion while Salvador Allende was in power from 1970 to 1973. When Pinochet came to power in 1973, however, he and his military regime severely tightened the definition of therapeutic abortions, and they passed legislation making abortion illegal under any conditions just before leaving power in 1989. The military regime's intolerance for abortion affected health professionals' actions. One hospital handed over to the government a list of women its doctors had treated whom they *suspected* of having had clandestine abortions, and some doctors even removed women's IUDs without their knowledge, let alone their consent. Once this was done there was little that a woman could do if she became pregnant afterwards.[29] Many countries make it difficult for a woman to get even a legal abortion, because laws require that two or three doctors agree that the woman's life is in danger.

Given the legal obstacles to abortion, combined with difficulty that many women have getting access to affordable and reliable contraceptives, the rate of illegal abortions is very high in Latin America. Women use a variety of methods, either at home alone or through the assistance of someone who performs abortions for a charge. Techniques that women use, particularly on their own, include the infliction of voluntary trauma (like falls), oral or vaginal administration of teas or herbal infusions, laxatives, or the insertion of medical objects, such as a catheter, into the cervix in order to induce contractions and expulsion of the embryo or fetus.[30] In many cases, women resort to increasingly dangerous methods, as one Chilean woman described:

> First, I had two injections of Methergin. Afterwards, for three days, I drank before breakfast red wine boiled with borage and rue, to which I added nine aspirins. My body was full of pimples but I did not abort. A few days later I drank cement water. It did not work either. Then I went to a lady who inserted a rubber catheter into me. I had to use it, after all the things I did I could not keep the child because he could have malformations.[31]

Given the unsafe and unhygienic conditions in which the majority of these illegal abortions occur, numerous women end up hospitalized after the fact, many of them with life-threatening infections. The maternal death rate from these complications remains very high (and probably underreported, given the illegal nature of the abortions), and obstetric departments in hospitals bear very high costs for treating women for infection and injuries from illegal abortions. Not all illegal abortions are equally dangerous, however. A middle-class or elite woman who wishes to get an abortion has a greater ability to find out about an underground clinic run by doctors who use safe methods and tools. Even if poor women could find out about these clinics, they could not afford them.

Therefore, it is primarily poor women whose lives or health are at risk with illegal abortions.[32]

Conflict over abortion has escalated since the 1960s, when many feminist organizations began to identify a woman's right to birth control and abortion as part of her fundamental individual rights. At the same time, and in response to rising use of abortion and birth control, the Catholic Church hardened its opposition to abortion. Both feminist abortion rights advocates and Catholic opponents of abortion cite individual rights as the basis for their arguments. Feminists view abortion as part of a woman's essential right to control her own body, while Catholic opponents argue that abortion compromises the rights of the fetus as an individual life-in-the-making. Divisions hardened under the leadership of Pope John Paul II in the late twentieth century, and the conflict over abortion became a worldwide struggle.[33]

Although the Church hierarchy has taken a clear position against abortion in all its forms, not all Latin American Catholics adhere to or agree with their church's stance. Many women simply do not comply with Catholic teachings on abortion. The majority of women in Latin America are self-proclaimed Catholics, and this includes the vast majority of women who get abortions. Faced with unwanted pregnancies, women often make decisions according to the practical considerations of their lives rather than the teachings of their church. A minority of Catholics are open critics of the Church's policies regarding birth control and abortion. Católicas por el Derecho a Decidir (CDD) has not only strongly advocated making birth control available and affordable, but it also published a book on sexuality and abortion in 1989 and it was one of the groups that helped to achieve abortion on demand for Mexico City in 2007.[34]

Despite the large number of dangerous and costly illegal abortions in Latin America and open protests calling for reform, abortion laws often became stricter in the late twentieth and early twenty-first centuries. In some cases, as with Chile, this occurred under military governments that upheld so-called traditional family values and sought Church support. However, stricter abortion laws – or more rigorous enforcement of existing laws – have occurred under democratic and even socialist regimes. Daniel Ortega, Nicaragua's Sandinista president of the 1980s who regained the presidency in 2007, never supported women's reproductive rights strongly.[35] Ortega became more outspoken against abortion while he was out of office, shifting his stance to identify with traditional and conservative Catholic values and embracing many antifeminist platforms. Just before he was elected president in 2007, the legislature passed a law making even therapeutic abortions illegal. Although Ortega was not yet in power when the law came into being, he never contested it once he was in office. Nor does having a woman president necessarily advance women's reproductive or abortion rights. Violeta Chamorro in Nicaragua adamantly opposed abortion, including in cases of rape. Even a supportive female president cannot guarantee increased reproductive rights: for example, Michelle Bachelet approved distribution of the "morning-after pill" in 2006, but the Chilean Constitutional Tribunal later suspended the program.

It is unclear what will happen with abortion in Latin America. Many experts agree that having greater access to available, cheap, reliable birth control would help to reduce the number of abortions used as a method of birth control in the region. Data would seem to support this view, because when birth control has been more readily available, abortion rates have usually dropped. Yet because birth control is expensive, and there is strong Catholic Church opposition to it, it seems unlikely that this will happen in the near future. There are many obstacles to overcome, and much negotiation that needs to be engaged, in order to find a solution.

Latin American Reproduction: Global Considerations

Sex and reproduction are profoundly private matters, and women who become pregnant experience changes in their bodies, income potential, and status within society. Yet as personal as these matters are, they have become the source of international political and moral disputes with both sides seeing them in absolutist terms, especially with regard to abortion. The controversies over birth control and abortion throughout the world, and particularly in Latin America, often lead to stereotypes that reinforce images of Latin American "backwardness." However, if one takes various forms of data into account, this impression of backwardness proves to be unsustainable.

First, one must pay careful attention to the sources of information that describe Latin America as "backwards" or "lagging behind" other parts of the world with regard to reproductive rights. While Latin American women definitely face serious challenges regarding their reproductive rights, these have often developed in profoundly modern contexts, and their problems have frequently been exacerbated rather than relieved by international intervention. US and western European scholars and politicians who worried about overpopulation in Latin America from the 1930s to 1970s often ignored data that suggested that structural problems, not population growth, accounted for problems of poverty in Latin America and other parts of the world. Moreover, comparative data on birth control use suggest that Latin American women actively seek ways to limit family size, even if they often use different methods than women in the United States or Europe. Nor do Latin American women cling to supposedly backwards traditional methods any more than women in all other parts of the world, including Europe.

Latin American women have been caught between tradition and modernity with regard to birth control and abortion, just as they have been with regard to other aspects of modernization in Latin America. This was not due to women's reluctance to use birth control methods, but rather to the relative difficulty that the majority of women have had in accessing affordable and reliable birth control. Their story is as much a modern story as in any other part of the world. In fact, it is often caught up in histories of urbanization and globalization, including when Latin American women's bodies have been used as testing grounds for birth control products before they were introduced in the United States. Even recent dilemmas and controversies over abortion have resulted from political and moral conflicts that are very much modern. With no clear answers available to them, Latin American women will continue to piece together solutions as best they can in order to meet the demands of modern life and to win some control over their reproductive destinies. Many of them, like Gabriela, pay a very high personal price for the contradictions in Latin American family planning policies.

Document 1: Puerto Rican Feminists Object to "Population Control"[36]

The following excerpt is from a group of Puerto Rican feminists who presented the history of birth control in Puerto Rico as part of "international crimes against women" at a 1976 international women's meeting in Brussels. How and why did they see the history of birth control in Puerto Rico as "criminal," and what evidence did they offer? How do their arguments compare and contrast with evidence presented in this chapter?

WE ACCUSE the United States of America, a state by which our country is dominated.

WE ACCUSE, simultaneously, their intermediaries on the island and the exploitative economic interests that both represent:

FIRST: they denied us the right to control our own bodies, using us as objects for their population control plans without the least respect for our integrity as human beings.

SECOND: they experimented with we Puerto Rican women with drugs that are still in an experimental stage as if we were guinea pigs or laboratory animals.

THIRD: they sterilized 35 percent of the female population of reproductive age.

FOURTH: they burdened Puerto Rican women with the sole responsibility for population control, at the same time benefiting from and perpetuating machista values in our society.

FIFTH: They assured the interests of great economic powers at the expense of woman.

SIXTH: They united behind the cultural premise of the Puerto Rican people that the women is solely responsible for procreation [and] the belief that the excess population is the direct cause of poverty, and can thus direct all methods of birth control to women's use [of them].

[. . .]

SUMMARY AND CONCLUSIONS:

For the year 2000, Puerto Rico will have, if it continues this rate of births, a population density around 1,600 persons per square mile, which is the basis for the necessity of establishing a population control program.

Our opposition is not against controlling the birth rate per se, but rather that it utilizes woman as a principal object for controlling the population offering this alternative as a remedy to resolve poverty, lack of housing, lack of efficient education or a high level of unemployment. We oppose that population control is separated from the necessity of a better distribution of wealth and the termination of an economic system based on exploitation of the majority in order to benefit the few.

Using woman in the population programs is also based on the subordination of a group, in this case the feminine sector, to the domination of another group, thus maintaining the sexist situation at the base of our society. [. . .]

The case of sterilized women in Puerto Rico has been a unique historical phenomenon. The high number of steriliza-tions labeled "voluntary," has been achieved by psychological coercion rather than physical force. Sterilization has been done under the recommendation of doctors without the woman being fully conscious of the necessity of it, and it was the principle reason that women consented to and submitted to the operation. Respect for a doctor's opinion has a great deal of weight at decision making time, and the physician was prejudiced in favor of sterilization; we should [therefore] doubt that this decision was made freely by the woman. Women have actually come to see it as natural to be sterilized after having two or three children. This is the extent to which sterilization has been inculcated into the Puerto Rican men-tality." [. . .]

Document 2: Declaration of the Catholic Women in Support of the Right to Choose[37]

What does this declaration show about the variety of "Catholic responses" to birth control and abortion in Latin America? How do their demands contradict claims that Latin Americans are "backwards" with regard to reproductive issues?

APPENDIX A: DECLARATION OF PRINCIPLES OF THE NETWORK CATÓLICAS POR EL DERECHO A DECIDIR EN AMÉRICA LATINA:

We are an autonomous movement of Catholics committed to social justice and the transformation of the existing cultural and religious parameters of our societies.

We promote women's rights, especially sexual and reproductive rights.

We are in a process of collective construction, working in a democratic and participatory manner.

We affirm

1. The right of women to have autonomy to control their own bodies and the pleasurable enjoyment of their sexuality, regardless of class, race/ethnicty, creed, age, and sexual orientation.
2. The moral agency of women and men to make responsible decisions about their lives, particularly about their sexuality and reproduction.
3. A theological thought that acknowledges the moral value of women's reproductive decisions without assigning blame to them, even in the case of abortion.
4. Respect for plurality, diversity, and difference, as essential factors in achieving freedom and justice.

We propose to

1. Create ecumenical spaces for ethical and religious reflection to promote public dialogues on sexuality, religion, and human reproduction, in societies and churches.
2. Debate on voluntary pregnancy termination, broadening the ethical, medical, and legal aspects of the discussion.
3. Exert influence on society so as to give women the right to free, voluntary motherhood and to decrease the number of abortions, as well as maternal mortality.
4. Continue our efforts to decriminalize abortion.
5. Involve and sensitize civil society, especially legislators and the groups working in reproductive and sexual health, education services, human rights, and commu-

nications, about the need to change the cultural patterns of our society.

We demand that the state

1. Comply with the commitments made at the United Nations conferences in Cairo (1994) and Beijing (1995).
2. Implement sex education programs with a sexual and reproductive rights perspective.
3. Implement legislation, public policies, and affordable health services of high quality so as to ensure access to all women, especially poor women, to fully enjoy their sexual and reproductive health.

Notes

1 María Rosa Cevallos, *El temor encarnado: Aborto en condiciones de riesgo en Quito* (Quito: FLACSO, 2013). Gabriela's story appears primarily on pp. 75–77, 79, and 91. I have also used evidence from this book about hospital conditions for and staff attitudes toward women who induce abortions or go to clandestine practitioners only to have to go to the hospital due to incomplete or botched abortions.

2 Cevallos, p. 58.

3 Cevallos, p. 90. The Minister of Public Health calls for vacuum aspiration rather than curettage.

4 John M. Paxman, Alberto Rizo, Laura Brown and Janie Benson, "The Clandestine Epidemic: The Practice of Unsafe Abortion in Latin America," *Studies in Family Planning* 24:4 (July–August 1993), pp. 205–226.

5 Mala Htun, *Sex and the State: Abortion, Divorce, and the Family Under Latin American Dictatorships and Democracies* (New York: Cambridge University Press, 2003), pp. 12–14.

6 Susan K. Besse, *Restructuring Patriarchy: The Modernization of Gender Inequality in Brazil, 1914–1940* (Chapel Hill: University of North Carolina Press, 1996), p. 105.

7 Karin Alejandra Rosemblatt, *Gendered Compromises: Political Cultures & the State in Chile, 1920–1950* (Chapel Hill: University of North Carolina Press, 2000), p. 213.

8 Asunción Lavrin, *Women, Feminism, and Social Change in Argentina, Chile, and Uruguay, 1890–1940* (Lincoln: University of Nebraska Press, 1995), pp. 174–175.

9   For a study on the dangers of illegal abortions, see Paxman *et al.*

10   Htun, pp. 55–56, 143–146.

11   Gabriela Soto Laveaga, *Jungle Laboratories: Mexican Peasants, National Projects, and the Making of the Pill* (Durham, NC: Duke University Press, 2009), pp. 42–46.

12   Laura Briggs, *Reproducing Empire: Race, Sex, Science, and U.S. Imperialism in Puerto Rico* (Berkeley: University of California Press, 2002), pp. 13, 18–19, 85, 94–97, 103, 107.

13   Briggs, pp. 87–88.

14   Heidi Tinsman, *Partners in Conflict: The Politics of Gender, Sexuality, and Labor in the Chilean Agrarian Reform, 1950–1973* (Durham, NC: Duke University Press, 2002), p. 158.

15   Briggs, chapter 5.

16   Mooney, pp. 83–84, 68–69; Tinsman 160–161, 165.

17   Maryssa Navarro and María Consuelo Mejía, "The Latin American Network of Católicas por el Derecho a Decidir," in Elizabeth Maier and Nathalie Lebon, eds, *Women's Activism in Latin America and the Caribbean: Engendering Social Justice, Democratizing Citizenship* (New Brunswick, NJ: Rutgers University Press, 2010), pp. 306–318.

18   References to Puerto Rico are from Briggs, pp. 76–79, 147–151; references and quotes on Chile are from Jadwiga E. Pieper Mooney, *The Politics of Motherhood: Maternity and Women's Rights in Twentieth-Century Chile* (Pittsburgh: University of Pittsburgh Press, 2009), pp. 106–108, 110, 118, 127.

19   Domitila Barrios de Chungara with Moema Viezzer, *Let Me Speak! Testimony of Domitila, A Woman of the Bolivian Mines* (New York: Monthly Review Press, 1978), pp. 199–200.

20   Information on indigenous peoples and family planning in Latin America is from Anne Terborgh, James E. Rosen, Roberto Santiso Gálvez, Willy Terceros, Jane T. Bertrand, and Sheana E. Bull, "Family Planning Among Indigenous Populations in Latin America," *International Family Planning Perspectives* 21:4 (1995), pp. 143–150.

21   The United Nations has an easy-to-read chart on these statistics from 2011 at: http://www.un.org/esa/population/publications/contraceptive2011/wallchart_graphs.pdf (last accessed November 15, 2013).

22   Soto LaVeaga, pp. 72–73.

23   Soto LaVeaga, p. 53–54.

24   Briggs, pp. 111, 131, 136–137.

25   Briggs, p. 129 for the quote, also 116, 119–120.

26   Briggs, p. 139.

27   Mooney, pp. 56–60.

28 For an especially good discussion of military governments and gender or family reform law, see Htun.

29 Mooney, pp. 123, 142–143, 186–187.

30 Davida Becker, Sandra G. García, and Ulla Larson, "Knowledge and Opinions about Abortion Law Among Mexican Youth," *International Family Planning Perspectives* 28:4 (December 2002), p. 206.

31 Paxman *et al.*, p. 208.

32 For a description of clinic conditions that middle- and upper-class women can afford, see Jennifer Strickler, Angela Heimburger, and Karen Rodriguez, "Clandestine Abortion in Latin America: A Clinic Profile," *International Family Planning Perspectives* 27:1 (March 2001), pp. 34–36.

33 Htun, pp. 23, 29–34, 39, 149–153.

34 Navarro and Mejía, pp. 310, 314.

35 Katherine Isbester, *Still Fighting: The Nicaraguan Women's Movement, 1977–2000* (Pittsburgh, PA: University of Pittsburgh Press, 2001), p. 84.

36 This was a presentation by the Puerto Rican Feminist group Mujer Integrante Ahora (MIA) to the International Tribunal of Crimes Against Women in Brussels in March 1976, and it was reprinted in Ana Irma Rivera Lassen and Elizabeth Crespo-Kebler, eds, *Documentos del feminismo en Puerto Rico: facisimiles de la historia* (University of Puerto Rico Press, 2001), pp. 296–306.

37 This declaration appears, translated into English, in Navarro and Mejía, p. 316.

10

Motherhood Transformed?
History, Gender, and the Shift into the Twenty-First Century

Brazil, Beauty, and the Rejection of Motherhood?

In Brazil, where fertility rates have plummeted in recent decades, aesthetic plastic surgery is on the rise. Though the trend began with elite women, plastic surgery is now common among women of middling and even some working classes. There are women in Brazil who will save scarce money in order to have plastic surgery done for so-called vanity reasons. Most common among these women's motives for seeking plastic surgery is to reverse the impact of child bearing and breastfeeding on their bodies. Both patients and plastic surgeons in Brazil see these operations as "postpartum corrections" even if a surgery occurs years after a woman's last pregnancy. Brazilian women blame pregnancy or breastfeeding for a wide range of complaints about the shape of their bodies, from droopy breasts to thickened waists to fat, and they often described their bodies as "finished" or "fallen." Anthropologist Alexander Edmonds describes women as active participants rather than as passive victims in the rise of plastic surgery in Brazil, emphasizing that most women who get plastic surgery seek it out. While this is true, one cannot forget different kinds of pressure on these women to conform to particular beauty standards, and how doctors themselves reinforce the plastic surgery trend. "Michelle" told Edmonds that her gynecologist frightened her into

Mothers Making Latin America: Gender, Households, and Politics Since 1825,
First Edition. Erin E. O'Connor.
© 2014 John Wiley & Sons, Inc. Published 2014 by John Wiley & Sons, Inc.

considering plastic surgery when he told her that her extra weight in the belly would not go away with exercise, only with plastic surgery. In the end, she was happy with her surgeries. Edmonds suggests that most doctors usually only make friendly suggestions or referrals about plastic surgery, rather than harsh criticisms or judgments of women's bodies. Even so, one wonders how judgmental a so-called friendly suggestion feels to a woman who is bombarded with images of young thin women in the media and already sensitive about changes in her body that have occurred over time.[1]

On the surface, Brazilian society seems to be trending away from the identification of women with motherhood that one finds woven throughout Latin American history. Rapidly falling fertility rates in the country imply that women's lives are less consumed by the labor of mothering. On top of this, President Dilma Rousseff won the presidency without presenting herself as a maternal figure, suggesting that the glass ceiling in politics has shattered. Meanwhile, Brazilian women – like women in many Latin American countries – are earning higher educational degrees and entering the formal wage labor force in unprecedented numbers. They are also more likely to divorce than they ever have been. All of these factors would seem to indicate that there is a major gender shift occurring in the country, and Brazilian women's experiences of motherhood are transforming as a result.

Below the surface, the question of Brazilian women's empowerment in general, and of motherhood experiences more specifically, is more complex. Although having a woman president was an important step with regard to gender norms and women's political potential, the Brazilian legislature is still overwhelmingly male. Brazil placed at 121 out of 141 country rankings for the percentage of women in its legislature. Women hold only 8.6% of legislative seats, despite the fact that Brazil is one of many Latin American countries with a gender quota system for elections.[2] Furthermore, although there are more educated women and more women in the job market in Brazil than ever before, they still tend to make less money than men. Finally, one has to wonder if the traditional family is really dissolving in Brazil, even with lower fertility and higher divorce rates. Particularly problematic in making such a claim is the fact that although the Brazilian constitution upholds the principle of equality, Brazilian civil law identified men as the legal heads of conjugal and family units, with the right to act as legal representatives for their wives and children, and to manage family finances, until 2002.[3]

Nor does a lower fertility rate necessarily mark a clear liberation for Brazilian women. Evidence about plastic surgery reveals that Brazilian women are increasingly anxious to erase the impact that motherhood has had on their bodies. Edmonds rightly identifies this as both a sign of increasing market logic in medical practices and a rejection of the maternal body in favor of a supposedly "sexy" one. Although women elect these surgeries themselves, surgical intervention on women's maternal bodies serves as a means of gender-specific social control and of passing judgment on women. All women who opt for plastic surgery are responding to social judgments on the maternal body. These judgments are not only those that men make about women, but that elites of both sexes make toward women of lower classes as well. Brazilian elites often pass judgment on working-class women who save up for plastic surgery, claiming that poor women should be spending their money in a more responsible way on their basic and family needs.

To what extent have recent developments around gender and motherhood marked a dramatic change from earlier periods in Latin American history, versus a continuation or culmination of patterns in the past? How does this complex set of advancements and problems for women in Brazil compare to women's issues and motherhood in other parts of Latin America? Although such a broad questions would require their own book to answer, this chapter will point to several general categories for readers to consider when weighing the state of gender and motherhood in Latin America in the early twenty-first century, with particular attention to changes and continuities since the mid- to late twentieth century. Trends in factors such as in fertility rates, female participation in the labor force, and women's involvement in politics indicate that the early twenty-first century is a moment of transition, but not necessarily one that is clearly and definitively putting an end to women's identification with motherhood (let alone to gender inequality more generally).

In addition to helping one interrogate recent developments, the history of motherhood in Latin America also offers insights about gender history, Latin America, and the meaning of motherhood in general. This book opened with a few key questions. Why have Latin American women often embraced and utilized maternalism, even though it set limits on them? What can motherhood teach us about the course of Latin American history? What can Latin American history teach us about the topic of motherhood? There are no simple answers to these questions, just as there are none to the question of whether (or how much) women's lives have changed in Latin America during the twenty-first century. Yet both sets of questions are crucial, and both are explored briefly in the sections to follow. My aim in this last chapter, then, is to provide food for thought rather than full-fledged (let alone absolute) answers.

Returning to the Questions of Gender and History

Motherhood reveals diversity, struggle, and agency in Latin American history since independence. It highlights not only women's initial exclusion from political participation based on gender norms centered on motherhood, but it also reveals that the categories of "woman" and "mother" were never unified. The impact of gender norms, and the experiences of motherhood, varied across regional, class, and racial divides. The very act of mothering differed dramatically for poor versus wealthy women in the nineteenth century. Wealthier women not only had access to better nutrition for their children, but they could afford to hire (or own, in the case of slaves) other women to tend to some of their mothering tasks. This flexibility enabled many middle- and upper-class women to contribute to charities in which they played the role of social mothers to poor families. Poor women's lives were far different. Unlike wealthy women, poor mothers of the nineteenth century had to attend to both home and work. In the best cases, the work that they did was adequate to keep their children healthy and allowed mothers to keep children with them during the day. Often this did not happen, and poor mothers had to give up children in order to find domestic work, or put them in orphanages because they could not afford to raise them. As Latin American countries modernized in the early to mid-twentieth century, mothering changed, but it still differed across class and race lines. Puericulture, or scientific motherhood, was emphasized for all women in the early twentieth century, but its impact was far more positive on middle- and upper-class women than on poor women. For women of means, modern motherhood methods offered them not only new ways to raise their children, but also new avenues for public activity, such as jobs in health care or social services. For poor women, new emphases on scientific child rearing and hygiene were more mixed. Sometimes, new government concerns with poverty and infant mortality enabled poor mothers to obtain much-needed state financial support. Even when financial assistance, educational programs, or social services helped them, however, they also placed poor mothers (and their methods of child rearing) under greater scrutiny and criticism than ever before.

Change over time mattered. Although one can find continuity over time in some of the ideas that associated women with motherhood, the meaning and impact of these ideas was far from stagnant. Nineteenth-century statesmen identified women with motherhood as a way to deny them the right to vote. They also used stereotypes about poor, indigenous, and Afro-Latin American women as bad mothers in order to justify ongoing race and class exploitation. By the late nineteenth century, women's rights advocates used notions that women were naturally mothers in order to argue that women needed better education and experience in the world (at least before marriage). In the early twentieth century, they used ideas about motherhood to seek positions in new welfare agencies (if middle class) or to obtain benefits from these agencies on their own terms (if poor). As the twentieth century advanced, motherhood reflected women's different engagements with political and social change. Some women, like the Mothers of the Disappeared in Argentina, used traditional notions about their motherhood in order to speak out against a government that made it almost impossible to protest. Others, like Michelle Bachelet in Chile and Dilma Rousseff in Brazil have not denied their motherhood, but they have not made it central to their political platforms, either.

Examining the history of motherhood in Latin America breaks down the myth that more democratic governments advance women's rights while right-wing governments limit them. Instead, both democratic (even radical) and authoritarian governments had a mix of advancements and limitations with regard to women's and motherhood issues. Mexican, Cuban, and Nicaraguan histories show, for example, that revolutions neither eradicated gender inequalities nor simply reinforced traditional notions about women and motherhood, but rather they often did both depending on the issue at hand. And while conservative regimes typically supported traditional gender norms and identified women as mothers, they sometimes also expanded women's rights within the family and in some cases (notably Frei's moderately conservative administration in 1960s Chile) provided more reliable and affordable birth control than more liberal governments did.

A focus on motherhood also reveals limitations in supposedly gender neutral history. If one were to assess independence, revolutions, or urbanization without attending to gender and motherhood, the meaning and course of those events would look much different. On one level, motherhood is a way of bringing in a social history perspective. If one were simply to read constitutions or political leaders' ideas about good government in the nineteenth century, he or she would likely conclude that independence brought equality before the law and an end to racial distinctions. Attention to motherhood helps to reveal not only the exclusion of women from these rights, but also how dominant gender norms were similar to (and sometimes reinforced) race and class ideas that excluded poor and nonwhite men from voting. Examining revolutions through motherhood similarly highlights not only men's and women's often distinct experiences of warfare, but it also indicates that reforms and benefits resulting from revolutionary state building tended to benefit men much more than women. Motherhood therefore allows the historian to understand historical events and issues more fully and to appreciate more deeply how other forms of divisions (along class and race lines) influenced the course of historical events also. Lines of alliance and opposition were not always neatly drawn, nor were the lines between winners and losers. In some cases, women shared certain common problems and concerns, and in a few they benefited across class, race, and regional divisions. At other times, women viewed men of the same class, race, and region as allies, and those outside of their group (including other women) as enemies or, at least, as groups unconcerned with their particular agendas.

Latin American history exposes the complexity of motherhood in ways that can be applied to evaluate other world regions and societies as well. Latin American history offers important lessons about how motherhood has been neither inherently limiting nor liberating. Over time, and in a variety of ways, Latin American women have taken the seeming disadvantages of their association with motherhood and domesticity and used it to advance interests unintended by powerful men. One sees this in the nineteenth century when feminists turned to social motherhood in order to argue for rights, and in the early to mid-twentieth century when Eva Perón identified herself as mother to Argentines in order to advance her own and (especially) her husband's political power. Perhaps most unexpected, however, were the ways in which mothers in authoritarian regimes became politicized, and had significant impacts on politics, when their children disappeared or died at the hands of government or military officials.

Latin American motherhood also offers good examples of how feminism was and is diverse rather than uniform, and how cultural and world regional differences have led to different relationships between women and feminism. The history of politicized motherhood in Latin America reveals that it was not only in Europe that relational feminism (discussed by Karen Offen) developed. Unlike the United States and Britain, where individualist feminists sought equality of rights based on a male model, Latin American feminists, similar to their counterparts in France, tended more toward relational feminism in which the goal was still advancing women's rights, but with an emphasis on women's differences from rather than similarities to men. Yet Latin American relational feminism was not simply a copy of European feminisms, as has often been assumed by nonacademics or even some scholars of Europe and the United States.[4] Instead, Latin American relational feminism developed out of the particular economic, political, and social contexts of the region, and they were influenced (but not determined) by Spanish and Portuguese colonial gender foundations. As individualist feminism came to predominate worldwide feminist discourses, however, this led many Latin American women – including those deeply concerned with winning greater rights – to reject the term "feminism" altogether. One sees this most prominently with poor women and those who became involved in leftist or ethnic-based activist movements who associated feminism with war against men or with the interest of wealthy women in Latin America, the United States, and western Europe. The history of motherhood in Latin America not only teaches one to look beyond a single definition of feminism, but it also highlights how class, race, and international power differentials have made many Latin American women, especially those who are poor and of indigenous or African descent, to be reluctant to identify with feminism at all.

An examination of Latin American motherhood shows that the public and private spheres were never entirely distinct except in the writings of certain intellectuals. Motherhood was never completely separate from politics and, in fact, has often been intertwined with political and economic developments. Perhaps it was the intricately intertwined natures of the domestic and political that led many Latin American women to embrace rather than reject motherhood over the course of Latin American history. Because Latin American political leaders identified motherhood with the national good – not just in the nineteenth century, but also in twentieth-century populist and authoritarian eras – women found this supposedly traditional and limiting identity a useful tool for advancing their interests and agendas. This does not mean that women necessarily manipulated maternalist ideas consciously. Instead, it is more likely that their political and personal lives were already so tightly interwoven, and motherhood already so deeply politicized, that they did not even think much about combining the two. Furthermore, rejecting motherhood identity did not necessarily improve the lives of most women – especially the majority of poor women. Until motherhood is reconsidered and resolved in a way that cuts across not only gender, but also class, race, and regional divides, it will likely continue to hold an important place in the course of Latin American history. With that in mind, the rest of this chapter explores a few twenty-first century issues facing women and mothers.

Considering Fertility

The media have made much of Latin America's – especially Brazil's – falling birth rates, but the press sometimes overlooks the deeper causes and possible consequences of the trend.[5] As noted in Chapter 1, not all Latin American countries have experienced the same level of decline in birth rates. Brazil is on one end of the spectrum, with the most dramatic drop. Guatemala is on the other end and, although birthrates there have declined, the population there might double by 2050 resulting in further economic strain in a country that is already quite poor.[6] Birth rates vary widely even within Latin American countries. Class, locality, and ethnicity all influence the extent to which fertility rates are falling. Urban women of the middle and upper classes (and some who aspire to enter the middle class) are having far fewer children in the early twenty-first century than they did in the 1970s. However, poor urban and rural women often continue to have large families. Sometimes, this difference is due to the difficulty and expense of obtaining reliable birth control among poorer populations. Cultural traditions and beliefs can also be a factor, particularly within rural indigenous communities.[7]

One must also consider the reasons that fertility rates are dropping in many countries, and their various impacts on women's lives. There is a correlation between higher education and lower fertility rates among Latin American women, primarily in the middle classes. Thus, it is likely that some middle- and upper-class women are opting to have fewer children in order to pursue professional (or other personal) opportunities. In this case, lower fertility rates indicate advances and greater freedom of choice for urban women of wealth, particularly those with enough money to hire servants to tend to domestic chores. Some urban dwellers who aspire to improve their status also appear to be limiting family size in hopes of entering the ranks of the middle classes. Among these urban folk, there is sometimes more emphasis on freeing up money to buy consumer goods than there is on freeing women to make more of their own choices in life.[8] Even these data, however, address only the reasons for a relatively privileged urban population.

One of the causes of reduced fertility in Latin America is one that the media rarely discuss: economic crises. Beginning in the 1980s, many Latin American countries faced mounting foreign debts and international pressures to get their economies under control. In response, many governments embraced neoliberal economic policies that cut back dramatically on social services, privatized many nationally owned business and utilities, and lowered tariffs on trade with other countries. These policies had a devastating impact on the poor, who lost much-needed services and assistance, and who often lost jobs when factories closed because they could not compete with low-priced goods coming into their countries from multinational corporations. More recently, the international recession starting in 2008 also hit poor families hard. In circumstances like these, many couples felt that they had no choice but to limit family size, whether they wanted to or not. This decision rarely had the result of freeing women from childcare or household responsibilities. Instead, wives and mothers often spent more time and energy than before trying to find affordable clothes and food, and mending or making their own clothes, than they had previously. Therefore, while they had fewer children, women were often equally burdened with home and reproductive labors that still went unremunerated.[9]

Nor have declining fertility rates necessarily meant that women became free from maternalist expectations in their societies. As Gabriela's story in the last chapter showed, women in Ecuador (and likely in other countries of Latin America) are often harshly judged if they opt out of motherhood, especially if they choose to terminate a pregnancy. Moreover, women's lower fertility rates and higher participation in the labor force have not changed the fact that Latin American women are, by and large, still responsible for the majority of housework and childcare – even when their husbands/male partners are out of work. Women therefore still face high demands on their time and bodies for (broadly defined) reproductive and domestic contributions to their families, even if they are not having as many children as their mothers and grandmothers did.

Women's bodies, especially with regard to maternity, are still the terrain on which struggles over gender norms and social changes are played out. For women without much money or access to reliable birth control, abortions are often their solution for limiting family size. Not only does the law define individuals who get or perform abortions as criminal, but women – especially poor women – often pay a high physical price for terminating their pregnancies in the way of infection from amateur procedures or treatment in hospitals after the fact. Although on the surface it seems quite different, women's quest for aesthetic plastic surgery in Brazil also notes ongoing pressures on women around maternity. In this case, rather than demanding women bear many children and fulfill an ages-old maternal social role throughout life, urban women feel a great deal of pressure to reverse and minimize the impact of maternity on their bodies. Women might choose plastic surgery, but their choices are determined by socioeconomic forces and pressures to conform to particular beauty and class ideals. The naturally aging maternal body is not deemed "good enough" to measure up. But measure up for whom, and for what purpose? Mostly, it is a modern, urban, male notion of the ideal woman to which these women are trying to force their bodies to conform. When anthropologist Alexander Edmonds asked a relatively poor woman vendor why she wanted to save enough money to get plastic surgery, he reported that "the answer is so obvious to her that she looks at me for a second, to see if the question is sincere. 'To find a husband.' "[10] Rather than feel pressure to put their bodies through strain by bearing many children, urban Brazilian women feel pressure to put their bodies through unnecessary surgical interventions in order to avoid appearing too maternal. The maternal discourse and ideals may have shifted, but they still have a tremendous impact on women's lives, choices, and bodies.

LGBT Rights and the Family

Lesbians have been one of the least visible groups in Latin American society, and the lives and families of lesbians are only beginning to be documented. Though we know that Amelio Robles (Chapter 7) lived with other women and adopted a child, most authorities recognized

Robles as a man. This allowed Robles to live as he pleased, and it allowed authorities to evade the conflict between Robles's life and rules of *heteronormativity*. Heteronormativity refers to "the tendency of societies to organize social relations and citizen rights based on the notion that reproductive heterosexuality is ideal."[11] In this sense, whether or not lesbians become mothers (either biologically or through adoption), the limits to their rights and protections within society are based on dominant gender norms that emphasize heterosexuality in general, and heterosexual motherhood in particular.

Lesbian, gay, bisexual, and transgender (LGBT) issues have become more visible in Latin America in the twenty-first century, and LGBT activists have made important progress regarding their political rights in several Latin American countries. For example, several countries have passed antidiscrimination laws that now include sexual orientation in their wording. Other countries have debated, and a few have passed, civil union laws that allow LGBT couples the same or similar rights as heterosexual couples who live together without formally marrying. Uruguay was the first country to do so, allowing couples (whether heterosexual or LGBT) who cohabited together for at least five years to enjoy health benefits, inheritance, parenting, and pension rights. In 2009, the Colombian Constitutional Court upheld a lower court decision that allowed same-sex couples the same benefits as heterosexual couples in common-law marriages, including pensions, survivor benefits, and property rights. Most Latin American nations, however, have fallen short of allowing civil union rights to gay couples, and as of this writing it is only in particular cities, such as Buenos Aires and Mexico City, that allow gay and lesbian couples to marry legally.[12]

LGBT parenthood has been one of the most difficult issues in Latin America. Though some countries or cities have antidiscrimination laws or even allow civil union rights to LGBT couples, some of these also restrict LGBT family rights. For example, the Brazilian "Partnership Bill" of 1995 legally recognized homosexual partnerships, but it also vetoed "any agreement on adoption, tutelage, or warding of children and adolescents [to gays or lesbians], even if they are the children of one of the partners." However, when same-sex couples try to adopt or get custody of children, Brazilian judges sometimes use the Child and Adolescent Statute in order to justify and grant them rights to do so on an individual basis.[13] Rather than representing an LGBT right to family and parenthood, however, this practice leaves the couple's fate up to the whim of the judge assigned to their case. Similarly, Ecuador's 2008 constitution recognized lesbians' and gays' rights to civil unions, but it also specified that marriage was the union of a man and a woman, and that only two people of the opposite sex can adopt.[14]

Things do appear to be moving forward, as a recent case from Chile shows. Karen Atala, a lesbian mother and Chilean judge, lost a case for custody of her children in the Chilean court system. Refusing to accept this decision, she brought her custody case to the Inter-American Court for Human Rights and won. As a result, the Chilean government (by court order) apologized to Atala in December 2012. At the same time, it appears that a civil union law might have a chance of passing in Chile.[15] In some cases, forward movement has come in the aftermath of brutality against LGBT people, as in when the Ecuadorian constitutional court declared it unconstitutional in 1997 when police arrested 14 gay men in a bar in Cuenca, Ecuador based on article 516 in the penal code, and tortured many of the prisoners. In Chile, a national nondiscrimination law was passed after the murder of the country's first openly gay politician, Daniel Zamudio.[16]

It is difficult to predict what will happen next with LGBT rights more generally, or the rights of lesbian mothers specifically, in Latin America. Although some governments are starting to pass laws protecting the lives or rights on LGBT individuals and couples, social attitudes have not necessarily changed toward homosexuality or so-called alternate families. This leaves lesbian and gay couples and parents vulnerable, particularly if police officials do not enforce antidiscrimination laws. Gradually, many feminist organizations are allying with LGBT activists, and the Argentine Mothers of the Disappeared have also participated symbolically in a few LGBT demonstrations.[17] Regardless of how these efforts for LGBT rights move forward, activists' hopes rest on redefining dominant notions of families, motherhood, and fatherhood that have held sway in Latin America for centuries, and that have been embedded in Latin American legal codes since independence.

Women, Work, and Motherhood

Since the 1990s, Latin American women have entered the formal labor force and politics at previously unprecedented levels. A 2009 United Nations report noted that while Latin American women only accounted for 32% of the labor market in 1990, they accounted for 53% of it in 2008; this was on top of already rising female participation in the workforce.[18] The World Bank has also estimated that women's rising workforce participation accounted for 30% of the recent drop in poverty rates in the region.[19] As noted earlier, the reasons for women's expanding employment vary: declining fertility and rising education rates are crucial, but economic crises that hit male employees hardest also drive women into the labor force.

Yet despite women's higher participation in the formal workforce, gender gaps remain that indicate that women's advancements with work – although important – are limited. First is the fact that domestic work continues to fall on women's shoulders, perpetuating the double work day for most of them. Second, women in Latin America (like women in the United States and other parts of the world) still only make about 70% as much in wages as men. This has partly to do with women's association with the low-paying service sector. However, the World Bank report found that the widest gap between men and women in both employment and pay were in the highest paying professional jobs. One does see more women finding their way into highly paid professional jobs, but they typically have more education than men doing the same jobs, and their pay is generally lower. The World Bank study suggested that one of the main reasons that women's pay is lower than men's in these fields is that many women seek part-time or flex-time work once they are married and have children, whereas men do not. Furthermore, the study suggested that Latin American women are often not able to take advantage of education and job opportunities because of factors like gender-based violence and teen pregnancy, both of which remain high in the region.[20]

Does greater activity in the wage labor force mean that women are identifying less than they once did with motherhood? The answer appears to be class-specific. Many middle- and upper-class women, who are more likely attain higher levels of education and get better jobs, have experienced a shift in how they understand their identities. These women's identities are often equally, sometimes more, caught up in their professions as they are in their experiences as mothers. These are also the women who can afford to hire others to tend to housework and childcare when their jobs require them to be away from the home. Poor women who work mainly in low-paying, low-status service sector or domestic jobs have not experienced the same shift in how they self identify. For them, work brings little pay and probably also little satisfaction. They also have to continue to take care of housework in their own homes, and many of them identify more strongly with their roles as mothers than with the work that they must do in order to keep their families afloat.[21]

Gender and Politics

Women's achievements in the realm of politics are also mixed. There has definitely been growth in Latin American women's political participation, particularly at the grassroots level, and women have made gains with national-level political positions. While such improvements are most obvious with women in prominent executive or cabinet positions, there also have been achievements for women in national legislatures. Though the percentage of women in national government remains low in Brazil, there has been considerable expansion of women holding legislative seats in other Latin American nations. Cuba (48.9%), Nicaragua (40.2%), Costa Rica (38.6%), Argentina (37.4%), and Mexico (36.8%) were all ranked in the top 20 world nations for the number of women in their legislatures. This is significantly higher than Canada (24.7%), the United Kingdom (22.5%), or the United States (17.8%), and it was on par with many Northern European countries.[22] These numbers indicate that although Latin American countries (like all world countries, except for Rwanda and Andorra) have yet to fill the gender gap in national politics, they are making headway.

Many of these achievements have been products of gender quotas in politics. Argentina was the first Latin American nation where political parties were required (rather than simply encouraged) to comply with a law that mandated that 1/3 of their party candidates had to be female. In some cases, a *closed-list system* is used, in which voters select their preferred party, rather than individuals. Depending on the number of votes that the party wins, they advance a certain number of candidates to fill elected seats. Three of the five Latin American nations that were listed among the top 20 for the number of women in their legislatures (Argentina, Costa Rica, and Mexico) use a closed-list system. Other countries use *open-list quota systems*, in which parties still have to have a certain percentage of female candidates, but voters elect individuals for seats, rather than selecting their preferred party only.[23] Though opponents have sometimes attacked gender quotas claiming that they would allow supposedly unqualified women to gain political offices, data from Latin American elections suggest otherwise. In most cases, the women who benefited from quotas were as qualified as men. Moreover, because politics was formerly a male domain, many "men's networks" developed (and still function) in Latin American politics, as they do in other parts of the world. These male networks mean that processes of candidate selection were gender biased even before the introduction of quotas.[24] Thus, while many experts do not assume that gender quotas are a panacea for achieving greater gender parity in political posts, they do seem to decrease gender gaps in Latin American politics.

Some scholarly findings on gender and politics have been a bit surprising. Political scientist Magda Hinojosa's extensive study on candidate selection, for example, found that political parties with more exclusive systems with top-down decision-making tend to result in more women becoming candidates and holding office than those that openly embrace inclusive, democratic processes.[25] This is also reflected in the earlier discussion in which higher rates of women gaining office when voters select parties rather than individuals. Again, this has partly to do with long-standing male domination of political parties. Without powerful individuals within the party deciding that they need to recruit women actively and advance them as candidates, male networks tend to produce male candidates and officials. Moreover, many Latin American women are reluctant to self-promote and advance themselves as candidates if they are not specifically recruited. This has a great deal to do with gender norms that make women (but not men) feel that promoting themselves is in poor taste.[26] Although such gender norms are not exclusively or specifically linked to motherhood, they are certainly linked to legacies of gender ideologies that emphasized women as self-sacrificing mothers who never put their own needs first. Even if Latin American women's lives did not always meet this ideal, there was and remains a certain social stigma that leaves many women reluctant to self promote openly.

Women's advancements in Latin American politics must also take into account which women are moving into political positions, and how thoroughly they are integrated into political networks in their countries. Although, as Chapter 8 discussed, poor women have been (and remain) very active in grassroots movements, few of them have made the transition into elected office. Instead, it is mainly middle- and upper-class educated women who benefit most from quota systems and elections.

Also, although women have made important gains in national elections in Latin America, they remain marginalized in local and regional politics. On average, women hold 1/7 of the legislative positions in Latin America, but only 1/20 of mayoral positions. They are also vastly underrepresented on municipal councils.[27] Motherhood might also play a role in women's political advancement. Among powerful women politicians, most are either childless or have children who are already grown and out of the house. Precisely why this phenomenon occurs and what it means for both politics and motherhood is a topic that requires further exploration.

The Question of Empowerment

In their book on gender in Latin America at the turn into the twenty-first century, geographer Sylvia Chant and political scientist Nikki Craske note that it is difficult to gauge whether recent changes have empowered Latin American women. First, what exactly does "empowerment" mean? Second, is it permanent or simply temporary change that we see occurring? Overall, Chant and Craske conclude that, at the very least, empowerment indicates women's ability to make choices in their lives.[28] Their questions and criteria, though broad-based, offer important guidelines for assessing the transitions that one finds in Latin American gender relations and motherhood in the early twenty-first century. Furthermore, because the category of women and meanings of motherhood are experienced differently among women of different regions, races, and classes, there are no simple answers to whether Latin American women have been empowered by recent changes.

Whether considering issues of fertility, employment, or politics, it is middle- and upper-class women who have seen the most changes in their identities and opportunities. Because they have greater access to education, they can get jobs that make motherhood only one of several aspects of their identity that they might choose to emphasize. Moreover, they have access to and can afford the most reliable forms of birth control and, if these do not work, safer (if still clandestine) abortions. They are also the women most likely to benefit from gender quotas in politics. Although further research needs to be done, it would also seem that it is these wealthier women who experience the greatest pressure to overcome the impact of maternity on the body. Whether they try to fight nature with plastic surgery or diets, many of these women feel pressed to conform to very specific beauty ideals.

Probably poorer women are influenced by media that uphold slender, young women as the beauty ideal as well, but other concerns often take precedent in their lives. Poor urban and rural women have not gained as much through the expansion of education, the job force, or political opportunities as their wealthy urban counterparts. Though they do achieve higher levels of education than previously, most of them are still stuck in lower-paying service sector jobs. Many of them identify more strongly with motherhood as a core feature of their identities as well. While many poor women are politically active and have sometimes had an important influence on local, national, or even international politics, they have most often done so through grassroots organizations rather than through formal party politics or elected positions.

The relative strength of national economies also determines Latin American women's opportunities and choices. The greatest changes have been in Latin American nations whose economies are strongest and growing the fastest, such as Brazil, Mexico, and Argentina. Changes are slower – and opportunities more rare – in poorer countries such as Guatemala or Bolivia. Yet many of these poorer countries are doing a better job of advancing female candidates for political office than their wealthier neighbors.

All of these changes suggest that motherhood is in a state of flux in twenty-first-century Latin America. The changes are clearly strongest for wealthy women in wealthier countries, but they can be found throughout the region to some extent. What has not happened – and does not seem likely to happen in the near future – is a reversal of ideologies that identify women with motherhood and the domestic sphere. These associations are stronger or weaker depending on where a particular woman lives, what her class and race are, and her government's relative commitment to gender equality. There is certainly a basis for change, but it is not yet clear the extent to which this potential will be realized. Whatever happens, Latin American women are likely to continue, as they have in the past, to embrace particular gender norms that are useful or meaningful to them, ignore or get around those that they oppose, and adapt to and alter those that only partially suit their needs. They will, in other words, continue to be active agents rather than passive subjects in the processes of historical change. This includes (though it is not limited to) the meaning of motherhood in Latin American politics and society.

Notes

1 Alexander Edmonds, *Pretty Modern: Beauty, Sex, and Plastic Surgery in Brazil* (Durham, NC: Duke University Press, 2010), particularly his chapter titled "Aesthetic Medicine and Motherhood."

2 Inter-Parliamentary Union, "Women in National Parliaments," http://www.ipu.org/wmn-e/classif.htm (last accessed November 13, 2013).

3 Sylvia Chant with Nikki Craske, *Gender in Latin America* (New Brunswick, NJ: Rutgers University Press, 2003), p. 167.

4 Karen Offen, "Defining Feminism: A Comparative Historical Approach," *Signs* 14:1 (Autumn 1988), pp. 119–157.

5 For example, see Juan Forero, "Birth Rate Plummets in Brazil," *Washington Post*, December 29, 2011. Available at http://articles.washingtonpost.com/2011-12-29/world/35286762_1_fertility-rate-demographic-shift-silva (last accessed November 13, 2013).

6 Samuel Schleier, "Latin America's Demographic Divergence" (6/12/12), available at http://www.newgeography.com/content/002874-latin-america%E2%80%99s-demographic-divergence (last accessed November 13, 2013).

7 Chant and Craske, pp. 73–74.

8 See "Falling Fertility Rate No Cause for Cheer," which first appeared via *Reuters* from *Indian Express* on March 14, 2012, and is available online at http://www.newgeography.com/content/002874-latin-america%E2%80%8099s-demographic-divergence (last accessed November 13, 2013). Although this short article focuses mostly on India, it does also mention Brazil and other parts of the world.

9 Chant and Craske, pp. 61, 180–181.

10 Edmonds, "Introduction," 5% (accessed on Kindle, no page numbers available).

11 Javier Corrales and Mario Pecheny, "Introduction: The Comparative Politics of Sexuality in Latin America," in Javier Corrales and Mario Pecheney, eds, *The Politics of Sexuality in Latin America: A Reader on Lesbian, Gay, Bisexual, and Transgender Rights* (Pittsburgh, PA: University of Pittsburgh Press, 2010), 2% (read on kindle). This book is an excellent collection of essays, and timelines, on LGBT movements and rights in the twenty-first century, and it is the basis for my discussion of these issues here.

12 *The Politics of Sexuality in Latin America*, 92–93%.

13 Adriana R.B. Vianna and Sergio Carrera, "Sexual Politics and Sexual Rights in Brazil: A Case Study," in *The Politics of Sexuality in Latin America*, 29%.

14 Selena Xie and Javier Corrales, "LGBT Rights in Ecuador's 2008 Constitution: Victories and Setbacks," in *The Politics of Sexuality in Latin America*, 50–51%.

15 "Chile Apologizes to Lesbian Mother," http://aftermarriageblog.word press.com/2012/12/17/chile-apologizes-to-lesbian-mother/ (last accessed November 13, 2013).

16 Xie and Corrales, 50%, and "Chile Apologizes to Lesbian Mother," respectively.

17 Stephen Brown, "Con Descriminación y Represión No Hay Democracia: The Lesbian and Gay Movement in Argentina," in *The Politics of Sexuality in Latin America*, 23%.

18 "Working Women Changing Traditional Roles in Latin America and Caribbean: UN Report," available at: http://www.un.org/apps/news/story.asp ?NewsID=31111&Cr=women&Cr1=labour#.UZEt47XFU_4 (last accessed November 13, 2013).

19 World Bank, "The Effect of Women's Economic Power in Latin America and the Caribbean" (August 2012), available online at: http://www.bancomundial .org/content/dam/Worldbank/document/PLBSummer12latest.pdf   (last accessed November 13, 2013).

20 World Bank, pp. 24–29.

21 Chant and Craske, p. 186.

22 Inter-Parliamentary Union, "Women in National Parliaments."

23 Chant and Craske, pp. 40–41.

24 Magda Hinojosa, *Selecting Women, Electing Women: Political Representation and Candidate Selection in Latin America* (Philadelphia: Temple University Press, 2012), pp. 139–148.

25 Hinojosa. See particularly Hinojosa's introduction for a good overview of her argument and supporting evidence.

26 Hinojosa, p. 151.

27 Hinojosa, p. 5; also see Chant and Craske, p. 44.

28 Chant and Craske, pp. 68–69.

Bibliography

Abbassi, Jennifer and Sheryl L. Lutjens, eds, *Rereading Women in Latin America and the Caribbean: The Political Economy of Gender*. New York: Rowman & Littlefield Publishers, 2002.

Abercrombie, Thomas A. (2000) "Affairs of the Courtroom: Fernando de Medina Confesses to Killing his Wife," in Richard Boyer and Geoffrey Spurling, eds, *Colonial Lives: Documents on Latin American History, 1550–1850*. New York: Oxford University Press, 54–75.

Adsera, Alicia and Alicia Menendez. "Fertility Changes in Latin America in the Context of Economic and Political Uncertainty," 2005. http://paa2006 .princeton.edu/papers/61407. Last accessed November 15, 2013.

Agosín, Marjorie and Isabel Allende. *Tapestries of Hope, Threads of Love: The Arpillera Movement in Chile*, 2nd ed. New York: Rowman and Littlefield, 2007.

Amadeo, Tomás. *La función social*. Buenos Aires: Imprenta Oceana, 1929.

Anderson, Benedict. *Imagined Communities: Reflections on the Origins and Spread of Nationalism*, revised ed. New York: Verso, 1992 [1983].

Anderson, Jon Lee. *Che Guevara: A Revolutionary Life*. New York: Grove Press, 2010.

Andrade, Raul Francisco. *Gender, Marriage Markets and the Family*. Ann Arbor, MI: ProQuest, 2007.

Archivo del Museo Nacional de Medicina (Quito): Junta Central de Asistencia Pública. Sección Servicios Sociales, Casos Sociales del Año de 1947, AP-1216, "Gordillo.".

Arrom, Sylvia M. *The Women of Mexico City, 1790–1857*. Stanford, CA: Stanford University Press, 1992.

Mothers Making Latin America: Gender, Households, and Politics Since 1825,
First Edition. Erin E. O'Connor.
© 2014 John Wiley & Sons, Inc. Published 2014 by John Wiley & Sons, Inc.

Arrom, Sylvia M. (1994) "Changes in Mexican Family Law in the Nineteenth Century," in Gertrude M. Yeager, ed., *Confronting Change, Challenging Tradition: Women in Latin American History*. Wilmington, DE: SR Books, 87–102.

Atuesta, Gustavo. *La Mujer Moderna ante Diós, En la Sociedad, y Ante el Derecho*. Bucaramanga: M.A. Gómez, 1940.

Bakewell, Liza. *Madre: Perilous Journeys with a Spanish Noun*. Albuquerque: University of New Mexico Press, 2012.

Baldez, Lisa. (2001) "Nonpartisanship as a Political Strategy: Women Left, Right, and Center in Chile," both in Victoria González and Karen Kampwirth, eds, *Radical Women in Latin America, Left and Right*. University Park: Pennsylvania State University Press, 273–298.

Barragán Romano, Rosanna. *Indios, mujeres y ciudadanos: Legislación y ejercicio de la ciudadanía en Bolivia (Siglo XIX)*. La Paz: Fundación Diálogo, 1999.

Barrios de Chungara, Domitila with Moema Viezzer. *Let Me Speak! Testimony of Domitila, a Woman of the Bolivian Mines*. Trans. by Victoria Ortiz. New York: Monthly Review Press, 1978.

Bayard de Volo, Lorraine. *Mothers of Heroes and Martyrs: Gender Identity and Politics in Nicaragua, 1979–1999*. Baltimore, MD: Johns Hopkins University Press, 2001.

Becker, Davida, Sandra G. García, and Ulla Larson. "Knowledge and Opinions about Abortion Law among Mexican Youth." *International Family Planning Perspectives* 28:4 (2002), pp. 205–213.

Becker, Marc. *Indians and Leftists in the Making of Ecuador's Modern Indigenous Movements*. Durham, NC: Duke University Press, 2008.

Beezley, William H. and Judith Ewell, eds. *The Human Tradition in Latin America: The Twentieth Century*. Wilmington, DE: SR Books, 1987.

Berryman, Phillip. *Liberation Theology*. Philadelphia: Temple University Press, 1987.

Besse, Susan K. *Restructuring Patriarchy: The Modernization of Gender Inequality in Brazil, 1914–1940*. Chapel Hill: University of North Carolina Press, 1996.

Black, Chad Thomas. *The Limits of Gender Domination: Women, the Law, and Political Crisis in Quito, 1765–1830*. Albuquerque: University of New Mexico Press, 2010.

Bliss, Katherine Elaine. *Compromised Positions: Prostitution, Public Health, and Gender Politics in Revolutionary Mexico City*. University Park: Pennsylvania State University Press, 2002.

Blum, Ann S. *Domestic Economies: Family, Work, and Welfare in Mexico City, 1884–1943*. Lincoln: University of Nebraska Press, 2009.

Briggs, Laura. *Reproducing Empire: Race, Sex, Science, and U.S. Imperialism in Puerto Rico*. Berkeley: University of California Press, 2002.

Briggs, Laura. *Somebody's Children: The Politics of Transracial and Transnational Adoption*. Durham, NC: Duke University Press, 2012.

Brown, Stephen. (2010) "Con Descriminación y Represión No Hay Democracia: The Lesbian and Gay Movement in Argentina," in Javier Corrales and Mario Pecheney, eds, *The Politics of Sexuality in Latin America: A Reader on Lesbian, Gay, Bisexual, and Transgender Rights*. Pittsburgh, PA: University of Pittsburgh Press, 86–101.

Buck, Sarah A. (2007) "The Meaning of the Women's Vote in Mexico, 1917–1953," in Stephanie Mitchell and Patience A. Schell, eds, *The Women's Revolution in Mexico 1910–1953*. New York: Rowman and Littlefield, 73–98.

Burgos-Debray, Elisabeth and Rigoberta Menchú. *I . . . Rigoberta Menchu: An Indian Woman in Guatemala*. Trans. Ann Wright. London: Verso, 1984.

Burns, E. Bradford. *The Poverty of Progress: Latin America in the Nineteenth Century*. Berkeley: University of California Press, 1980.

Burns, Kathryn. *Colonial Habits: Convents and the Spiritual Economy of Cuzco, Peru*. Durham, NC: Duke University Press, 1999.

Campolieti, Roberto. *Conciencia Social de la mujer, su responsabilidad frente a la crisis moderna y al comunismo*. Buenos Aires: Editorial Tor, 1938.

Cano, Gabriela. (2006) "Unconcealable Realities of Desire: Amelio Robles's (Transgender) Masculinity in the Mexican Revolution," in Jocelyn Olcott, Mary Kay Vaughan, and Gabriela Cano, eds, *Sex in Revolution: Gender, Politics, and Power in Modern Mexico*. Durham, NC: Duke University Press, 35–56.

Caulfield, Susan. *In Defense of Honor: Sexual Morality, Modernity, and Nation in Early-Twentieth-Century Brazil*. Durham, NC: Duke University Press, 2000.

Cervone, Emma. (2002) "Engendering Leadership: Indigenous Women Leaders in the Ecuadorian Andes," in Rosario Montoya, Lessie Jo Frazier, and Janise Hurtig, eds, *Gender's Place: Feminist Anthropologies of Latin America*. New York: Palgrave MacMillan, 179–196.

Cevallos, María Rosa. *El temor encarnado: Aborto en condiciones de riesgo en Quito*. Quito: FLACSO, 2013.

Chambers, Sarah C. *From Subjects to Citizens: Honor, Gender, and Politics in Arequipa, Peru, 1780–1854*. University Park: Pennsylvania State University Press, 1999.

Chambers, Sarah C. "Republican Friendship: Manuela Sáenz Writes Women into the Nation, 1835–1856." *The Hispanic American Historical Review* 81:2 (2001), pp. 225–257.

Chaney, Elsa M. and Mary Garcia Castro, eds. *Muchachas No More: Household Workers in Latin America and the Caribbean*. Philadelphia: Temple University Press, 1989.

Chant, Sylvia with Nikki Craske. (2003) *Gender in Latin America*. New Brunswick, NJ: Rutgers University Press.

Cherpak, Evelyn. (1978) "The Participation of Women in the Independence Movement in Gran Colombia, 1780–1830," in Asunción Lavrin, ed., *Latin American Women: Historical Perspectives*. Westport, CT: Greenwood Press, 219–234.

Chéves, J. Adeláida. *Llave de Oro: Compendio de economía doméstica para uso de las niñas Centro-Americanas*. New York: La Revista Ilustrada de Nueva York Pub. Co., 1887.

Christian, Shirley. *Nicaragua: Revolution in the Family*. New York: Vintage Books, 1986.

Christiansen, Tanja. *Disobedience, Slander, Seduction,and Assault: Women and Men in Cajamarca, Peru, 1862–1900*. Austin: University of Texas Press, 2004.

Clark, A. Kim. *Gender, State, and Medicine in Highland Ecuador: Modernizing Women, Modernizing the State, 1895–1950*. Pittsburgh, PA: University of Pittsburgh Press, 2012.

Clark, A. Kim and Marc Becker, eds, *Highland Indians and the State in Modern Ecuador*. Pittsburgh, PA: University of Pittsburgh Press, 2007.

Clendinnen, Inga. *Aztecs: An Interpretation*. New York: Cambridge University Press, 1995.

Corrales, Javier and Mario Pecheney. *The Politics of Sexuality in Latin America: A Reader on Lesbian, Gay, Bisexual, and Transgender Rights*. Pittsburgh, PA: University of Pittsburgh Press, 2010a.

Corrales, Javier and Mario Pecheney. (2010b) "Introduction: The Comparative Politics of Sexuality in Latin America," in Javier Corrales and Mario Pecheney, eds, *The Politics of Sexuality in Latin America: A Reader on Lesbian, Gay, Bisexual, and Transgender Rights*. Pittsburgh, PA: University of Pittsburgh Press, 1–32.

Criquillon, Ana. (1995) "The Nicaraguan Women's Movement: Feminist Reflections from Within," in Minor Sinclair, ed., *The New Politics of Survival: Grassroots Movements in Central America*, New York: Monthly Review Press, 209–237.

Damas y damitas. Año VIII, No. 386, 20 Noviembre de 1946.

Decoud, A. López. *Sobre el feminismo*. Asunción: Imp. De Luis Tasso, 1902.

Deere, Carmen Diana and Magdalena León. "Women and Land in the Latin American Neo-Liberal Counter-Reforms," Working Paper No. 264, MSU, 1997. Available online at: http://gencen.isp.msu.edu/documents/Working _Papers/WP264.pdf. Last accessed November 15, 2013.

Deere, Carmen Diana and Magdalena León. "Liberalism and Married Women's Property Rights in Nineteenth-Century Latin America." *The Hispanic American Historical Review* 85:4 (2005), pp. 627–678.

de Erauso, Catalina. *Lieutenant Nun: Memoir of a Basque Transvestite in the New World*. Boston: Beacon Press, 1997.

de Jesus, Carolina Maria. *Child of the Dark: The Diary of Carolina Maria de Jesus.* Trans. David St. Clair. New York: Signet Classic, 2003 [1962].

de la Cadena, Marisol. *Indigenous Mestizos: The Politics of Race and Culture in Cuzco, Peru, 1919–1991.* Durham, NC: Duke University Press, 2000.

de la Cruz, Sor Juana Inés. *The Answer / La Respuesta.* Trans. Electa Arenal and Amanda Powell. New York: The Feminist Press, 2009.

De Los Reyes Castillo Bueno, María, Daisy Rubiera Castillo, and Anne McLean. *Reyita: The Life of a Black Cuban Woman in the Twentieth Century.* Durham, NC: Duke University Press, 2000.

Departamento de Salubridad Pública. "Alforismos para la radio, durante la semana de hygiene: 'La Madre y el Niño.'" Mexico, 1940.

De Queiros Mattoso, Katia M. *To Be a Slave in Brazil, 1550–1888.* Trans. Arthur Goldhammer. New Brunswick, NJ: Rutgers University Press, 1987.

de Reyes, Julia B. "Llamamiento que Alianza Femenina Ecuatoriana dirige a las mujeres del pais." *El Comercio* 8 (1944).

de Wilson, Baronesa. *Perlas del Corazón: Deberes y aspiraciones de la mujer en su vida íntima y social.* Quito: Fundación de Tipos de Manuel Rivadeneira, 1880.

Di Marco, Graciela. (2010) "The Mothers and Grandmothers of the Plaza de Mayo Speak," in Elizabeth Maier and Nathalie Lebon, eds, *Women's Activism in Latin America and the Caribbean: Engendering Social Justice, Democratizing Citizenship.* New Brunswick, NJ: Rutgers University Press, 95–110.

Dias, Maria Odila Silva. *Power and Everyday Life: The Lives of Working Women in Nineteenth-Century Brazil.* New Brunswick, NJ: Rutgers University Press, 1995.

Dore, Elizabeth. (2000) "One Step Forward, Two Steps Back: Gender and the State in the Long Nineteenth Century," in Elizabeth Dore and Maxine Molyneux, eds, *Hidden Histories of Gender and the State in Latin America.* Durham, NC: Duke University Press, 3–32.

Dore, Elizabeth. *Myths of Modernity: Peonage and Patriarchy in Nicaragua.* Durham, NC: Duke University Press, 2006.

Dore, Elizabeth and Maxine Molyneaux. *Hidden Histories of Gender and the State in Latin America.* Durham, NC: Duke University Press, 2000.

Earle, Rebecca. (2000) "Rape and the Anxious Republic: Revolutionary Colombia, 1810–1830," in Elizabeth Dore and Maxine Molyneux, eds, *Hidden Histories of Gender and the State in Latin America.* Durham, NC: Duke University Press, 127–146.

Eckstein, Susan, ed., *Power and Popular Protest: Latin American Social Movements.* Berkeley: University of California Press, 2001.

Edmonds, Alexander. *Pretty Modern: Beauty, Sex, and Plastic Surgery in Brazil.* Durham, NC: Duke University Press, 2010.

"Educación de las Hijas." *Aljaba* (Buenos Aires) No. 6, 3 de Diciembre de 1830.

"Falling Fertility Rate No Cause for Cheer." *Reuters from Indian Express* on March 14, 2012. http://www.newgeography.com/content/002874-latin-america%E2%80%99s-demographic-divergence. Last accessed November 15, 2013.

Farnsworth-Alvear, Ann. *Dulcinea in the Factory: Myths, Morals, Men, and Women in Colombia's Industrial Experiment, 1905–1960.* Durham, NC: Duke University Press, 2000.

Fiol-Matta, Licia. *Queer Mother for the Nation: The State and Gabriela Mistral.* Minneapolis, MN: University of Minnesota Press, 2002.

Fisher, Jo. *Mothers of the Disappeared.* Boston: South End Press, 1989.

Foote, Nicola. "Manuela Saenz and the Independence of South America." *World History Connected,* February 2010. http://worldhistoryconnected.press.illinois.edu/7.1/foote.html. Last accessed November 15, 2013.

Forero, Juan. "Birth Rate Plummets in Brazil." *Washington Post,* December 29, 2011. Available at http://articles.washingtonpost.com/2011-12-29/world/35286762_1_fertility-rate-demographic-shift-silva. Last accessed November 15, 2013.

Fowler-Salamini, Heather and Mary Kay Vaughan, eds. *Women in the Mexican Countryside, 1850–1990.* Tucson: University of Arizona Press, 1994.

Franceschet, Susan. "El triunfo de Bachelet y el ascenso politico de las mujeres." *Nueva Sociedad* 202 (2006), pp. 13–22.

Frasier, Nicholas and Marysa Navarro. *Evita: The Real Life of Eva Perón.* New York: W.W. Norton, 1996.

French, John D. and Daniel James, eds. *The Gendered World of Latin American Women Workers: From Household and Factory to the Union Hall and Ballot Box.* Durham, NC: Duke University Press, 1997.

Freyre, Gilberto. *New World in the Tropics: The Culture of Modern Brazil.* New York: Alfred A. Knopf, 1959.

Freyre, Gilberto. *The Masters and the Slaves: A Study in the Development of Brazilian Civilization.* 2nd English-language ed. Trans. Samuel Putnam. New York: Alfred A. Knopf, 1970.

Gauderman, Kimberly. *Women's Lives in Colonial Quito: Gender, Law, and Economy in Spanish America.* Austin: University of Texas Press, 2003.

González de Fanning, Teresa. *Educación Femenina: Coleccion de artículos pedagógicos, morales, y sociológicos.* Lima: Tipografía de "El Lucero, 1905.

González, Victoria and Karen Kampwirth, eds. *Radical Women in Latin America, Left and Right.* University Park: Pennsylvania State University Press, 2001.

Gotkowitz, Laura. (2000) "Commemorating the Heroínas: Gender and Civil Ritual in Early-Twentieth-Century Bolivia," in Elizabeth Dore and Maxine Molyneaux, eds, *Hidden Histories of Gender and the State in Latin America.* Durham, NC: Duke University Press, 215–237.

Gotkowitz, Laura. *A Revolution for our Rights: Indigenous Struggles for Land and Justice in Bolivia, 1880–1952*. Durham, NC: Duke University Press, 2008.

Grandin, Greg. *The Blood of Guatemala: A History of Race and Nation*. Durham, NC: Duke University Press, 2000.

Grez, Vicente. *Las mujeres de la independencia*. Santiago: Imp. de la "Gratitud Nacional", 1910.

Gutiérrez, Gustavo. *A Theology of Liberation: History, Politics, and Salvation*. Maryknoll, NY: Orbis Books, 1988.

Guy, Donna J. *Women Build the Welfare State: Performing Charity and Creating Rights in Argentina, 1880–1955*. Durham, NC: Duke University Press, 2009.

Guzmán Bouvard, Marguerite. *Revolutionizing Motherhood: The Mothers of the Plaza de Mayo*. Wilmington, DE: SR Books, 1994.

Hahner, June E. *Women in Latin American History: Their Lives and Views*. Los Angeles: UCLA Latin American Center Publications, 1976.

Hammond, Gregory. *The Women's Suffrage Movement and Feminism in Argentina from Roca to Peron*. Albuquerque: University of New Mexico Press, 2011.

Hart, Diane Walta. (1987) "Leticia: A Nicaraguan Woman's Struggle," in William H. Beezley and Judith Ewell, eds, *The Human Tradition in Latin America: The Twentieth Century*, Wilmington, DE: SR Books, 259–273.

Hartmann, Heidi I. "The Unhappy Marriage of Marxism and Feminism: Towards a More Progressive Union." *Capital and Class* 3:2 (1979), pp. 1–33.

"Higiene. Dedicado a las madres de familia." *Hijas del Anáhuac*, Año I, Tomo I, Núm. 10, 5 febrero 1888.

Haslanger, Sally, Nancy Tuana, and Peg O'Connor. "Topics in Feminism," in Edward N. Zalta, ed., *Stanford Encyclopedia of Philosophy*, 2013. Available at: http://plato.stanford.edu/archives/fall2013/entries/feminism-topics. Last accessed November 15, 2013.

Hijas del Anáhuac. Año I, Tomo I: Núm. 1, 11 diciembre de 1887; Núm. 10, 5 febrero de 1888; Núm. 24, 20 mayo de 1888.

Hinojosa, Magda. *Selecting Women, Electing Women: Political Representation and Candidate Selection in Latin America*. Philadelphia: Temple University Press, 2012.

Htun, Mala. *Sex and the State: Abortion, Divorce, and the Family Under Latin American Dictatorships and Democracies*. New York: Cambridge University Press, 2003.

Hunefeldt, Christine. *Liberalism in the Bedroom: Quarreling Spouses in Nineteenth-Century Lima*. University Park: Pennsylvania State University Press, 2000.

Inter-Parliamentary Union. "Women in National Parliaments." 2013. http://www.ipu.org/wmn-e/classif.htm. Last accessed November 15, 2013.

Isbester, Katerine. *Still Fighting: The Nicaraguan Women's Movement, 1977–2000*. Pittsburgh, PA: University of Pittsburgh Press, 2001.

James, Daniel. *Doña María's Story: Life History, Memory, and Political Identity.* Durham, NC: Duke University Press, 2000.

Jefatura Política del Primer Cantón del Estado de Jalisco, *Reglamento de Domésticos* (1888).

Kampwirth, Karen. (2001) "Women in the Armed Struggles in Nicaragua: Sandinistas and Contras Compared," in Victoria González and Karen Kampwirth, eds, *Radical Women in Latin America, Left and Right.* University Park: Pennsylvania State University Press, 79–110.

Kampwirth, Karen. (2002) "The Mother of the Nicaraguans: Doña Violeta and the UNO's Gender Agenda," in Jennifer Abbassi and Sheryl L. Lutjens, eds, *Rereading Women in Latin America and the Caribbean: the Political Economy of Gender.* New York: Rowman & Littlefield Publishers, 179–196.

Kampwirth, Karen. (2010) "Gender Politics in Nicaragua: Feminism, Antifeminism, and the Return of Daniel Ortega," in Elizabeth Maier and Nathalie Lebon, eds, *Women's Activism in Latin America and the Caribbean: Engendering Social Justice, Democratizing Citizenship.* New Brunswick, NJ: Rutgers University Press, 111–126.

Kellogg, Susan. *Weaving the Past: A History of Latin America's Indigenous Women from the Prehispanic Period to the Present.* New York: Oxford University Press, 2005.

Klubock, Thomas Miller. (1997) "Morality and Good Habits: The Construction of Gender and Class in the Chilean Copper Mines, 1904–1951," in John D. French and Daniel James, eds, *The Gendered World of Latin American Women Workers: From Household and Factory to the Union Hall and Ballot Box.* Durham, NC: Duke University Press, 232–263.

Klubock, Thomas Miller. *Contested Communities: Class, Gender, and Politics in Chile's El Teniente Copper Mine, 1904–1951.* Durham, NC: Duke University Press, 1998.

Kuznesof, Elizabeth Anne. "Household Composition and Headship as Related to Changes in Mode of Production: Sao Paulo 1765 to 1836." *Comparative Studies in Society and History* 22:1 (1980), pp. 78–108.

Kuznesof, Elizabeth Anne. "From Family Clans to Class Alliance: The Relationship of Social Structure to Economic Development in 19th Century Sao Paulo." *Revista da SBPH* 3 (1986/1987), pp. 29–46.

Kuznesof, Elizabeth Anne. (1989) "A History of Domestic Service in Spanish America (1492–1980)," in Elsa M. Chaney and Mary Garcia Castro, eds, *Muchachas No More: Household Workers in Latin America and the Caribbean.* Philadelphia: Temple University Press, 17–35.

Kuznesof, Elizabeth Anne. "The Construction of Gender in Colonial Latin America." *Colonial Latin American Review* 1:1–2 (1992), pp. 253–270.

Kuznesof, Elizabeth Anne. "Ethnic and Gender Influences on 'Spanish' Creole Society in Colonial Spanish America." *Colonial Latin American Review* 4:1 (1995), pp. 153–176.

Lauderdale Graham, Sandra. *House and Street: The Domestic World of Servants and Masters in Nineteenth-Century Rio de Janeiro.* Austin: University of Texas Press, 1988.

Lauderdale Graham, Sandra. *Caetana Says No: Women's Stories from a Brazilian Slave Society.* New York: Cambridge University Press, 2002.

Laveaga, Gabriela Soto. *Jungle Laboratories: Mexican Peasants, National Projects, and the Making of the Pill.* Durham, NC: Duke University Press, 2009.

Lavrin, Asunción, ed. *Latin American Women: Historical Perspectives.* Westport: Greenwood Press, 1978.

Lavrin, Asunción, ed. *Sexuality and Marriage in Colonial Latin America.* Lincoln: University of Nebraska Press, 1992.

Lavrin, Asunción. *Women, Feminism, and Social Change in Argentina, Chile, and Uruguay, 1890–1940.* Lincoln: University of Nebraska Press, 1995.

Lewis, Oscar. *Pedro Martínez: A Mexican Peasant and His Family.* New York: Random House, 1964.

Lipsett-Rivera, Sonya and Lyman L. Johnson. *The Faces of Honor: Sex, Shame, and Violence in Colonial Latin America.* Albuquerque: University of New Mexico Press, 1998.

Lyons, Barry J. *Remembering the Hacienda: Religion, Authority, and Social Change in Highland Ecuador.* Austin: University of Texas Press, 2006.

Maier, Elizabeth and Nathalie Lebon, eds. *Women's Activism in Latin America and the Caribbean: Engendering Social Justice, Democratizing Citizenship.* New Brunswick, NJ: Rutgers University Press, 2010.

Mallon, Florencia. *Peasant and Nation: The Making of Postcolonial Mexico and Peru.* Berkeley: University of California Press, 1995.

Mangan, Jane E. *Trading Roles: Gender, Ethnicity, and the Urban Economy in Colonial Potosí.* Durham, NC: Duke University Press, 2005.

March, Aleida. *Remembering Che: My Life with Che Guevara.* Minneapolis, MN: Ocean Press, 2012.

Martínez, Nela. *Yo siempre he sido Nela Martínez Espinosa: Una autobiografía hablada.* Quito: CONAMU-UNIFEM, 2006.

Martínez Alier, Verena. *Marriage, Class, and Colour in Nineteenth-Century Cuba: A Study of Racial Attitudes and Sexual Values in a Slave Society.* Ann Arbor, MI: University of Michigan Press, 1989.

Matto de Turner, Clorinda. *Torn from the Nest.* Trans. John H.R. Polt. New York: Oxford University Press, 1998.

McGee Deutsch, Sandra. "Gender and Sociopolitical Change in Twentieth-Century Latin America." *The Hispanic American Historical Review* 71:2 (1991), pp. 259–306.

Mehta, Uday S. "Liberal Strategies of Exclusion." *Politics and Society* 18:4 (1990), pp. 427–454.

Méndez de Cuenca, Laura. *El Hogar Mexicano: Nociones de Economía Doméstica.* 2a parte. Mexico: Herrero Hermanos, 1907.

Mellibovsky, Matilde, ed. *Circle of Love Over Death: Testimonies of the Mothers of the Plaza de Mayo.* Willimantic, CT: Curbstone Press, 1997.

Metcalf, Alida C. "Women and Means: Women and Family Property in Colonial Brazil." *Journal of Social History* 24:2 (1990), pp. 277–298.

Migden Socolow, Susan. *The Women of Colonial Latin America.* New York: Cambridge University Press, 2000.

Milanesio, Natalia. "'The Guardian Angels of the Domestic Economy': Housewives' Responsible Consumption in Peronist Argentina." *Journal of Women's History* 18:3 (2006), pp. 91–117.

Milanich, Nara. *Children of Fate: Childhood, Class, and the State in Chile, 1850–1930.* Durham, NC: Duke University Press, 2009.

Miller, Francesca. *Latin American Women and the Search for Social Justice.* Hanover, NH: University Press of New England, 1991.

Ministerio de Agricultura de la Nación. *Informe del Curso Temporario del Hogar Agrícola para Mujeres.* Buenos Aires: Talleres Gráficas del Ministerio de Agricultura de la Nación, 1921.

Mitchell, Stephanie and Patience A. Schell, eds. *The Women's Revolution in Mexico, 1910–1953.* New York: Rowman and Littlefield, 2007.

Molyneaux, Maxine. (2000) "State, Gender, and Institutional Change: The Federación de Mujeres Cubanas," in Elizabeth Dore and Maxine Molyneaux, eds, *Hidden Histories of Gender and the State in Latin America*, Durham, NC: Duke University Press, 291–321.

Montoya, Rosario, Lessie Jo Frazier and Janise Hurtig, eds. *Gender's Place: Feminist Anthropologies of Latin America.* New York: Palgrave MacMillan, 2002.

Mooney, Jadwiga E. Pieper. *The Politics of Motherhood: Maternity and Women's Rights in Twentieth-Century Chile.* Pittsburgh, PA: University of Pittsburgh Press, 2009.

Movimiento Autónomo de Mujeres. http://www.movimientoautonomode mujeres.org. Last accessed November 15, 2013.

Mujeres de CONAIE. *Memorias de las jornadas del foro de la mujer indígena del Ecuador.* Quito: CONAIE-UNFPA, 1994.

Murray, Pamela S. "'Loca' or 'Libertadora'? Manuela Sáenz in the Eyes of History and Historians, 1900–c. 1990." *Journal of Latin American Studies* 33:2 (2001), pp. 291–310.

Murray, Pamela S. "Of Love and Politics: Reassessing Manuela Sáenz and Simón Bolívar, 1822–1830." *History Compass* 5:1 (2007), pp. 227–250.

Murray, Pamela S. *For Glory and Bolívar: The Remarkable Life of Manuela Sáenz.* Austin: University of Texas Press, 2010.

Navarro, Marysa. (1994) "Juan and Eva Perón: A Family Portrait," in John Charles Chasteen and Joseph S. Tulchin, eds, *Problems of Modern Latin American History: A Reader.* Wilmington, DE: SR Books, 103–113.

Navarro, Marysa. (2001) "The Personal Is Political: Las Madres de Plaza de Mayo," in Susan Eckstein, ed., *Power and Popular Protest: Latin American Social Movements*. Berkeley: University of California Press, 241–258.

Navarro, Marysa. (2002) "Against Marianismo," in Rosario Montoya, Lessie Jo Frazier, and Janise Hurtig, eds, *Gender's Place: Feminist Anthropologies of Latin America*. New York: Palgrave MacMillan, 257–272.

Navarro, Maryssa and María Consuelo Mejía. (2010) "The Latin American Network of Católicas por el Derecho a Decidir," in Elizabeth Maier and Nathalie Lebon, eds, *Women's Activism in Latin America and the Caribbean: Engendering Social Justice, Democratizing Citizenship*. New Brunswick, NJ: Rutgers University Press, 306–318.

Nazzari, Muriel. "Parents and Daughters: Change in the Practice of Dowry in São Paulo (1600–1770)." *The Hispanic American Historical Review* 70:4 (1990), pp. 639–665.

Nazzari, Muriel. (1998) "An Urgent Need to Conceal," in Lyman L. Johnson and Sonya Lipsett-Rivera, eds, *The Faces of Honor: Sex, Shame, and Violence in Colonial Latin America*. Albuquerque: University of New Mexico Press, 103–126.

O'Connor, Erin. *Gender, Indian, Nation: The Contradictions of Making Ecuador, 1830–1925*. Tucson: Arizona University Press, 2007.

O'Connor, Erin E. and Leo J. Garofalo, eds. *Documenting Latin America, Volume 2: Gender, Race, and Nation*. Upper Saddle River, NJ: Prentice Hall/Pearson, 2011.

Offen, Karen. "Defining Feminism: A Comparative Historical Approach." *Signs* 14:1 (1988), pp. 119–157.

Olcott, Jocelyn, Mary Kay Vaughan, and Gabriela Cano, eds. *Sex in Revolution: Gender, Politics, and Power in Modern Mexico*. Durham, NC: Duke University Press, 2006.

Olcott, Jocelyn H. "'Worthy Wives and Mothers': State-Sponsored Women's Organizing in Postrevolutionary Mexico." *Journal of Women's History* 13:4 (2002), pp. 106–131.

Olcott, Jocelyn H. *Revolutionary Women in Postrevolutionary Mexico*. Durham, NC: Duke University Press, 2006.

Paxman, John M., Alberto Rizo, Laura Brown, and Janie Benson. "The Clandestine Epidemic: The Practice of Unsafe Abortion in Latin America." *Studies in Family Planning* 24:4 (1993), pp. 205–226.

Peniche Rivero, Piedad. (1994) "Women, Bridewealth and Marriage: Peonage and Social Reproduction in the Henequen Hacienda of Yucatán, Mexico," in Heather Fowler-Salamini and Mary Kay Vaughan, eds, *Women in the Mexican Countryside, 1850–1990*. Tucson: U of Arizona Press, 74–89.

Perón, Eva. *My Mission in Life*. New York: Vantage Press, 1953.

Pescatello, Ann, ed. *Female and Male in Latin America.* Pittsburgh, PA: Pittsburgh University Press, 1973.

Piccato, Pablo. *City of Suspects: Crime in Mexico City 1900–1931.* Durham, NC: Duke University Press, 2001.

Pilcher, Jeffrey M. *Que vivan los tamales! Food and the Making of Mexican Identity.* Albuquerque: University of New Mexico Press, 1998.

Porter, Susie S. *Working Women in Mexico City: Public Discourses and Material Conditions, 1879–1931.* Tucson: University of Arizona Press, 2003.

Postero, Nancy Grey and Leon Zamosc, eds. *The Struggle for Indigenous Rights in Latin America.* Brighton: Sussex Academic Press, 2004.

Power, Margaret. (2001) "Defending Dictatorship: Conservative Women in Pinochet's Chile and the 1988 Plebiscite," in Victoria González and Karen Kampwirth, eds, *Radical Women in Latin America, Left and Right.* University Park: Pennsylvania State University Press, 299–324.

Power, Margaret. *Right Wing Women in Chile: Feminine Power and the Struggle Against Allende, 1964–1973.* University Park: Pennsylvania State Press, 2002.

Powers, Karen Vieira. *Women in the Crucible of Conquest: The Gendered Genesis of Spanish American Society, 1500–1600.* Albuquerque: University of New Mexico Press, 2005.

Prats de Sarratea, Teresa. *Educación doméstica de las jóvenes.* Santiago: Imprenta A. Eyzaguirre I Ca., 1909.

Premo, Bianca. *Children of the Father King: Youth, Authority, and Legal Minority in Colonial Lima.* Chapel Hill: University of North Carolina Press, 2005.

Pribilsky, Jason. *La Chulla Vida: Gender, Migration, and the Family in Andean Ecuador and New York City.* Syracuse, NY: Syracuse University Press, 2007.

Prieto, Mercedes, Clorinda Cuminao, Alejandra Flores, Gina Maldonado, and Andrea Pequeño. "Respeto, discriminación y violencia: mujeresIndígenas en Ecuador, 1990–2004." n.d. http://www.flacso.org.ec/docs/respeto.pdf. Last accessed November 25, 2013.

Radcliffe, Sarah A., Nina Laurie, and Robert Andolina. "TheTransnationalization of Gender and Reimagining Andean Indigenous Development." *Signs* 29:2 (2004), pp. 387–420.

Randall, Margaret. *Cuban Women Now.* Toronto: Dumon Press, 1974.

Randall, Margaret. *Sandino's Daughters.* Toronto: New Start Books, 1981.

Rendón de Mosquera, Zoila. *La mujer en el hogar y en la sociedad*, 3ra ed. Quito: Editorial Universitaria, 1961 [1923].

República del Ecuador. *Anales de Senadores*, Congreso Ordinario de 1911. Cámara del senado, September 15. 1911.

Ríos Tobar, Marcel. "Chilean Feminism and Social Democracy from the Democratic Transition to Bachelet." *NACLA Report on the Americas* 40:2 (2007), p. 25.

Rodas Morales, Raquel. *Crónica de un sueño: Las escuelas indígenas de Dolores Cacuango*. Quito: Proyecto EBI-GTZ, 1998a.

Rodas Morales, Raquel. *Dolores Cacuango*. Quito: Proyecto EBI-GTZ, 1998b.

Rodas Morales, Raquel. *Dolores Cacuango: Gran líder del pueblo indio*. Quito: Banco Central del Ecuador, 2005.

Romero, Oscar. *The Violence of Love*. Trans. James R. Brockman. Maryknoll, NY: Orbis Books, 2004.

Rosemblatt, Karin Alejandra. *Gendered Compromises: Political Cultures and the State in Chile, 1920–1950*. Chapel Hill: University of North Carolina Press, 2000.

Rubenstein, Anne. (2006) "The War on *Las Pelonas*: Modern Women and Their Enemies in Mexico City, 1924," in Jocelyn Olcott, Mary Kay Vaughan, and Gabriela Cano, eds, *Sex in Revolution: Gender, Politics, and Power in Modern Mexico*. Durham, NC: Duke University Press, 57–80.

Salas, Elizabeth. (1994) "Soldaderas in the Mexican Revolution: War and Men's Illusions," in Heather Fowler-Salamini and Mary Kay Vaughan, eds, *Women of the Mexican Countryside, 1850–1990*. Tucson: University of Arizona Press, 74–92.

Sanders, Nichole. (2007) "Improving Mothers: Poverty, the Family, and 'Modern' Social Assistance in Mexico, 1937–1950," in Stephanie Mitchell and Patience A. Schell, eds, *The Women's Revolution in Mexico, 1910–1953*. New York: Rowman and Littlefield, 187–203.

Schleier, Samuel. "Latin America's Demographic Divergence." 2012. http://www.newgeography.com/content/002874-latin-america%E2%80%99s-demographic-divergence. Last accessed November 15, 2013.

Schroeder, Susan, Stephanie Wood, and Robert Haskett, eds. *Indian Women of Early Mexico*. Norman: University of Oklahoma Press, 1999.

Schwartz, Stuart B. *Sugar Plantations in the Formation of Brazilian Society: Bahia, 1550–1835*. New York: Cambridge University Press, 1985.

Scott, Joan Wallach. *Gender and the Politics of History*. New York: Columbia University Press, 1988.

Shelton, Laura M. *For Tranquility and Order: Family and Community on Mexico's Northern Frontier, 1800–1830*. Tucson: University of Arizona Press, 2010.

Silverblatt, Irene. *Moon, Sun, and Witches: Gender Ideologies and Class in Inca and Colonial Peru*. Princeton, NJ: Princeton University Press, 1987.

Sinclair, Minor, ed. *The New Politics of Survival: Grassroots Movements in Central America*. New York: Monthly Review Press, 1995.

Sinha, Mrinalini. *Gender and Nation*. Washington, DC: American Historical Association and Committee on Women Historians, 2006, pp. 1–40.

Smith, Lois M. and Alfred Padula. *Sex and Revolution: Women in Socialist Cuba*. New York: Oxford University Press, 1996.

Soto, Shirlene. *Emergence of the Modern Mexican Woman: Her Participation in Revolution and Struggle for Equality, 1910–1940*. Denver: Arden Press, 1990.

Stein, Stanley. *Vassouras: A Brazilian Coffee County, 1850–1900: The Roles of Planter and Slave in a Plantation Society*, 2nd ed. Princeton, NJ: Princeton University Press, 1986.

Stepan, Nancy Leys. *The Hour of Eugenics: Race, Gender, and Nation in Latin America*. Ithaca, NY: Cornell University Press, 1991.

Stephenson, Marcia. *Gender and Modernity in Andean Bolivia*. Austin: University of Texas Press, 1999.

Stern, Steve J. *The Secret History of Gender: Women, Men, and Power in Late Colonial Mexico*. Chapel Hill: University of North Carolina Press, 1995.

Stevens, Evelyn P. (1973) "*Marianismo*: The Other Face of Machismo," in Ann Pescatello, ed., *Female and Male in Latin America*. Pittsburgh, PA: Pittsburgh University Press, 89–101.

Stone, Elizabeth, ed. *Women and the Cuban Revolution: Speeches and Documents by Fidel Castro, Vilma Espin, and Others*. New York: Pathfinder Press, 1981.

Strickler, Jennifer, Angela Heimburger, and Karen Rodriguez. "Clandestine Abortion in Latin America: A Clinic Profile." *International Family Planning Perspectives* 27:1 (2001), pp. 34–36.

Swanson, Kate. *Begging as a Path to Progress: Indigenous Women and Children and the Struggle for Ecuador's Urban Spaces*. Athens: University of Georgia Press, 2010.

Taylor, William B. *Drinking, Homicide, and Rebellion in Colonial Mexican Villages*. Stanford, CA: Stanford University Press, 1979.

Terborgh, Anne, James E. Rosen, Roberto Santiso Gálvez, Willy Terceros, Jane T. Bertrand, and Sheana E. Bull. "Family Planning Among Indigenous Populations in Latin America." *International Family Planning Perspectives* 21:4 (1995), pp. 143–150.

Tinsman, Heidi. *Partners in Conflict: The Politics of Gender, Sexuality, and Labor in the Chilean Agrarian Reform, 1950–1973*. Durham, NC: Duke University Press, 2002.

Tinsman, Heidi. "A Paradigm of Our Own: Joan Scott in Latin American History." *The American Historical Review* 113:5 (2008), pp. 1357–1374.

Townsend, Camilla. *Malintzin's Choices: An Indian Woman in the Conquest of Mexico*. Albuquerque: University of New Mexico Press, 2006.

Tula, María Teresa. *Hear My Testimony: Maria Teresa Tula, Human Rights Activist of El Salvador*. Ed. and trans. by Lynn Stephen. Boston: South End Press, 1994.

Tutino, John. "The Revolution in Mexican Independence: Insurgency and the Renegotiation of Property, Production, and Patriarchy in the Bajío, 1800–1855." *The Hispanic American Historical Review* 78:3 (1998), pp. 367–418.

Valle, Don Manuel. *Inauguración del Servicio: Discurso Oficial.* Guatemala: Tipografía Nacional, 1907.

Vasconcelos, José. *The Cosmic Race/La raza cósmica.* Baltimore, MD: Johns Hopkins University Press, 1989.

Vaughan, Mary Kay. *Cultural Politics in Revolution: Teachers, Peasants, and Schools in Mexico, 1930–1940.* Tucson: University of Arizona Press, 1997.

Vaughan, Mary Kay. (2000) "Modernizing Patriarchy: State Policies, Rural Households, and Women in Mexico, 1930–1940," in Elizabeth Dore and Maxine Molyneaux, eds, *Hidden Histories of Gender and the State in Latin America.* Durham, NC: Duke University Press, 194–214.

Veccia, Theresa R. (1997) "My Duty as a Woman": Gender Ideology, Work, and Working-Class Women's Lives in São Paulo, Brazil, 1900–1950," in John D. French and Daniel James, eds, *The Gendered Worlds of Latin American Women Workers: From Household and Factory to the Union Hall and Ballot Box.* Durham, NC: Duke University Press, 100–146.

Vianna, Adriana R.B. and Sergio Carrera. (2010) "Sexual Politics and Sexual Rights in Brazil: A Case Study," in Corrales Javier and Mario Pecheney, eds, *he Politics of Sexuality in Latin America: A Reader on Lesbian, Gay, Bisexual, and Transgender Rights.* Pittsburgh, PA: University of Pittsburgh Press, 122–134.

Warren, Kay B. and Jean E. Jackson, eds. *Indigenous Movements, Self-Representation, and the State in Latin America.* Austin: University of Texas Press, 2002.

Weinstein, Barbara. (1997) "Unskilled Worker, Skilled Housewife: Constructing the Working-Class Woman in São Paulo, Brazil," in John D. French and Daniel James, eds, *The Gendered Worlds of Latin American Women Workers: From Household and Factory to the Union Hall and Ballot Box.* Durham, NC: Duke University Press, 72–99.

Weismantel, Mary. *Food, Gender, and Poverty in the Ecuadorian Andes.* Philadelphia: University of Pennsylvania Press, 1988.

Weismantel, Mary. *Cholas and Pishtacos: Stories of Race and Sex in the Andes.* Chicago: University of Chicago Press, 2001.

World Bank. "The Effect of Women's Economic Power in Latin America and the Caribbean." August 2012. http://www.bancomundial.org/content/dam/Worldbank/document/PLBSummer12latest.pdf. Last accessed November 15, 2013.

Xie, Selena and Javier Corrales. (2010) "LGBT Rights in Ecuador's 2008 Constitution: Victories and Setbacks," in Javier Corrales and Mario Pecheney, eds, *The Politics of Sexuality in Latin America: A Reader on Lesbian, Gay, Bisexual, and Transgender Rights.* Pittsburgh, PA: University of Pittsburgh Press, 224–232.

Yashar, Deborah. *Contesting Citizenship in Latin America: The Rise of Indigenous Movements and the Postliberal Challenge.* New York: Cambridge University Press, 2005.

Yeager, Gertrude M., ed. *Confronting Change, Challenging Tradition: Women in Latin American History.* Wilmington, DE: SR Books, 1994.

Zulawski, Ann. *Unequal Cures: Public Health and Political Change in Bolivia, 1900–1950.* Durham, NC: Duke University Press, 2007.

"Working Women Changing Traditional Roles in Latin America and Caribbean: UN Report." 2009. http://www.un.org/apps/news/story.asp?NewsID=31111 &Cr=women&Cr1=labour#.UZEt47XFU_4. Last accessed November 15, 2013.

Subject Index

Note: Figures in *italics*, boxes in **bold**

Mothers Making Latin America: Gender, Households, and Politics Since 1825,
First Edition. Erin E. O'Connor.
© 2014 John Wiley & Sons, Inc. Published 2014 by John Wiley & Sons, Inc.